NICHOLSON

THE ORDNA SURVEY GU THE WATERWAYS

3 NORTH

Series editor: David Perrott

Robert Nicholson Publications

Also available in this series:

Nicholson/Ordnance Survey Guide to the Waterways 1. South
Nicholson/Ordnance Survey Guide to the Waterways 2. Central
Nicholson/Ordnance Survey Guide to the River Thames (and Wey)

*The indication of a towpath in this book
does not necessarily imply a public right
of way. If you are in any doubt, check
before you proceed with the latest published
Ordnance Survey map.*
Pathfinder Series (1:25 000 scale or 2½ in to
1 mile). These OS walker and rambler maps show the
countryside in great detail, including rights
of way in England and Wales.
Landranger Series (1:50 000 scale or about 1¼ in
to 1 mile). This OS series covers the country
in 204 sheets and is ideal for detailed
exploring by car or on foot.

First published 1983 by **Robert Nicholson
Publications Limited**, 17 Conway Street,
London W1P 6JD and **Ordnance Survey**,
Romsey Road, Maybush, Southampton SO9 4DH.

2nd edition 1985

© Text, Robert Nicholson Publications Limited 1985

© The maps in this publication are reproduced from
Ordnance Survey maps with the permission of the
Controller of HMSO. Crown Copyright Reserved.

Original research: Paul Atterbury, Andrew Darwin
and David Perrott

Thanks are extended to the Electric Boat Association,
who supplied information on recharging points,
and the staff of the British Waterways Board who
helped with the preparation of this guide.

Cover photograph: Derek Pratt

Great care has been taken throughout this book
to be accurate, but the publishers cannot accept
any responsibility for any errors which appear.

Typeset by Rowland Phototypesetting Ltd,
Bury St Edmunds, Suffolk
Printed in Great Britain by
Chorley & Pickersgill Ltd,
Leeds and London

ISBN 0 905522 75 3

INTRODUCTION

The canals and navigable rivers of Britain were built as a system of new trade routes at a time when roads were virtually non-existent. After their boom period in the late 18th and early 19th centuries, they gradually declined in the face of fierce competition from the new railway companies, and large-scale commercial carrying ended by the time of the Second World War, when many of the routes had slipped into decay and ruin. It is true that in a few areas goods continue to be carried profitably to this day, but for the majority of canals it was the new traffic of pleasure boats that provided the impetus for rescue and restoration.

The founding of the Inland Waterways Association by L.T.C. Rolt and Robert Aickman in 1946 brought together enthusiasts from all over the country who were to campaign to save and restore these 2000 miles of navigable waterways that are so much a part of our history. More and more people are now realising that what had been abandoned as little more than a muddy ditch and a convenient place to dump rubbish can be transformed into a linear park, full of interest and a place of recreation for all.

There is something for everyone in the canals: engineering feats like aqueducts, tunnels and flights of locks (all of which amazed a world that had seen nothing like it since Roman times); the brightly decorated narrow boats which used to throng the waterways; the wealth of birds, animals and plants on canal banks; the mellow, unpretentious architecture of canalside buildings like pubs, stables, lock cottages and warehouses; and the sheer beauty and quiet isolation that is a feature of so many canals.

Use this book to discover the waterways for yourself; it is one of four volumes covering the South, Centre and North of England and the rivers Thames and Wey, published jointly by Nicholson and the Ordnance Survey, in response to public demand.

CONTENTS

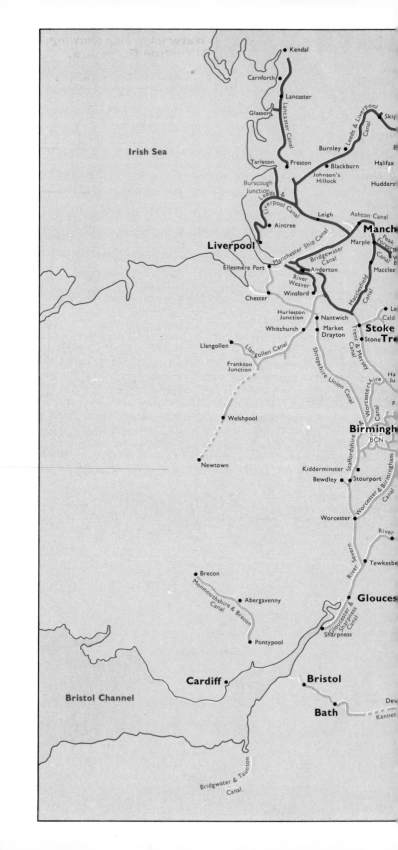

Waterways Map showing Nicholson Guide Areas

Waterways covered in this guide
Waterways covered in other guides in the series
Other Waterways
Waterways unnavigable at present time

The North East Waterways are shown at reduced scale only

Ripon

Ripon Canal

York

River Ouse

ds

Aire & Calder Navigation

Castleford

Wakefield

Selby Canal

Selby

Pocklington Canal

Market Weighton Canal

Hull

River Hull

Goole

Keadby

North Sea

Stainforth

Sheffield & South Yorkshire Navigation

Doncaster

River Idle

River Ancholme

heffield

Rotherham

Worksop

Chesterfield Canal

West Stockwith

Gainsborough

Torksey

Lincoln

River Trent

Fossdyke & Witham Navigations

Newark

Erewash Canal

Gunthorpe

Boston

Mersey Canal

n upon Trent

Nottingham

Kings Lynn

Loughborough

Grand Union Canal

River Soar

Wisbech

rth

Leicester

Peterborough

River Nene

Ashby Canal

Foxton

entry

Rugby

Grand Union Leicester Section

Market Harborough

River Nene

River Great Ouse

Bedford Rivers

Welford

Oxford Canal

wood Junc

Union

Canal

Crick

Norton Junction

River Cam

apton

unction

Braunston Turn

Gayton Junction

Northampton

Cambridge

d-

ron

Stoke Bruerne

Cosgrove

Banbury

Grand Union Canal

Bishops Stortford

Oxford Canal

Leighton Buzzard

Marsworth

Hertford

River Stort

Thrupp

Aylesbury

Berkhamstead

Lee Navigation

Oxford

Watford

LONDON

River Thames

Slough

River Thames

Hungerford

Reading

Newbury

River Medway

Chatham

Guildford

River Wey

Maidstone

HOW TO USE THIS GUIDE

The maps are drawn at a scale of two inches to one mile. Adjacent to each map section is a description of the countryside and places of interest together with a commentary on the course of the canal or river. Details of boatyards correspond to the symbol ⑧ on the map, and pubs ● near the waterway are also named and in some cases described. Those with a restaurant are indicated by the symbol ✕ and wine bars and licensed premises by ▾. Other symbols used on the maps are:

28 8′ 8″	Locks, with number and 'rise'. The symbol points uphill.
	Staircase locks.
197	Bridge and its number. Many are named.
	Tunnel—often described in the text.
) (	Aqueduct—often described in the text.
	Winding hole—turning point for boats longer than the ordinary width of the canal (it's pronounced as in the wind that blows). Canal junctions are also good places to 'wind'.
Towing Path	Weir.

R is refuse disposal, **S** is sewage or 'Elsan' disposal, **W** is a water point, **P** is petrol, **D** is diesel and **E** is electric boat recharge. Many of these facilities are often available at boatyards; 'pump-out' toilet emptying machines may also be available—see the text entry for each boatyard.

A feature of these guides is the 'milestone' which appears on every map thus:

22¼M	22L
Napton	
Oxford	
27M	17L

This performs many useful functions. It reminds you of your direction of travel—in this example **up** the page is towards Napton, **down** the page is towards Oxford; it denotes distances and indicates the number of locks between the milestone and strategic points (usually junctions) along the waterway—in this example, Napton is 22¼ miles (M) with 22 locks (L) from the 'milestone', and Oxford is 27 miles and 17 locks from the milestone. By deducting the miles and locks on one milestone from those on the next, distances from page to page can be accurately estimated. Using the 'lock-miles' system (see **Planning a cruise**, page 13) the time your journey will take can be calculated, and with a little experience based on your speed of travel and lock operation, your own time formula can be arrived at.

Where this device occurs on a map it simply means that the actual route of the waterway would not fit neatly onto the page, so the cartographer has 'bent' the map, using two north points. The navigator on the water, or the walker on the bank, will notice nothing amiss. Distances in this book should be measured along the thick blue line only, not including these gaps.

LOCKS AND THEIR USE

The different locks and their attendant machinery are a source of endless fascination for all waterway users. Understanding why they are there and the principle upon which they work will help you in their use.

A lock is a device for transporting craft from a higher water level to a lower level, or vice versa, for example when a canal crosses a range of hills. It consists of a box with gates at each end, and a separate means of letting water in at the top (higher level) and out at the bottom (lower level). This is controlled by paddles. These paddles may simply open and shut holes in the gates (gate paddles), or they may open and shut underground culverts (ground paddles). A windlass (carried on the boat) is used to wind the paddles open and shut. Whilst locks differ in detail, the following instructions will apply in the case of the vast majority of *narrow* canal locks. Some extra points regarding wide locks are covered later.

A typical narrow lock

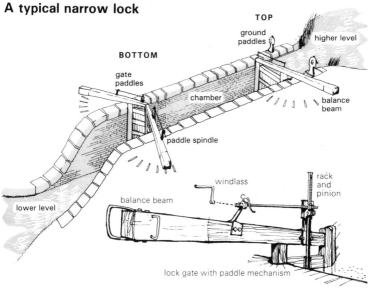

How to go through a lock

PRELIMINARIES

Stop the boat well outside the lock and secure it. If members of your crew can get off the boat before the lock (at the narrow point under a bridge for example) and run ahead to prepare the lock, this will save time.

GOING UP IN A LOCK (LOCKING UP)

Lock empty—ie water at lower level

Open bottom gate(s)
Drive boat in
Close bottom gate(s)
Check bottom paddles closed
Keep boat near to the bottom of lock
Open top paddles to fill lock
Open top gate(s) when lock is full
Drive boat out
Close top gate(s)
Close top paddles

Lock full—ie water at higher level

Check top gate(s) and paddles closed
Open bottom paddles to drain lock
Open bottom gate(s)
Drive boat in
Close bottom gate(s) and paddles
Keep boat near to the bottom of lock
Open top paddles to fill lock
Open top gate(s) when lock is full
Drive boat out
Close top gate(s)
Close top paddles

GOING DOWN IN A LOCK (LOCKING DOWN)

Lock full—ie water at higher level	Lock empty—ie water at lower level
Open top gate(s)	Check bottom gate(s) and paddles closed
Drive boat in	Open top paddles to fill lock
Close top gate(s)	Open gate(s)
Check top paddles closed	Drive boat in
Keep boat near to the bottom of the lock	Close top gate(s) and paddles
Open bottom paddles to empty lock	Keep boat near to the bottom of the lock
Open bottom gate(s)	Open bottom paddles to empty lock
Drive boat out	Open bottom gate(s)
Close bottom gates and paddles	Drive boat out
	Close bottom gate(s) and paddles

If you have to drain or fill a lock in order to enter it, make sure there is no boat approaching that could usefully use the lock before you. Always try to conserve water, which is being continually passed down the canal from its summit and thus requires constant replenishment at a higher level.

SOME GENERAL DO'S AND DONT'S AT LOCKS

Do not leave your windlass slotted onto the paddle spindle—if something slips it could be thrown off and cause injury.

Always leave all gates and paddles closed when you leave, but look out for notices which may give other instructions for the proper operation of a particular lock.

Always wind the paddles down—letting them drop is bad practice, and causes damage.

Beware of protrusions in the side walls of the lock chamber that may damage the boat, and don't use fenders in narrow locks—they may jam.

When opening and closing lock gates, keep to the landward side of the balance beam.

Don't rush around at locks, especially in wet weather, when the sides are slippery. Never jump across partly opened gates.

Always make the safety of the crew and boat your prime concern and remember that if things do start to go wrong, you can stop everything by closing the paddles.

There is no reason why your children, wearing buoyancy aids and properly supervised, should not help at locks—it is all part of the fun, after all—but impress upon them the potential dangers, and establish some commonsense rules. You have no authority over other people's children, and their participation should be discouraged. Great difficulties could ensue should they be injured in any way.

Beware of fierce top gate paddles, especially in wide locks.

Don't leave your windlass behind; hundreds are lost this way each year.

WIDE LOCKS

Taking a narrow boat (7ft beam) through a wide lock (14ft) can present special difficulties, especially when locking up. If all the top paddles were to be opened fully at the same time, the boat would be buffeted considerably. The diagram below illustrates one method of ensuring a smooth passage. The stern line held ashore will provide added security.

Locking up in a wide lock
(a suggested technique)

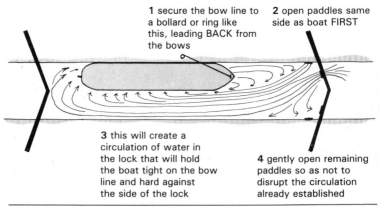

1 secure the bow line to a bollard or ring like this, leading BACK from the bows

2 open paddles same side as boat FIRST

3 this will create a circulation of water in the lock that will hold the boat tight on the bow line and hard against the side of the lock

4 gently open remaining paddles so as not to disrupt the circulation already established

STAIRCASE LOCKS

Where the top gates of one lock are the bottom gates of the next. Usually there is a board nearby giving operating instructions—read it carefully and make sure you understand it before you start. And remember: in a narrow staircase you can't pass a boat coming the other way.

Even young children can help, if properly supervised, but you must make sure life jackets are worn all the time when near the water. *David Perrott.*

GENERAL CRUISING INFORMATION

The vast majority of the waterways covered in this series are controlled by the British Waterways Board. All craft using BWB canals must be licensed and those using BWB rivers must be registered. Charges are based on the length of the boat and a canal craft licence covers all the navigable waterways under the Board's control. Permits for permanent mooring on the canals are also issued by the Board. Apply in each case to:

Craft Licensing Office,
Willow Grange,
Church Road,
Watford WD1 3QA.
(Watford 26422).

The Licensing Office will also supply a list of all BWB rivers and canals. Other river navigation authorities relevant to this book are mentioned where appropriate.

Getting afloat

There is no better way of discovering the joys of canals than by getting afloat. The best thing is to hire a boat for a week or a fortnight from one of the boatyards on the canals. (Each boatyard has an entry in the text, and most of them offer craft for hire; brochures may be easily obtained from such boatyards.)

General cruising

Most canals are saucer-shaped in section and so are deepest in the middle. Very few have more than 3–4ft of water and many have much less. Try to keep to the middle of the channel except on bends, where the deepest water is on the *outside* of the bend. When you meet another boat, the rule is to keep to the right, slow down, and aim to miss the approaching boat by a couple of yards: do not steer right over to the bank or you will most likely run aground. The deeper the draught of the boat, the more important it is to keep in the middle of the deep water, and so this must be considered when passing other boats. If you meet a loaded working boat, keep right out of the way. Working boats should always be given precedence, for their time is money. If you meet a boat being towed from the bank, pass it on the outside rather than intercept the towing line. When overtaking, keep the other boat on your starboard, or right, side.

Speed

There is a general speed limit of 4mph on most British Waterways Board canals. This is not just an arbitrary limit: there is no need to go any faster, and in many cases it is impossible to cruise even at this speed. Canals were not built for motor boats, and so the banks are easily damaged by excessive wash and turbulence. Erosion of the banks makes the canal more shallow, which in turn makes running aground a more frequent occurrence. So keep to the limits and try not to aggravate the situation. It is easy to see when a boat is creating excessive turbulence by looking at the wash—if it is 'breaking' or causing large waves, you are going too fast and should slow down.

Slow down also when passing moored craft, engineering works and anglers.

Slow down when there is a lot of floating rubbish on the water: old planks and plastic bags may mean underwater obstacles that can damage a boat or its propeller if hit hard. Try to drift over obvious obstructions in neutral.

Slow down when approaching blind corners, narrow bridges and junctions.

Running aground

The effective end of commercial traffic on the narrow canals has resulted in canals being shallower than ever. Running aground is a fairly common event, but is rarely serious, as the canal bed is usually soft. If you run aground, try first of all to pull the boat off by gently reversing the engine. If this fails, use the pole as a lever against the bank or some solid object, in combination with a tow rope being pulled from the bank. Do not keep revving the engine in reverse if it is obviously having no effect. Another way is to get your crew to rock the boat from side to side while using the pole or mooring lines. If all else fails, lighten your load; make all the crew leave the boat except the helmsman, and then it will often float off quite easily.

Remember that if you run aground once, it is likely to happen again as it indicates a particularly shallow stretch—or that you are out of the channel. If you are continually bumping the bottom in a shallow stretch, it may be that you are going too fast, causing the boat to 'dig in' at the back. Going less fast may make things more comfortable.

In a town it is common to run aground on sunken rubbish; this is most likely to occur near bridges and housing estates. Use the same methods, but be very careful as hard objects can very easily damage your boat or propeller.

Remember that winding holes are often silted up—do not go further in than you have to.

Mooring

All boats carry metal stakes and a mallet. These are used for mooring when there are no rings or bollards in sight, which is usually the case. Generally speaking you may moor anywhere to

BWB property but there are certain basic rules. Avoid mooring anywhere that could cause an obstruction to other boats; do not moor on a bend or a narrow stretch; do not moor abreast boats already moored. Never moor in a lock, and do not be tempted to tie up in a tunnel or under a bridge if it is raining. Pick a stretch where there is a reasonable depth of water at the bank, otherwise the boat may bump and scrape the canal bed—an unpleasant sensation if you are trying to sleep. For reasons of peace and quiet and privacy it is best to moor away from main roads and railway lines.

Never stretch your mooring lines across the towpath; you may trip someone up and face a claim for damages.

There is no need to show a riding light at night, except on major rivers and busy commercial canals.

Beware of mooring at unrecognised sites in cities—you may attract the unwelcome attention of vandals.

So long as you are sensible and keep to the rules, mooring can be a pleasant gesture of individuality.

Knots

A simple and easy way of securing a rope to a bollard or mooring stake is to use a couple of round turns and a half hitch made with a loop and pulled tight. This can be released quickly by pulling the loose end, which will have been left tidily coiled.

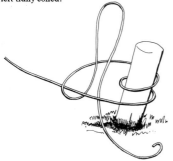

When leaving a mooring, coil all the ropes up again. They will then be out of the way, but ready if needed in a hurry. Many a sailor has fallen overboard after tripping on an uncoiled rope.

Fixed bridges

At most bridges the canal becomes very narrow, a means of saving building costs developed by the engineers. As a result, careful navigation is called for if you are to avoid hitting either the bridge sides with the hull or the arch with the cabin top. As when entering a lock, the best way to tackle 'bridgeholes' is to slow down well in advance and aim to go straight through, keeping a steady course. Adjustments should be kept to a minimum for it is easy to start the boat zig-zagging, which will inevitably end in a collision. One technique is to gauge the width of the approaching bridgehole relative to the width of the boat, and then watch one side only, aiming to miss that side by a small margin—say 6in; the smaller you can make the margin, the less chance you have of hitting the other side of

the bridge. If you do hit the bridge sides when going slowly it is not likely to do much damage; it will merely strengthen your resolve to do better next time.

Moveable bridges

Swing and lift bridges are an attractive feature of some canals and cannot be ignored as they often rest only 2 or 3ft above the water. They are moved by being swivelled horizontally, or raised vertically. Operation is usually manual, although some have gearing to ease the movement. There are one or two mechanised versions; these have clear instructions at control points. Before operating any bridge make sure that approaching road traffic is aware of your intention to open the bridge. Use protective barriers if there are any and remember to close the bridge again after you.

Some *lift bridges are very unstable*, and could close while your boat is passing underneath, with disastrous consequences. For this reason it is prudent to have your strongest (or heaviest) crew member hold it open until the boat is clear. Many swing bridges are very heavy to operate, and require two strong people to move them.

Tunnels

Many people consider a canal incomplete without one or two tunnels, and certainly they are an exciting feature of any trip. Nearly all are easy to navigate, although there are a few basic rules:

Make sure your boat has a good headlight in working order and *always* use it.

If it is a narrow tunnel (ie 7ft) make sure there is no boat coming the other way *before* you enter. Craft of 7ft beam can pass in some wide tunnels—slow right down when you meet to lessen the almost inevitable bump.

In most tunnels the roof drips constantly, especially under ventilation shafts. Put on a raincoat and some form of hat before going in.

A notice on the tunnel portal will give its length, in yards, and will say whether unpowered craft are permitted to use it.

Where there are restrictions on time of entry, and one-way systems, these must be adhered to. To meet head on half way through a long narrow tunnel would create great difficulties.

Care of the engine

Canal boats are generally powered by either diesel, petrol or two-stoke engines. If you have a hire craft, the boatyard will give you instructions for your daily maintenance, which will no doubt include some or all of the following:

Every day before starting off, you should:

Check the oil level in the engine.
Check the fuel level in the tank.

If your engine is water-cooled, check that the filter near the intake is clean and weedfree. Otherwise the engine will over-heat, which could cause serious damage.

Check the level of distilled water in the battery, and ensure that it is charging correctly.

Lubricate any parts of the engine, gearbox or steering that need daily attention.

Check that the propeller is free of weeds, wire, plastic bags and any other rubbish. The propeller and the water filter should be checked whenever there is any suspicion of obstruction or overheating—which may mean several times a day.

Pump the bilges everyday

When navigating in shallow water, keep in mind the exposed position of the propeller. If you hit any underwater obstruction put the engine into neutral immediately. When running over any large floating object put the engine into neutral and wait for the object to appear astern before re-engaging the drive.

Fuel

Petrol engines and petrol/oil outboards are catered for by some boatyards and all road-side fuel stations. Fuel stations on roads near the canal are shown in the guide, and these should be considered when planning your day's cruise. Running out is inconvenient; remember you may have to walk several miles carrying a heavy can.

Diesel-powered craft, and narrowboats in particular, can usually cruise for over two weeks before needing to be refilled. Those using diesel-powered hire craft rarely need to be concerned about fuel. Those with their own boats, however, should bear in mind that boatyards are few and far between on some parts of the network, and should a diesel-powered boat run out of fuel, the system will need to be bled before the engine can run again. Most boatyards sell marine diesel (indicated D in the text), which is cheaper than the road fuel.

Electrically powered boats

These are becoming very popular on the inland waterways, in view of their quietness and lack of environmental pollution. Indicated E under the **BOATYARD** heading are those establishments known to offer recharging facilities—polite enquiry by electric boat users will certainly reveal more. If you are lucky enough to be using this form of power, please note the following:

All boats using this information are assumed to have a battery charger on board and 50 metres of cable fitted with standard 13 amp terminals. You are advised to offer a £2 fee (1984) for an overnight re-charge if not equipped to measure what you take.

It is essential for the safety of the boater, the owner of the supply and the general public that a proper residual current circuit breaker (RCD) be carried by the boat and fitted between the boat's cable and the supply unless the supply is already so protected. The RCD must be tested for correct operation before battery charging starts.

Water

Fresh water taps occur irregularly along the canals, usually at boatyards, BWB depots, or by lock cottages. These are marked on the maps in the guide. Ensure that there is a long water hose on the boat (BWB taps have a ½-inch slip-on hose connection). Fill up every day.

Lavatories

Some canal boats are fitted with chemical lavatories which have to be emptied from time to time. Never empty them over the side or tip them into the bushes. Use the sewage disposal points marked on the map S, for which you will need a BWB key, or at boatyards. Many boats now have pump-out toilets, which must be emptied with a special machine—usually at boatyards and indicated in the text. This symbol at the canalside indicates just such a 'pump-out station' (although not all boatyards with the facility display it). Expect to have to pay.

Some BWB depots and boatyards have lavatories for the use of boat crews; again, you may need your BWB key.

Litter

Some canals are in a poor state today because they have long been misused as unofficial dumps for rubbish, especially in towns. Out of sight is only out of mind until some object is tangled round your propeller. So keep all rubbish until you can dispose of it at a refuse disposal point, indicated R on the map, or at a boatyard equipped to deal with it.

Byelaws

Although no-one needs a 'driving licence' to navigate a boat, boat users should remember that they have certain responsibilities to others on the waterways. Prospective navigators are advised to obtain a copy of the byelaws relevant to the waterways on which they are to travel.

Stoppages

Although the BWB and other navigation authorities plan their maintenance for the winter months, it often becomes necessary to carry out repairs during the cruising season. Many of the structures on the canal system are beginning to show their age (especially the tunnels) and repairs are a lengthy and costly affair, sometimes resulting in stoppages lasting many years. A long dry spell can lower water levels and restrict lock operation, and of course a canal bank can breach at any time.

To avoid disappointment it is wise to check that your planned route is clear before you set off, and that there are no time restrictions on locks that may upset your schedule. Those using hire craft may be able to get this information from their boatyard, although some are surprisingly lax. It is best to check for yourself by ringing the BWB Area Amenity Assistants (listed on page 173) or the relevant navigation authority. News of any last minute stoppages is available on 'Canalphone', as a recorded message. Ring (01)-723 8486 for the North and Midlands, or (01)-723 8487 for the South and Midlands.

PLANNING A CRUISE

It is wise when planning a cruise to establish a means of calculating the time it takes to travel any given length of canal. This ensures that you can reliably work out whether you will reach a shop or pub before closing time. And of course for those who have hired their boat for a week, it is vital to return on time to the starting point.

The time taken to navigate any canal depends, of course, on the average cruising speed of your boat and the amount of time it takes to negotiate the locks along the way. Remember that there is in any case an overall legal speed limit of 4 mph on all canals. In practice, 3 mph is a realistic canal cruising speed for most boats and 2 mph is the maximum which can be achieved on shallow canals, such as the Peak Forest.

To the uninitiated, 3 mph may sound an unbearably slow rate of progress through the countryside; but a few hours of gentle cruising on a fine day is usually enough to convert most people to this pace. For only by proceeding at walking pace can you appreciate the peace and beauty of the countryside, watch the bird life, and see the scurry of voles, rats and other creatures as they suddenly notice the slowly approaching boat.

The length of time taken to work through a lock depends on several things: whether the lock is full or empty, wide or narrow, deep or shallow. It depends on the number and size of the paddles that control the sluices, on the presence or otherwise of other boats near the lock, and of course on the number and competence of the boat crew. Most people take around 10 minutes on average to work through a typical lock—or, to put it another way, they take as long to get through a lock as they would have taken to travel another ½ mile at 3 mph. Herein lies the basis for a simple method of estimating time required to travel along a given length of canal: take the number of miles to be travelled and add half the number of locks to be negotiated on the way. This gives the number of 'lock-miles'. Divide this by your average cruising speed, and the result is the approximate length of time it will take, in hours. Thus if you intend to travel 30 miles, and there are 42 locks along the way, the calculation is as follows: 30 + (42 divided by 2) = 30 + 21 = 51 lock-miles. 51 divided by 3 (mph) = 17 hours. So this particular journey will take you around 17 hours, assuming your average cruising speed to be 3 mph and assuming you take about 10 minutes to get through the average lock. (If you're a beginner, it might take a little longer than this to start with.) The length of your journey and the number of locks can easily be calculated using the 'milestones' that appear on every map in this series of guides. To refine the system, simply tailor it more closely to the actual cruising speed of your boat and the efficiency of your lock-operating technique.

An excellent fortnight's trip, for example, would be the circuit formed by the River Soar and Trent and Mersey, Coventry, Oxford and Grand Union (Leicester Section) canals. This is 170 miles and 74 locks long (about 70 hours cruising time), and takes you through some of the very best parts of Leicestershire. You will see the Foxton staircase locks, Braunston Tunnel and the delightful canal village of Shardlow, and if you have time to spare you can explore the lock-free Ashby Canal (22 miles long—2 days there and back) or the meandering course of the unspoilt Market Harborough arm, 5 miles long.

A good round trip in terms of contrasts would be the Grand Union main line, north Oxford, Coventry and Birmingham & Fazeley canals, which at 106 miles and 88 locks (about 50 hours cruising time) would be an energetic week's cruising. On this route you could see Braunston and Hillmorton, the long level of the north Oxford and Coventry Canals broken by the 11 locks at Atherstone, and then the industrial outpost of Fazeley. Once out in Warwickshire, you encounter the 5 wide but modern locks at Knowle and the 21 locks of the Hatton Flight. Then you are in the valley of the Warwickshire Avon, and after passing Warwick and Leamington Spa you start locking up out of the valley again to rejoin the Oxford Canal at Napton.

These are just two examples of the many circular cruising routes available—a glance at the planning map on pages 4 and 5 will reveal many more. Of course, there is also much to be said for a straight out and back cruise—it will all look different when you are coming the other way, and you can arrange to re-visit that favourite pub again. The whole secret is to allow plenty of time, for shopping, for exploring and for gentle cruising. Many a holiday has been spoilt by becoming a race against time.

See also 'Stoppages' in the **General Cruising Information** *section.*

The Chesterfield Canal at Clayworth. *Derek Pratt*

BRIDGEWATER CANAL

Maximum dimensions

Length: 70'
Beam: 14'
Headroom: 8'
Draught: 3"

Licences

Estates Officer, Manchester Ship Canal Company, Trafford Road, Manchester.
Enquiries: 061-872 7031.
All craft using the canal must be licensed and insured against normal third party risks. Any boat holding a normal BWB licence may cruise freely on the Bridgewater for up to 7 days.

Mileage

PRESTON BROOK to
Lymm: 9¾
Waters Meeting, junction with
Leigh Branch: 20½
Hulme Locks Branch: 23¼
CASTLEFIELD JUNCTION, start of
Rochdale Canal: 23½

No locks

DULCIE STREET JUNCTION, start of
Ashton Canal: 25 (Rochdale Canal, 9 locks)

Preston Brook to Runcorn: 5¾, no locks

Leigh Branch: 8½, no locks

The Bridgewater Canal, which received the Royal Assent on 23 March 1759, was the forerunner of all modern canals, following a route that was independent of all existing natural watercourses. It was built by Francis Egerton, third Duke of Bridgewater, to enable coal from his mines at Worsley to be transported to Manchester and sold cheaply. His engineers were James Brindley and John Gilbert, who designed a lockless contour canal which crossed the River Irwell on a stone aqueduct – a revolutionary concept and one that was ridiculed by many sceptics. However the line was open to Stretford by the end of 1765.

While the canal was under construction, there began the excavation of a remarkable system of underground canals to serve the Duke's mines, reached through 2 entrances at Worsley Delph. Eventually 46 miles of underground canal were built, some on different levels and linked by an ingenious inclined plane built along a fault in the sandstone. The craft used in the mines were known as 'starvationers', double-ended tub boats which could carry up to 12 tons of coal. This whole system remained in use until the late 19thC.

In 1762 the Duke received sanction to extend his canal to the Liverpool tideway at Runcorn – this was later amended in order to connect with the new Trent & Mersey Canal at Preston Brook. The route between Liverpool and Manchester was opened in 1776, although Brindley did not live to see its completion. In 1795 the Duke, then 60 years old, received the Royal Assent for the final part of the network, which linked Worsley to the Leeds & Liverpool Canal at Leigh. As a result of this enterprise, the Duke spent much of his life heavily in debt, although he finally recouped his investments to die, in 1803, a rich man.

The coming of the railways did not initially affect the prosperity of the canal, the Trustees going to great lengths in Parliament to protect their position. In 1872 the newly formed Bridgewater Navigation Company purchased the canal for £1,120,000, and they in turn sold it to the Manchester Ship Canal Company in 1885. The building of the new Ship Canal meant that Brindley's original stone aqueduct over the River Irwell would need to be replaced. Its successor, the Barton Swing Aqueduct, was no less outstanding than the original, being a steel trough closed by gates at each end, pivoting on an island in the ship Canal. The weight of water carried by the new aqueduct is 1500 tons.

The Bridgewater Canal is a tribute to its builders in that it continued to carry commercial traffic until 1974 – indeed its wide gauge, lock-free course and frequent use of aqueducts makes many later canals seem retrograde.

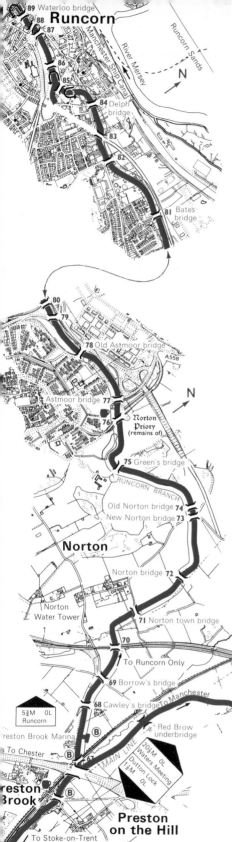

Preston Brook

Although the main line of the Bridgewater was originally to Runcorn, where it locked down to the Mersey, this is now a dead end, reached through the dull acres of the new town's expanding housing estates, although there are some attractive terraces and elegant iron bridges to enliven the journey. The locks down to the Mersey were closed in 1966. The route to Manchester bears to the right immediately after the big motorway bridge, and the canal's direct course to the south of the Mersey affords interesting views of the Manchester Ship Canal and industry to the north.

Runcorn
Ches. EC Wed. MD Tue, Thur, Sat. All Services. Runcorn's industrial growth began with the completion of the Bridgewater Canal in the latter part of the 18thC. The old town is to be found down by the docks, where the elegant curved 1092-ft single span of the steel road bridge (built 1961), with the railway beside, leaps over the Ship Canal and the Mersey. West of the bridge, by the Ship Canal, is Bridgewater House where the 'Canal Duke' spent much of his time while the docks were being built – it is now occupied by the Manchester Ship Canal Company. The massive flight of 10 double locks which connected the canal to the Mersey was finally abandoned in 1966, and filled in, much to the dismay of thousands of industrial archaeologists and canal enthusiasts. Since 1964 Runcorn has been a 'new town', its rapid growth being carefully planned. It is interesting to note that Runcorn, following recent local government reorganisation, is now part of Halton (which includes Widnes on the north bank of the Mersey), an echo of the time following the Norman Conquest when it was a dependent manor of the Barony of Halton.
Information Centre Church Street, Runcorn. (76776).
Norton Priory
The remains of a priory c1200, set in woodland, with a picnic area and museum. *Open Mon–Wed, Sat, Sun and B. Hol afternoons in summer – also Thur and Fri in Aug.*
Preston Brook
Ches. PO, tel, stores. A village that grew up to serve the canal, where goods were trans-shipped from the wide beam craft of the north west to the narrow boats of the Midlands. There is now little left to remind us of this activity, and a very different means of transport, the M56 motorway, dominates the area. To the south, on the Trent & Mersey Canal, is the 1239-yd long Preston Brook Tunnel (see page 149).

BOATYARDS
Ⓑ **Claymoore Navigation** The Wharf, Preston Brook. (Runcorn 717273). Ⓢ Ⓦ Ⓓ Pump-out, narrow boat hire, gas, boat fitting & repairs, mooring, chandlery, provisions, winter storage, toilets. Note: those negotiating the Cheshire ring in a clockwise direction should remember that the next pump-out station is at Macclesfield.
Ⓑ **Pyranha Watersports Centre** Marina Village, Preston Brook. (Runcorn 716666). Ⓟ Ⓓ Gas, wet dock, boat building & repairs, mooring, chandlery, showers, day boat hire, toilets.
Ⓑ **Preston Brook Marina** Preston Brook, Runcorn. (Runcorn 713074). Operated by the Pyranha Watersports Centre. Ⓢ Ⓦ Moorings.

PUBS
Plenty of pubs in Runcorn, including:
🍺 **Clarendon** Church Street, Runcorn.
🍺 **Egerton Arms** Bridge Street, Runcorn.
🍺 **Barge Hotel** Norton. By bridge 77.
🍺 **Red Lion** Preston Brook.

Daresbury

Industry is far enough away to the north to remain an interesting diversion rather than an ugly intrusion as the canal passes through pleasant countryside, punctuated initially by the tall white tower and pleasant landscaped grounds of the Science Research Laboratory at Daresbury, where nuclear research is carried out. By Moorefield Bridge there is one of the small cranes used to hoist stop planks into position, should a section of the canal need to be drained. The canal frontage at Moore is attractive, with moored boats and a shop and phone right by the canal, followed by a group of interesting red brick, bow-fronted cottages. A short rural stretch is interrupted by the estate village of Higher Walton, which can be seen among trees, and this is followed by a secluded tree-lined length in a shallow cutting before the outskirts of Stockton Heath are approached. There follows a pleasant example of urban canal, busy with fishermen and walkers. There are useful services at London Bridge.

Stockton Heath
Ches. EC Thur. Shops and services north of London Bridge. An outer suburb of Warrington, England's centre for vodka distilling. A useful place to victual.
Stockton Quay Bridge 15. The terminus of the canal from 1771 to 1776, before the Duke of Bridgewater completed his route from Manchester to Runcorn, and consequently a major trans-shipment point with stables, yards, wharves, warehouses and a canal company office. Passenger packet boat services also ran from here from 1771 to the mid 1880s, one of the craft being the renowned 'Duchess-Countess'.

Higher Walton
Ches. PO, tel, stores. A pretty, late Victorian estate village among trees. The gardens of Walton Hall are open to the public.

Daresbury
Ches. PO, tel, stores. Half a mile up the road from Keckwick Bridge. Appealing village on a hill, where Charles Lutwidge Dodgson, better known as Lewis Carrol, was born in 1832. His father was vicar of Daresbury (pronounced Darzby) and they lived until 1843 in the Old Parsonage, Newton-by-Daresbury, 2 miles south of the church. The home was burnt down in 1883 – the site is now marked by a plaque, standing in an open field on Glebe Farm. The church has a Lewis Carrol memorial window, bright and cheerful, where he is shown with characters from 'Alice in Wonderland.'

BOATYARDS
Ⓑ **Thorn Marine** London Bridge, Stockton Heath. (Warrington 65129). Ⓢ Ⓦ Gas, chandlery, sweets, ice cream.

PUBS
London Bridge Stockton Heath. Canalside.
Walton Arms Higher Walton. Food, garden.
Ring o' Bells Daresbury. Unspoilt old pub.

The Bridgewater Canal at Lymm. *Derek Pratt*

Lymm

Where the canal comes to only a ¼ mile from
the Manchester Ship Canal, the houses of
Stockton Heath merge into those of
Grappenhall crowded to the north, while to the
south the old village survives. The canal makes
a dog leg turn passes Thelwall and under the
M6 Motorway south of the vast and infamous
Thelwall Viaduct which climbs laboriously over
the ship canal. There are fine views of the
distant Pennines to the north before the canal
makes a very pleasing passage through the heart
of Lymm, whose cobbled streets come down
almost to the water's edge. There are
convenient temporary moorings here.

Lymm
*Ches. PO, tel, stores, banks, fish & chips,
launderette.* The 17thC Lymm Cross, with
replica wooden stocks close by, stands on a rock
out-crop just a few yards from the canal in the
centre of this hilly and attractive little town,
which has retained its intimate character in
spite of its proximity to Warrington. Craft of
the Lymm Cruising Club line the banks, and
there are several fine canalside residences.
Thelwall
Ches. A short walk north from Thelwall
underbridge will bring you to a ferry where, for
a minimal charge, you will be rowed across the
Ship Canal.
Grappenhall
Ches. PO, tel, stores. A fine group of buildings
on cobbled streets survive around the church of
St Wilfred, where the village stocks remain.
There are 2 pubs.

PUBS
🍺 **Golden Fleece** Lymm. Canalside. Food,
garden, children's room.
🍺 **Spread Eagle** Town centre, Lymm.
There are plenty of pubs in Lymm.
🍺 **Ram's Head** Grappenhall. Food.
🍺 **Parr Arms** Grappenhall. Food.

Bollington

The canal leaves Lymm, passes the village of
Outrington to the north and a row of smart new
houses to the south, each with a canalside
garden and barking dog, before entering
surroundings which are surprisingly rural.
Rows of moored boats, some in an advanced
state of decay, announce the presence of 2
useful boatyards. The fields then gently fall
away into the valley of the River Bollin, which
the Bridgewater crosses on a large
embankment, with fine views of the
Manchester Ship Canal and Dunham Park, the
last greenery before Sale and Manchester. The
Bollin Aqueduct is a new concrete and steel
construction, built to replace the original stone
trough which breached disastrously in August
1971 and resulted in a 2-year closure. It cost
£125,000 to repair. *PO, stores, fish and chips* are
south of Seamons Moss Bridge.

Dunham Massey Hall Until recently the seat
of the Earl of Stamford, now owned by the
National Trust. The beautiful 18thC house
stands in a wooded park, with deer and an
Elizabethan mill. Access is via Bollington, over
the footbridge near the Swan with Two Nicks.
Open daily except Fri, Apr–Oct. Restaurant &
shop. Admission charge.
Dunham Town
Gt Manchester. A small scattered farming
village.
Bollington
Ches. A compact and attractive village, with a
fine old pub.
Outrington
Ches. PO, tel, stores. A good place for supplies.

BOATYARDS

Ⓑ **Lymm Marina** Warrington Lane, Lymm.
(2945). ⓇⓌⒹ Gas, chandlery, repairs, service,
boat sales, slipway, toilets.
Ⓑ **Hesford Marine** Warrington Lane, Lymm.
(4639). ⓌⒹ Gas, moorings, slipway, crane,
chandlery, winter storage, boat & engine sales
and repairs, toilets.

PUBS

🍺 **Bay Malton** By Seamons Moss Bridge.
Food, bowling green, overnight mooring, Ⓡ.
🍺 **Axe & Cleaver** Dunham Town. Food,
garden.
🍺 **Swan with Two Nicks** Bollington. Fine old
pub with good food.
🍺 **Ye Olde No 3** Bollington Wharf. Food,
garden.

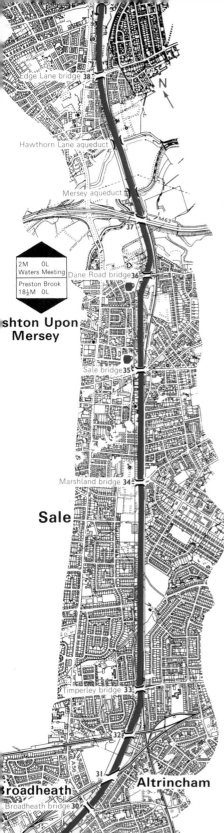

Sale

Beyond Seamons Moss Bridge the buildings close in on the canal, and the countryside disappears from view. Among the derelict buildings and graffiti stands the superb Victorian Linotype Factory, dated 1897, where metal printing type was manufactured. Moored by Timperley Bridge are assorted craft of the Sale Cruising Club. The electric suburban railway closes in from the south east and escorts the canal all the way through Sale and on into Stretford – as the trains hurry by you can enjoy a more relaxing 3mph. There are 2 convenient canalside pubs before the canal is crossed by the M63 motorway, and then itself crosses the River Mersey. A large expanse of graves heralds the entrance to Stretford, followed by the moorings of the Stretford Boat Club.

Sale
Gt Manchester. EC Wed. All Services. A residential suburb of Manchester, transformed from a farming community by the building in 1849 of the Altrincham to Manchester Railway – hence most of its buildings are Victorian or later. St Martin's Church is, however, 18thC and has a hammer beam roof. The clock tower of the town hall, built in 1914, is a prominent landmark. It is useful for supplies, which are conveniently close to Sale Bridge. The northern part of Sale merges into Ashton Upon Mersey, unremarkable except as the birthplace of Stanley Houghton (1881–1913) who wrote 'The Dear Departed' in 1908 and 'Hindle Wakes' in 1912.

Altrincham
Gt Manchester. EC Wed. A few black-and-white-timbered buildings remain in the market square of what was once a small market town. Later in the 18thC it became a textile manufacturing centre, and is now, inevitably, a dormitory town.

BOATYARDS

Ⓑ **Rathbone Bros** Longford Dry Dock, Longford Bridge, Stretford. (061-865 1880). Slipway, dry dock, boat building & repairs. *Closed winter weekends.*

PUBS

🍺 **Bridge Inn** Canalside at Dane Road Bridge. *Shop & launderette nearby.*
🍺 **The Railway** Canalside at Sale Bridge. Food.

Manchester

There are many bridges and
buildings, over the canal in
Manchester-these have been
omitted where they obscure
the canal.

Manchester

At Waters Meeting the original main line of the
canal is joined – to the north west is Barton,
Leigh and the connection with the Leeds &
Liverpool Canal which crosses the Pennines to
Leeds; to the east is the centre of the
Manchester and Rochdale Canal, which itself,
as the name implies, once crossed the hills to
Rochdale before it fell into disuse. It is now
time to make sure you know where the weed
hatch is – and if you have wire cutters and a
hacksaw so much the better. The Bridgewater's
route is now hemmed in by factory walls and
fences, which bear striking evidence of the local
spray paint suppliers success with those who
wish to declare publicly their allegiance to
MUFC (Manchester United Football Club) on
any relatively graffiti-free wall surface. The
floodlights of this famous football club tower
above the canal, which passes between the
ground and the massive (and almost empty)
docks of the Ship Canal. Old Trafford Cricket
ground, the home of Lancashire Cricket Club
and a Test Match venue is a little further south.
The Ship Canal is now very close – more empty
docks are passed before Hulme Lock Branch,
which connects the 2 canals, is reached. There
are moorings here on a narrow isthmus isolated
from the surrounding factories and roads – it is
not particularly attractive, and trains pass
frequently high above, but it is a safe spot to
spend the night before tackling the locks of the
Rochdale and Ashton Canals (after Castlefield
Junction the next mooring safe from the
attentions of the mischief makers is Fairfield
Junction). The Bridgewater ends and the short
navigable (most of the time) stretch of the
Rochdale begins at Castlefield Junction – the
first of the 9 wide locks is just after the bridge.
The lock gear is anti-vandal locked (use the
BWB anti-vandal key) and heavy to operate –
this first lock is opened by winding chains over
a roller. Some of the ratchets have no stops –
but there is plenty of rubbish lying around, so it
is not too difficult to wedge the paddles open
(mind your fingers). The canal now creeps
between the backs of tall buildings festooned
with steaming pipes where the clear water
reveals a prodigious amount of rubbish, some
of it defying decent description. There is,
however, a certain faded grandeur about the
elaborate railway arches, and tantalising
glimpses of Victorian buildings invite
exploration – but unfortunately this is no place
to leave the boat. Finally the canal crawls under
an 18 storey office block where a lock lurks
among concrete pillars, dim lights and heaps of
rubbish. The Rochdale Canal Office (see page
23) is next to the top lock, and here, if you
haven't already done so, you can pay a hefty
licence fee for navigating these 2 miles of city
centre canal. Sharp right and sharp left turns
bring you to the start of the Ashton Canal, and
the climb to Fairfield Junction (see page 120).

Manchester
All services. It is a pity that Manchester does
little to welcome canal travellers. The provision
of safe moorings would allow navigators to visit
what is one of Britain's finest Victorian cities, a
monument to 19thC commerce and the textile
boom. There is an incredible wealth of
Victorian buildings still surviving in spite of
redevelopment – the Town Hall and the
surrounding streets being a particularly rich
area (north of Oxford Street Bridge). St Peter's
Square, by the Town Hall, was the site of the
'Peterloo Massacre' in 1819, when a meeting
demanding political reform was brutally
dispersed by troops carrying drawn sabres.
Eleven people were killed and many more were
injured. The Free Trade Hall, home of the
Hallé Orchestra, is a little further along the
road. Built in 1856 on the site of the original
Free Trade Hall, it was badly damaged in
World War II, but was subsequently rebuilt to
its original Palladian design. There is theatre,
ballet and cinema, art galleries, a wealth of
interesting buildings and the superb North
Western Museum of Science and Industry in
Grosvenor Street. Victorian shopping arcades,
many pubs with an excellent choice of good
beer, many excellent restaurants – one being an

Indian Tandoori house, in Sackville Street, between the sixth and seventh lock up, all a short walk from the canal. What a pity that most navigators feel safest if they charge through as quickly as possible.

Information Centres In Portland Street, not far east of Ducie Street Junction, and in the Town Hall.

Manchester Ship Canal
The Harbour Master, The Port of Manchester, Manchester Ship Canal Co, Dock Office, Manchester. (061-872 2411). The canal was opened in 1894 at a cost of £15½ million and carries ships up to 15,000 tons displacement. It is 36 miles long and connects the tidal Mersey at Eastham to Manchester. The Weaver Navigation, the Bridgewater and the Shropshire Union connect with it.
Unfortunately the upper 23 miles are due to be closed to commercial traffic in 1987, since it is only the 13 miles from Eastham to Runcorn which remain viable.
Pleasure craft wishing to navigate on the Ship Canal must complete an application form demanding stringent standards of

seaworthiness (and third party insurance for £50,000), and return it to the Harbourmaster at the above address at least 48 hours before entering the canal.

BOATYARDS

Rochdale Canal Company 75 Dale Street, Manchester. (061-236 2456). Licences for their 2-mile stretch of canal cost £17 if bought in advance (1985 prices), and £2 more if bought on the day. The flight is *usually open Mon–Sat 09.30–17.00 and Sun mornings*, with last entry into the flight *at 15.15* (the top lock is padlocked outside these times). In practice these times may be changed from day to day and there are often chronic water shortages due to vandalism, so it is a good idea to ring and check before you attempt your passage.

PUBS

There are many fine pubs in Manchester.
🍺✗ **Westward Ho!** A floating pub and restaurant on the Ship Canal, to the north of Cornbrook Bridge.

The Rochdale Canal passes through the heart of Manchester, heemed in by high walls and tall buildings. *David Perrott*

Worsley

This is a very interesting section of canal, well worth visiting. What was the original line of the canal leaves Waters Meeting through the vast Trafford Park Industrial Estate to cross the Manchester Ship Canal on the impressive Barton Swing Aqueduct (*open 09.00–17.00 every day*). There is a useful boatyard just to the north of the aqueduct – the closest canal services to the city centre. Curving through the suburbs of Salford the navigation reaches the village of Worsley and the entrance to the underground mines which provided its *raison d'être*. It is now possible to navigate into the Delph to view the entrance tunnels where iron ore colours the water bright ochre. After Worsley the M62 motorway and its attendant slip roads cross the canal, which then heads west through parkland on its way to Leigh.

Worsley
Gt Manchester. EC Wed. PO, tel, stores, garage.
Originally an estate village dating from the 18th–19thC, now recognised as the birthplace of British canals. Coal had been mined in Worsley since the 14thC, originally from the surface, and later by sinking shafts. It is thought that a drainage sough, common in underground workings, may have provided the germ of the idea for an underground canal network to bring the coal out. John Gilbert, the Duke of Bridgewater's agent, probably designed the system, which included an inclined plane on a 1 in 4 gradient. Work started at the same time as the building of the canal to Manchester, and eventually 46 miles of tunnels were hewn out. A particular kind of double ended tub boat was used underground, called a 'starvationer', carrying up to 12 tons of coal. The old canal basin at Worsley Delph, with its entrance tunnels to the mines, is still intact, and full length narrow boats can enter the wind – smaller craft can navigate the entrance tunnels. The basin is overlooked by Worsley Old Hall (now a restaurant), the half-timbered Court House and the Lantern Gallery. The church, by George Gilbert Scott, 1846, has a spire decorated with crockets and gargoyles – inside there is a rich collection of Duke of Bridgewater monuments.

Salford
Gt Manchester. Although now merged with Manchester, Salford was granted its charter 80 years before that of its now larger neighbour. It has a fine new university, built in 1967, and a Roman Catholic cathedral dating from 1855. It is, however, most widely known as being the subject of many paintings by the artist L. S. Lowry (1887–1976). It is less widely known that he gained his inspiration by walking the streets of Salford for many years as a rent collector, only painting in the evenings and at weekends – a fact to which he would never willingly admit. There is a wonderful collection of his paintings in Salford Art Gallery, Peel Park.

Eccles
Gt Manchester. EC Wed. All services. Monks Hall Museum, Wellington Road, contains an important collection of Nasmyth machine tools and relics. *Closed Sun.*

Patricroft
Gt Manchester. All services. Here are the Bridgewater Mills, established in 1836 by Nasmyth, who invented the steam hammer. Now a Royal Ordnance factory.

Barton upon Irwell
Gt Manchester. PO, tel, stores, garage. In an interesting position overlooking the 2 canals. The richly decorated Catholic church is by Pugin, 1867.

Barton Aqueduct One of the wonders of the waterways, it carries the Bridgewater Canal over the Manchester Ship Canal. Designed by Sir Edward Leader Williams, it was built in the early 1890s. Gates seal off the 234ft-long 800 ton section that swings at right angles to the Ship Canal over a central island. It replaced Brindley's earlier aqueduct over the Irwell. The aqueduct operates *daily 09.00–17.00.*

To Waters Meeting (page 22)

BOATYARDS

Ⓑ **Worsley Dry Docks** The Boatyard, Worsley, Manchester. (061-793 6767). W̄ Moorings, drydock. Egerton Narrow Boats operate from here.

Ⓑ **Lorenz & Co** 26 Worsley Road, Worsley, Manchester. (061-794 1441). Based just north of the Barton Swing Aqueduct at Barton Yard. R̄W̄D̄ P̄ and gas close by). Boat building and repair, engine repairs, overnight moorings. The closest boatyard to the centre of Manchester.

BOAT TRIPS

Lorenz & Co Address as above. Run regular summer Sunday afternoon trips from Worsley, other trips from Timperley and Manchester by arrangement.

PUBS & RESTAURANTS

🍺 **Bridgewater Hotel** Worsley. Canalside.

✗ **Worsley Old Hall** Restaurant. James Brindley stayed in this building while working on the new canal.

🍺 **Wellington Inn** Patricroft. Canalside.

🍺 **Dutton Arms** Barton. Canalside.

Worsley, on the Bridgewater Canal. Iron ore colours the water bright ochre here. *Derek Pratt*

Leigh

After the excitement of Barton and Worsley, the canal now passes through open farmland towards the mill town of Leigh, and its junction with the Leeds & Liverpool Canal. Raised canal banks beyond Boothshall Bridge reveal the problems of subsidence in this area, caused by mine workings. The colliery village of Astley Green is passed, and an industrial wasteland is entered. Soon the mill chimneys of Leigh appear, and the canal becomes the Leeds & Liverpool beyond Leigh Bridge. The familiar stop plank cranes of the Bridgewater finish here, and signs announce you are back in BWB territory. Wigan is 7¼ miles away (see page 81).

Leigh
Gt Manchester. EC Wed. All services. An archetypal mill town, dominated by the tall chimneys and brick edifices of the old textile industry. The largest is Alder Mill, built in red and yellow brick and terracotta, richly decorated. It dates from 1907. The fine Edwardian baroque Town Hall, 1904–7, faces the battlemented church of St Mary across the Market Place.

Astley Green
Gt Manchester. PO, tel, stores. Canalside colliery village dominated by a gaunt red brick Victorian church.

PUBS
🍺 **Eagle & Hawk** Chapel Street, Leigh. Food.
🍺 **Railway Twist** Lane, Leigh.
🍺 **Cart & Horses** Manchester Road, Astley Green.

CHESTERFIELD

Maximum dimensions

Length: 72′
Beam: 7′
Headroom: 7′ 6″
(Craft of 8′ 6″ beam *may* be able to proceed as
far as Clayworth, depending on the height of
the superstructure).

Mileage

WEST STOCKWITH to
Drakesholes Tunnel: 6½
Hayton: 12
Retford lock: 15¼
Oberton lock: 22¼
WORKSOP Town lock: 25½

Locks: 16

The Chesterfield Canal was surveyed and largely built by James Brindley, who did not survive to see its opening. He called a public meeting in Worksop in 1769 to launch his project, which was estimated to cost £100,000 and to take 4 years to build. Its object was to provide trade outlets for the industries based on lead, coal and other resources in the Chesterfield area. Up to then, products from the area had to go by pack mule to Bawtry and then down the River Idle to West Stockwith on the Trent.

Construction of the canal was authorised by Act of Parliament in 1771, and work started in July that year. Owing to the difficulty of building the 2895-yd tunnel at Norwood, the work exceeded the 4-year estimate and the navigation was not opened until the 12 September 1777. Meanwhile the estimated cost of £100,000 rose to an actual £152,000 as a result of fraudulent dealings by the Company's agent John Varley and the main contractor, Hugh Henshall (James Brindley's brother-in-law). Traffic built up steadily to a peak of over 200,000 tons in 1848, but in that year the canal was bought by the Manchester & Lincoln Union Railway (later the Great Central). Traffic immediately began to fall off, and 10 years later was down to 110,000 tons. Mining subsidence hastened the decline of the waterway – Norwood Tunnel was particularly vulnerable – and the heavily locked section from Worksop to Chesterfield was unnavigable by 1896. By 1906, only 40 boats were left working the canal, and by 1939 a mere 20,000 tons were carried annually. The navigation was temporarily resuscitated by the transport of munitions during the War, but came to an end in the 1950s, when the small traffic finished from Walkeringham brickworks (near Gringley) to the Trent.

During the 1960s voluntary working parties undertook an extensive programme of restoration, and now the navigation is in good condition for pleasure craft. The restored section, saved in the nick of time from complete decay, runs from Worksop to West Stockwith, and has 16 locks.

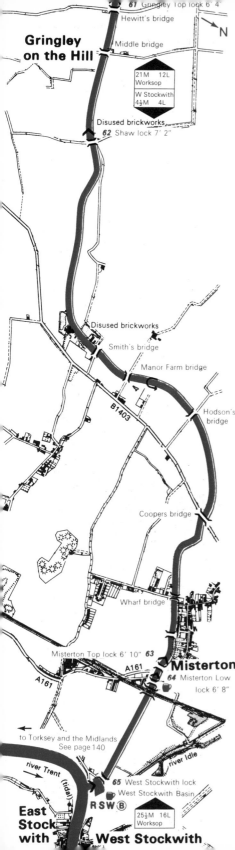

West Stockwith

The church spire of East Stockwith stands
opposite the entrance to the Chesterfield Canal,
just downstream of a sharp bend in the River
Trent. The lock here is operated by a lock
keeper. Just above the lock is a basin housing a
boatyard, a boat club, a slipway (apply to the
lock keeper), and plenty of moored pleasure
boats. A pub is nearby. This is obviously an
excellent safe mooring to keep a sea-going boat.
Leaving the basin for the gradual 15-lock rise to
Worksop, the navigator must notice the
tremendous contrast between the great tideway
of the River Trent and this little canal, picking
its way through the countryside. At Misterton
there are 2 locks close together, with a canalside
pub at the bottom. The canal's passage through
the village is a pleasant one. At the new
Cooper's Bridge the canal emerges into quiet
farmland, heading south towards and then
along the ridge of low hills that is capped by the
village of Gringley. There are 2 disused
brickyards along here – they supplied the canal
with its last commercial traffic, sending bricks
to Stockwith for the Trent. The yards were
closed down in 1948. The course of the canal is
entirely rural and pleasant, passing well
established but often decaying farm buildings
that are mostly built of the rich red brick that is
so common in north Nottinghamshire. At
Gringley top lock the little lock cottage has
a delightful garden, with creepers, climbing
roses and flowers on the towpath.

Navigational Note
The river lock at West Stockwith basin is
operated by a keeper. (Gainsborough 890204).
The operation of the lock is dependent on the
height of the tide, but a passage can usually be
made 2½ hrs before to 4½ hrs after high water.
For a passage between *22.00–08.00*, 24 hrs
notice should be given.

Gringley-on-the-Hill
Notts. PO, tel, stores, garage. Situated along the
top of a ridge of hills, the village is about a
mile's walk up from the canal. Its high situation
is emphasised by the tower of the old windmill.
Gringley is a quiet and attractive place with
plenty of handsome, mellow houses – and a
butcher's shop. The pretty stone church
commands the village. Its most striking aspect
inside is probably the north side of the nave,
whose arches are leaning drastically outwards.
A small rise on a level with the church tower
gives a good view – over the flat lands to the
north and the hills of Nottinghamshire to the
south. On a clear day the pinnacles of Lincoln
Cathedral can sometimes be seen, nearly 20
miles to the south east.

Misterton
*Notts. PO, tel, stores, garage, banks (with
irregular hours).* Although attractive from the
canal, this village is not really very fascinating.
The 2 pubs are in the older part, which
surrounds the curiously shaped church; a
stubby spire stands heavily beside its rather
low, flat nave roof. It was rebuilt in the 19thC
after being struck by lightning. The village also
has a thriving Methodist church, like most of
the places in this area. (John Wesley came from
nearby Epworth.)

West Stockwith
Notts. PO, tel, stores. An interesting riverside
village at the junction not only of the
Chesterfield Canal with the Trent but also of
the River Idle with the Trent. The Idle was
once a busy navigation up to Bawtry, so West
Stockwith must have been a very prosperous
port in days gone by. (Adventurous navigators
still penetrate occasionally up to Bawtry on the
flood tide in a suitable boat, having arranged
with the Severn Trent Water Authority for the
big steel floodgate in Stockwith to be raised.)
The village extends along the west bank of the
River Trent, although bank raising measures
over the years have shut out a view of the river
from ground level. The houses are old, and
remind one of a typical coastal village. The
plain 18thC brick church preserves the illusion.
East Stockwith is just across the river,
tantalisingly out of reach. The 2 communities
used to be connected by a ferry, but as so often
on this river, the ferry has vanished. In a way,
the total lack of communication with the other

village, only 50yds away, serves to enhance the
magical sense of remoteness that Stockwith
possesses – especially when one sees the big
barges appearing round the bend on every tide,
churning past the 2 villages and then as quickly
disappearing again.

BOATYARDS

Ⓑ **Trent Valley Narrowboats** The Yacht
Basin, West Stockwith, nr Doncaster, S. Yorks
(Gainsborough 890 450) Ⓡ Ⓢ Ⓦ Ⓓ Boat hire,
slipway, gas, boat building & repairs, mooring,
chandlery, winter storage, toilets.

PUBS

🍺 **White Hart** Gringley-on-the-Hill.
🍺 **Blue Bell** Gringley-on-the-Hill. *Evenings
only Mon–Fri.*
🍺 **White Hart** Misterton, near the church.
🍺 **Windmill** Misterton, near the church. Fish
& chips nearby.
🍺 **Packet Inn** Misterton. Canalside, at the foot
of the locks.
🍺 **Crown** Canalside, at West Stockwith Basin.
🍺 **Red Hart** West Stockwith. By the junction
of the Rivers Idle and Trent.

rakeholes Tunnel on the Chesterfield Canal. *Derek Pratt*

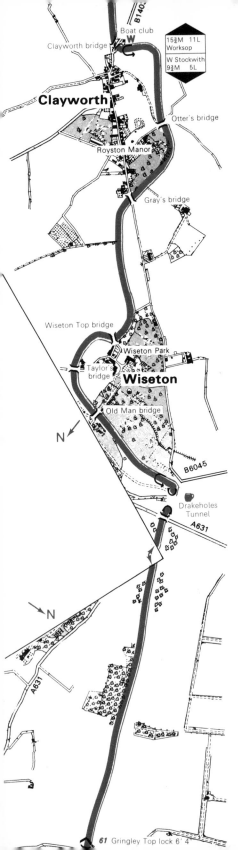

Clayworth

This is a thoroughly delightful stretch of canal.
Leaving Gringley Top Lock, the navigation
goes along the bottom of the ridge of hills,
before turning sharply south east and heading
for Drakeholes Tunnel. All the way from
Gringley to Drakeholes the canal is heavily
overhung by trees. Plenty of wild life lives here
near the water's edge, especially coots,
moorhens, water rats, and bats. It is very
secluded, but the intimate feeling of the thickly
wooded cutting preceding the tunnel has been
ruined by the construction of a large road
bridge. The tunnel, which is a mere 154yds
long, is cut through rock and is mostly unlined.
At the south end one emerges to find a sharp
corner at a mooring site, where there is also a
turning place for full-length narrow boats, and
a slipway owned by the Retford & Worksop
Boat Club. A handsome pub stands nearby.
Leaving Drakeholes, the canal is still
accompanied by woods as it reaches Wiseton
Park, passing the stern features of a bearded
man on the parapet of Old Man Bridge. The
canal then skirts the Park's kitchen garden and
heads off through a wooded cutting to
Clayworth. The straight road that crosses the
canal at Gray's Bridge is of Roman origin. The
navigation circles round the village, ending up
with a sharp turn to the right at Clayworth
Bridge. The white building by the bridge used
to be a pub (The White Hart). It is now a boat
club base, so a good lookout for other boats
should be maintained when negotiating the
bridge.

Clayworth
Notts. PO, tel, stores. A quiet and pleasant
village extending along a single main street.
The houses are of all periods, the new blending
well with the old. The Retford & Worksop Boat
Club is based at the old pub at Clayworth and
welcomes visitors to the clubhouse. There are
good moorings and a water tap here. In the old
days a passenger boat used to run every
Saturday from this pub to Retford, so that the
villagers of Clayworth, Hayton and
Clarborough could take their produce to
Retford Market. The goods were loaded into
the 'packet' boat on the Friday night, then the
people would return early on the Saturday
morning, leaving at 06.30 to reach Retford by
08.30. The boat used to return in the evening
when the market closed.

Wiseton
Notts. PO, tel. A superbly elegant estate village
set in a landscaped park, still clearly fulfilling
its original manorial function. Trees and grass
separate the various buildings, of which the
large stable with its handsome clock tower is
the most significant. The hall, a modern red
brick building which replaced the original in
1962, is well hidden behind high walls.

PUBS
- **Brewers Arms** Clayworth.
- **Blacksmiths Arms** Clayworth.
- **The Griff Inn** Drakeholes. Unusual shape
for a canal pub.

Hayton

The canal now leaves the woods and low hills to the north and heads southwards through more open farmland towards Retford. From Clayworth to Hayton there is a 2-mile stretch without a single bridge, only green fields and hedgerows accompanying the navigation on its quiet course. Approaching Hayton, there is a pub by the bridge but otherwise the only signs of the village are a succession of old farms and bridges – one of them extremely narrow. Near 1 of these bridges is the very ancient stone church. At Clarborough Wharf there is another canalside pub, with good moorings. South of here the railway embankment draws near as the canal arrives at the first lock for 9 miles. Whitsunday Pie Lock is apparently so called because a local farmer's wife baked a vast pie on Whit Sunday for the navvies who had that day completed construction of the lock. This lock is the last wide lock on the canal as one travels towards Worksop. The cottage near the lock was built this century, of bricks fired at the brickyards near Gringley and naturally brought to this site by canal boat. Yet another canalside pub is soon encountered, before the navigation begins to follow its circuitous course round East Retford.

Clarborough
Notts. PO, tel, stores, garage, fish & chips. An unexciting village straggling along the main road.
Hayton
Notts. Tel. A quiet farming village, stretching along the road parallel to the canal. The church is near the canal and dates from 1120.

PUBS
🍺 **Hop Pole Inn** Canalside, at Hop Pole Bridge (A620).
🍺 **Gate** Clarborough. Canalside, near Clarborough top bridge.
🍺 **Kings Arms** Clarborough. Fish & chips opposite.
🍺✕ **Boat** Hayton. Near Hayton low bridge. Fish & chips here.

Retford

The canal's twisting passage through Retford is
outstandingly pleasant – though not by design.
It just happens that almost all the way through
the town, the canal is accompanied by green –
either grazing fields, or common land, or water
meadows (however unkempt), or at the west
end of the town by a long and treelined
cemetery. In the town centre one encounters
the first of the narrow locks, with a large canal
warehouse beside it. West of here the canal
crosses 3 minute aqueducts, then a double bend
and an old iron foot bridge lead to West Retford
Lock, overlooked by large trees and old houses.
Beyond the main road bridge the canal is still
lined by trees and bushes as it invades the very
middle of the extensive cemetery. The busy
East Coast railway line crosses here, and while
the navigation now begins to meander through
open farmland, the noise of the frequent
express trains thundering along the track takes
a long time to recede. In the open countryside
along here are the 4 Forest Locks. At the third
one up is a BWB permanent mooring site; and
there is a water point right beside the top gate.
The straight road crossing at the nearby Barnby
Wharf Bridge was a Roman highway. It was, in
fact, the original course of the Great North
Road; but 200 years ago the citizens of Retford
got the road diverted to pass through their
town, thereby increasing its importance and
prosperity. They must now be equally relieved
to have rid themselves of it again.

East Retford
Notts. EC Wed, Mon. MD Sat. All services. A
market town with good railway connections
(passenger services in 4 directions) and light
industry. There is a funfair held on 23 March
and a sheep fair on 2 October. The market
square is the only area of any interest in
Retford, and this is indeed superb, with lots of
cheerfully uneven Georgian terraced houses
jumbled up with lesser, newer buildings. All
are put to shame by the flamboyant Town Hall
built in 1868. In front of it is a stone called the
Broad Stone, and when a plague raged in the
town many years ago people making cash
transactions would put their coins into a
vinegar-filled vessel on this pedestal. The
vendor picking the money out of the vinegar
thus ran less risk of catching the disease from
the purchaser, it was thought.
East Retford Church A splendid cruciform
structure of great dignity and elegance, all set
about with battlements, pinnacles, and fine
foliate ornament. The nave is tall, and
incorporates a generous clerestory giving light
to the interior, while there is a peal of 10 bells in
the tower. Outside, the church is guarded by a
mean-looking black 24-pounder cannon,
captured at Sevastopol in 1855.

BOAT TRIPS

Spitfire Narrow Boat Cruises Fourways,
Romper Road, Saundby, Retford. (Saundby
729). Run trips on the canal from various point
– public cruises and private charter.

PUBS

White Hart Hotel The Market Place,
Retford. Lunches and dinners daily. Ancient
coaching establishment.
Clinton Arms Retford, not far from Retford
Lock.
Hop Pole Retford. Canalside.
Packet Inn Canalside, at Gas House Bridge,
Retford. This used to be the terminus for the
weekly market boat from Clayworth.
Ship Wharf Road, Retford.

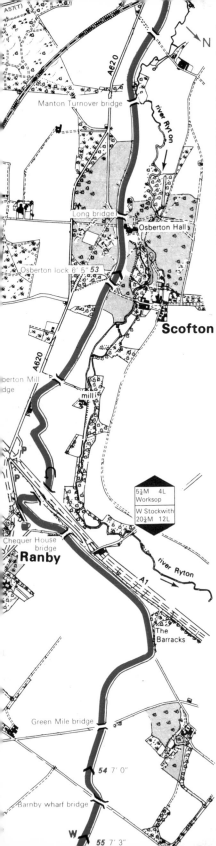

Osberton Park

Leaving Forest Top Lock, the canal now
wanders westwards before turning sharply
south as it meets the noisy A1 road. There used
to be a big army barracks here during the
1914–18 War, but now only a small cottage
survives as a reminder. The road follows the
canal very closely for over ½ a mile, and its
presence is deafening. Fortunately a thick
hedge serves to screen it. At Ranby the canal
begins once again to follow a winding course,
passing under the A1 before making for the
haven of Osberton Park. The little lock here,
where the towpath crosses over, introduces one
of the most attractive stretches of the whole
canal, for one passes through a country estate,
which looks as carefully maintained now as it
doubtless did in the 18thC. The canal goes
straight past the stables at Osberton Hall.
Manton railway viaduct, consisting of low but
heavily braced red brick arches dwarfs the little
accommodation bridge over the canal. Nearby
the long-standing pit heaps of Manton Colliery
have been landscaped and grassed.

Osberton Hall
Built in 1806 by James Wyatt and enlarged and
altered in 1853 (Private).

Scofton
This is the tiny estate village for Osberton Hall.
It looks decayed now, but the old stable block is
impressive. It is of course surmounted by a
clock tower. The church built in 1830 has been
completely restored, at great expense. All the
roof lead has been renewed, the windows have
been rebuilt, a new red carpet has been laid,
and central heating has been installed. The
inside of the church now looks brand new, and
for the visitor is a refreshing sight.

Ranby
Notts. Tel, garages (on A1). A small rambling
village which manages to retain some charm in
spite of being practically on top of the A1. The
willow trees that line the canal bank near the
village are the gesture of a local tree-loving
landowner. There is a pub on the canal, the
only one for miles in either direction.

PUBS

🍺 **Chequers** Ranby. Canalside.

Worksop

Leaving Manton Colliery the canal now negotiates 2 locks before reaching Worksop. The canal's course into Worksop is fairly open, as the towpath is also a minor public road. There is a canal pub along here, and a good place to tie up for the Canal Tavern is at either side of the old Pickford's warehouse that straddles the canal. One can still see the trapdoors above the water where the goods used to be hauled straight up out of the boats. The BWB yard is just through the warehouse, and this is a remarkable oasis of privacy and quiet in the town centre. Worksop Town Lock is by the yard. Just beyond the lock, the navigation is very narrow for a short stretch. The remaining 20 miles of the canal to Chesterfield are no longer a through navigation although parts have been restored, and a trip boat operates on the summit level near Kiveton Park station. At the turn of the century there was little trade on the canal and the 3100yd tunnel on the summit level at Norwood collapsed because of mining

Worksop

subsidence. There is an attractive walk along the towpath of the old canal, and there are good railway connections from Worksop and Retford with the canalside stations of Kiveton Park and Shireoaks. The unnavigable section of the canal still feeds water into the navigable section.

Navigational note

The winding hole above Worksop Town Lock is suitable for full length (70ft) craft.

Worksop

Notts. EC Thur. MD Wed, Sat. All services. An unlovely town in the centre of the north Nottinghamshire coal field – which has contributed much to the present prosperity and ugliness of the area. Old buildings of note in Worksop are the Priory and its gatehouse.
The Priory Near Prior Well Bridge. The church dates from the 12thC, although it suffered badly under Henry VIII's policy towards monasteries. Much rebuilding has taken place since then: in fact in 1970–2 the superstructure was added to, incorporating a new spire. There are interesting paintings and monuments inside the church, and a gruesome relic from Sherwood Forest – a skull with the tip of an arrow embedded in it.
14thC Gatehouse This was given to the priory under a trust by the Duke of Newcastle.
Worksop Museum Memorial Avenue. Displays showing the natural and local history of the Worksop area. Also on show is a portion of a high relief sculpture, originally part of the Great Altar of Pergamon in Asia Minor, c150 BC. In 1625 it formed part of the 'Arundel Marbles' and in the mid 18thC it was sent to Worksop Manor after being found 'dumped' beside the Thames. It was rediscovered in 1960 cemented to an outside wall of a house in Worksop. *Museum open daily except Thur and Sun.*
Information Centre (Worksop 475531, ext 431.)

Within a few miles of the town there are some interesting places and some beautiful countryside to visit, although a car or a bicycle is needed to reach them. All around are the surviving woods of Sherwood Forest, while to the south of the town is the area called the Dukeries, each of the adjacent estates of Thoresby, Clumber and Welbeck having been owned by a Duke. Welbeck is now an army college, Thoresby Hall and Park are open to the public. Clumber House was demolished in 1938 but the Park, owned by the National Trust, is one of its most visited properties. There are superb avenues of trees in this park. Three miles west of Worksop is an outstanding building well worth visiting. This is the tiny Steetley Chapel, which has been described by one expert as 'the most perfect and elaborate specimen of Norman architecture to be found anywhere in Europe'. There is a delightfully elaborate triple rounded porch and a beautiful apse. The windows are very narrow, so the interior is dark.

BOATYARDS

BWB Worksop Yard (Worksop 472788). RSW

PUBS

⬤ **Canal Tavern** Worksop. Near the BWB yard.
⬤ **Fisherman's Arms** Church Walk, Worksop.
⬤✗ **Lion Hotel** Bridge Street, Worksop.
⬤✗ **Royal Hotel** Bridge Street, Worksop.

EREWASH

Maximum dimensions

Trent Lock to Tamworth Road Bridge
Length: 78′
Beam: 14′ 3″
Headroom: 7′ 4″
Tamworth Road Bridge to Langley Mill
Length: 72′
Beam: 14′ 3″
Headroom: 6′

Mileage

TRENT LOCK to
Sandiacre Lock: 3¼
Stanton Ironworks: 5½
LANGLEY MILL: 11¾

Locks: 15

The Erewash is 1 of 5 canals built towards the end of the 18thC to carry coal from the pits of the Nottinghamshire/Derbyshire coalfield to the towns of the East Midlands. Completed in 1779 by the engineer John Varley, its success encouraged the promotion and construction, during the following decade, of the Cromford, Nottingham, Derby and Nutbrook Canals. The Erewash Canal is navigable for its entire 11¾-mile length from the River Trent to Langley Mill. Unlike its neighbours, the Cromford and Nottingham Canals, the Erewash never came under railway control but remained independent until its absorption into the Grand Union system in 1932.

Nationalisation of the canals in 1947 brought the Erewash Canal under the administration of the British Transport Commission and in 1962 this body closed to navigation the upper section from Gallows Inn to Langley Mill. The need to supply water to the lower section for navigation and industry, however, meant that the upper section had still to be maintained, and boats were allowed to navigate

it upon application to the Commission and subsequently to its successor, the British Waterways Board. With the cessation of narrow boat carrying in 1952, such boats had been few, but the growing interest in pleasure boating resulted in more and more craft venturing up the canal from the popular River Trent. With the increased use the canal gradually improved, and the news that the major portion of it was to be designated a 'remainder' waterway in the impending 1968 Transport Act was received locally with dismay. A public meeting led to the formation of the Erewash Canal Preservation and Development Association, a body consisting of representatives of boating and fishing interests, residents and local authorities. The need to convince local authorities of the value of the canal as an amenity was recognised at a very early stage and the association's efforts eventually met with success when in 1972 Derbyshire and Nottinghamshire County Councils agreed to share the cost, with the British Waterways Board, of the restoration of the canal to 'cruising waterway' standards.

An old photograph of Little Eaton Wharf on the now defunct Derby Canal, served by the Little Eaton Gangway.

Long Eaton

The Erewash Canal leaves the Trent Navigation at Trent Lock, a fascinating waterway junction. A long line of moored boats stretches from this junction for nearly ½ mile, including several houseboats nestling in the shade of the willow trees. To the south can be seen the towers of Ratcliffe Power Station, peeping over the top of Red Hill. At the 2 railway bridges is the concealed entrance to an interesting basin; once known as Sheet Stores Basin, this was an important railway depot where the tarpaulin sheets for covering railway wagons were made and repaired. (Nowadays, synthetic materials have rendered tarpaulin obsolete in this field). The basin was used for transhipment of coal between boats and trains; now it is full of pleasure boats, for a boatyard and a boat club are based here. North of this basin one sees the first of many canalside gardens that use the canal as a perfect background. Approaching Long Eaton, the canal passes under the A453 and then runs right beside it, a pleasant, tree-lined urban boulevard. The centre of Long Eaton is conveniently close. North of Long Eaton Lock the old lace mills with their ornamental capped chimneys overshadow the navigation. To the east, open country contains the extensive Toton railway sidings and the little River Erewash, which despite its name is not joined by the canal at any point. At Sandiacre is the only surviving lock cottage on the Erewash Canal (now the base of the ECPDA), and this lock is particularly significant because the Derby Canal used to branch off here. The Derby Canal Company shared this toll office until 1832, when they built their own lock house on the opposite bank of their canal, by the bridge. North of the big concrete bridge carrying the A52 is Sandiacre; just through the bridge is a delightfully landscaped free overnight mooring, with a properly kept lawn, flower beds and young trees. All services are nearby. Nearly a mile further on is Pasture Lock, in a pleasant setting between the partly hidden railway sidings and some water meadows.

Navigational note
Trent Lock should always be left *full*, with the top gates open, except when there is much traffic about. This will ensure that any flotsam coming down the canal is able to escape over the bottom gates. Boatmen intending to navigate the Erewash Canal should ensure they have a BWB anti-vandal key.

Sandiacre
Derbs. PO, tel, stores, garage, bank. These services are all conveniently near the canal, but there is not much of interest in this outskirt, except for the church, which is set on a rise called 'Stoney Clouds' (clearly visible from the canal at Pasture Lock). The church features some original Norman work inside, including carvings. The font is 600 years old.

The Derby Canal
The closure of the Derby Canal ended Derby's link with the navigable waterways which dated back to the time when the Danes sailed up the River Derwent to found the settlement of Deoraby. Navigation of the Derwent was never easy – the absence of navigation works and, later, the construction of water mills were obviously a great handicap – but it was not until 1796, with the completion of the canal, that navigation on the river ceased. The main line of the Derby Canal commenced at Swarkestone on the River Trent. Four locks, which like all the rest were built to take Upper Trent barges, lifted the canal to a junction with the Trent & Mersey Canal. A ¼-mile section of this canal was then used with the Derby Canal recommencing just before Swarkestone Lock. The main line then continued into Derby, where it crossed the Derwent on the level, and terminated at Little Eaton. A 9-mile long branch ran from Derby to connect with the Erewash Canal at Sandiacre, and a short

navigable feeder connected with the upper Derwent. The southern section (from Derby to the Trent) was an early casualty due to the double tolls payable on the Trent & Mersey, and the abandonment of the length to Little Eaton followed in 1935. The rest of the canal survived until 1964, when a Warrant of Abandonment was granted to the Derby Canal Company.

Long Eaton
Derbs. EC Thur. MD Fri, Sat. All services, plus a bingo hall and a speedway & stock car racing track. The town is an important junction for canals, railways and roads, and has little intrinsic character of its own. Its prosperity was based on the lace trade – nearby Nottingham has for a long time been the national centre of this industry. Long Eaton has an annual festival in May.

Trent Lock
An important waterway junction and a long-established boating centre. For motorists, Trent Lock is at the dead end of a narrow lane – but they flock there, for it has great charm and two fine pubs. Sailing clubs on the Trent fill and confuse the scene here; while across the river the steep wooded slopes of Red Hill are overlooked by the steaming towers of Ratcliffe Power Station. The busy railway line to the south disappears into the hill via 2 splendid blackened portals. Boats navigating the Trent in this rather complicated area should beware of straying too near Thrumpton Weir.

BOATYARDS
Ⓑ **Long Eaton Marina** Wyvern Avenue, Long Eaton, Nottingham. (Long Eaton 66539). Ⓡ Ⓦ Slipway, moorings and winter storage. Inboard engine repairs, welding and general metal work carried out. Do-it-yourself work encouraged.
Ⓑ **Mills Dockyard** Trent Lock, Long Eaton, Nottingham. (Long Eaton 3657). Ⓡ Ⓦ Moorings, dry-dock and chandlery.
Ⓑ **Davison's** Trent Lock, Long Eaton, Nottingham. (4643). Ⓢ Ⓦ Pump-out, hire cruisers, drydock, boat building and fitting out. *Closed Sun, and weekends in winter.*

PUBS
🍺 **Plough** Sandiacre, north of the main road bridge. Garden down to the canal bank.
🍺 **Red Lion** Sandiacre, by the main road bridge. The White Lion is next to it.
🍺 **Lord Nelson** Long Eaton by the A453 bridge.
🍺 **Royal Oak** Long Eaton by the A453 bridge.
🍺✗ **Steamboat Inn** Trent Lock, Sawley (Long Eaton 732606). Built by the canal company in 1791, when it was called the Erewash Navigation Inn, it is now a busy and popular venue. Handsome bars, restaurant and carvery, evening entertainment and Shipstones real ales. Garden, playground, children welcome. Their beer is delivered by narrowboat.
🍺✗ **Trent Navigation Inn** Trent Lock. Large popular pub facing the river. Huge garden. Meals available at The Carvery.

River Trent in Nottingham. *Derek Pratt.*

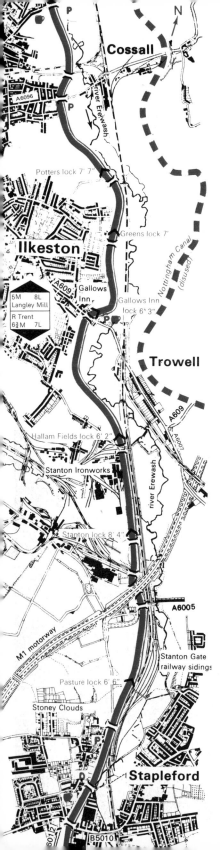

Ilkeston

At Stanton Gate the M1 motorway looms up
and then crosses the canal on its way to
Sheffield. On the west side, large spoil heaps
reveal a much older landmark – the Stanton
Ironworks. Between the ironworks and Stanton
Lock, a small pipe sticking out of the bank is
the only sign of the Nutbrook Canal, now filled
in. Beyond the ironworks, the outskirts of
Ilkeston loom up on the left side while, across
the shallow Erewash valley, the Nottingham
Canal appears from the east, twisting along the
contours of the hillside. Like the Erewash
Canal, its course is generally northerly, but the
2 waterways do not meet until Langley Mill.
Meanwhile the Erewash Canal passes extensive
low-lying playing fields before reaching the
Horse & Groom pub at Gallows Inn Lock.
North of Gallows Inn, the canal passes housing
estates on one side and water meadows and a
main line railway on the other. The town of
Ilkeston is on the hillside on the west side of the
canal. At the north end of the town is Common
Bottom Lock, whose balance beams, although
sturdy, are so crudely fashioned as to be
virtually uncarved tree trunks. A pub is near
the lock.

Ilkeston
Derbs. EC Wed. MD Sat. Cinema. A market
and textile town, with a compact main square.
The parish church of St Mary dates from 1150
and has an unusual 14thC stone screen. The
annual 3-day fair is held in the Market Place in
Oct.
Cossall
Notts. Tel. Cossall is a refreshing contrast to
Ilkeston, an attractive village built on top of a
hill, spreading gently down to the Nottingham
Canal. A narrow street winds among the
houses, all of which seem to be surrounded by
pretty gardens. The little church contains an
oak screen made by village craftsmen: in the
churchyard is a memorial to a soldier killed at
Waterloo. The remains of a moat are to be
found just to the east.
The Nutbrook Canal
This little branch off the Erewash Canal used to
lead for 4½ miles almost parallel to the
Erewash Canal and slightly west of it. But it has
been unnavigable since 1895 and is now totally
abandoned. The short section that used to pass
through the Stanton Ironworks was filled in in
1962 and is now quite untraceable.

PUBS
🍺 **Bridge** Canalside, below Common Bottom
Lock.
🍺 **Horse & Groom** Canalside, at Gallows Inn
Lock. Fish & chips, grocer and petrol nearby.

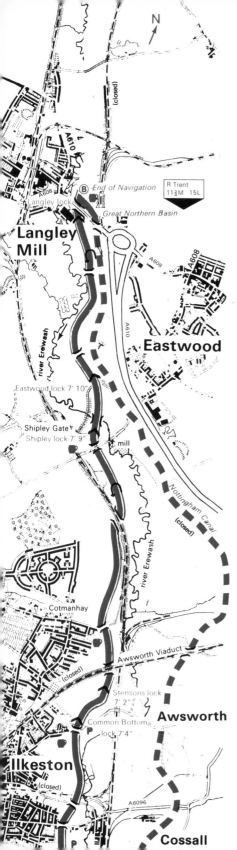

Langley Mill

The northernmost section of the Erewash Canal is more isolated than the rest, and is definitely more rural and attractive. As the tentacles of Ilkeston are left behind, a big trestle viaduct across the valley is passed; the inconspicuous River Erewash and beyond it the Nottingham Canal continue to wind their ways northwards. There are 2 pubs called The Bridge along here: the second is passed at Cotmanhay. The bridge it refers to is low (just over 6ft) because of mining subsidence. At Shipley Gate is the site of a long-abandoned railway and canal interchange wharf. There are 2 splendidly painted old canal buildings beside Shipley Lock – one was a stable and the other a slaughterhouse for worn-out canal horses. Just above the lock, the River Erewash creeps under the canal, which is carried above it on a very small aqueduct. Since this river is the county boundary between Derbyshire and Nottinghamshire, the canal now enters Nottinghamshire. The next lock – Eastwood Lock – features, like the lock further south, extremely crudely shaped wooden balance beams. Beyond the next very pleasant rural stretch is Langley Mill, where the canal terminates at the Great Northern Basin beyond the final lock. Boatmen who have navigated the whole of the Erewash to this point are invited to call at the cottage just above the old junction in order to obtain a free facsimile of the old Erewash Canal Company's bye laws.

Great Northern Basin
This restored basin once formed the junction of the Erewash, Cromford and Nottingham Canals. A feeder enters here from Moorgreen reservoir. Since it passes through a coal field on its way to the basin, it brings down a lot of coal silt – which over the years filled up the Great Northern Basin. Now the Erewash Canal Preservation & Development Association has restored the basin and lock, so that boats may reach a good mooring site with an enjoyable pub beside it. The Nottingham and Cromford Canals can never be restored here, for their closure was necessitated by mining subsidence – although substantial lengths of both canals are still in water, away from Langley Mill (the Cromford Canal Society runs horse drawn trips from Cromford Wharf during the summer (Wirksworth 3727)). Both canals pass through an interesting mixture of heavily industrial surroundings and quiet open countryside. The northern 5 miles of the Cromford Canal, from Ambergate to Cromford (a length still in water) is strongly recommended to all walkers, country lovers and especially industrial archaeologists. Explorers will find all kinds of exciting things, including 2 aqueducts and a fine old pumping station.
Langley Mill
Derbs. EC Wed. Near the head of the Erewash Canal, with the little Erewash river going past it, this is not a pretty place. Langley Mill stoneware pottery is made here in a very modern works.
Eastwood
Notts. EC Wed. PO, tel, stores, garage, bank.
Up on the hill east of the Great Northern Basin, this mining town is best known as the childhood home of D. H. Lawrence. He was born at 8A Victoria Street, and the early part of 'Sons and Lovers' is set in the town. At the Sun Inn a meeting in 1843 between local coal owners and iron masters led to the construction of the Midland Railway.

BOATYARDS

ⓑ **Langley Mill Boat Co** Great Northern Basin, Langley Mill. (Ilkeston 502525 or Derby 881 258). ⓡ ⓢ ⓦ ⓓ ⓔ Slipway, drydock, boat & engine repairs, mooring, toilets. *Open weekends.*

PUBS

🍺 **Great Northern** Canalside, at the junction. (The Great Northern Railway Company was at one time owner of the Nottingham Canal.)

🍺✕ **Shipley Boat Inn** Shipley Gate. Enormous modernised roadhouse 100yds from Shipley Lock. Lavish furnishings, several bars and a large restaurant.

🍺 **Bridge** Cotmanhay. Canalside, at the very low bridge.

Great Northern Basin, the terminus of the Erewash Canal. *Derek Pratt*

The famous Glory Hole in Lincoln. *Derek Pratt*

FOSSDYKE & WITHAM

Maximum dimensions

Fossdyke Navigation (Torksey to Lincoln)
Length: 75'
Beam: 15' 3"
Headroom: 12'
Witham Navigation (Lincoln to Boston)
Length: 75'
Beam: 15' 3"
Headroom: 9' 2"

Mileage

TORKSEY to
Saxilby: 5½
Brayford Pool, Lincoln: 11
Bardney: 20½
Southrey: 23¼
Kirkstead: 26¾
Dogdyke: 31¾
Antons Gowt: 40¼
BOSTON Grand Sluice: 42¾

Locks: 3

The Fossdyke Navigation was built in about 120 AD by the Romans, and is the oldest artificially constructed waterway in the country which is still navigable. It was designed to connect the River Witham (made navigable by the Romans) to the Trent and the Humber. The 2 navigations were used by the Danes when they invaded England, and later by the Normans to carry stone to build Lincoln Cathedral. Subsequently the Fossdyke and the Witham Navigations became the responsibility of various riparian landowners, and of the church. They gradually deteriorated and by the beginning of the 17thC were virtually impassable. But King James I transferred the Fossdyke to the Corporation of Lincoln, and from that time conditions improved. Acts of Parliament were passed in 1753 and 1762 for straightening and dredging both navigations, and in 1766 the Grand Sluice at Boston was built, to protect the Witham from the damaging effects of tides and floods. In the 18thC and 19thC further improvements were made, many related to the extensive drainage systems carried out throughout the Fenlands. Thus over a period of centuries the 2 navigations came to assume the wide, straight course that is so characteristic of them today.

In 1846 the navigations were leased to the Great Northern Railway Company, and immediately their revenue began to fall. Railway competition continued, and by the end of the 19thC both navigations were running at a loss. After a period of dormancy the Witham and Fossdyke became established as cruising waterways, as pleasure boats replaced the last surviving commercial operators.

Today their isolation and total lack of development attract many, while their survival preserves the pleasures of visiting Lincoln by boat; also Boston is one of the vital links between the inland waterway system and the open sea.

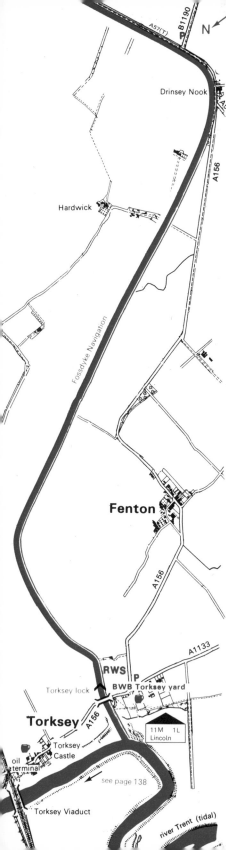

Torksey

The Fossdyke Navigation dates from Roman times and is the oldest artificial navigation in Britain. It leaves the tidal Trent at Torksey, ½ mile south of the railway viaduct. The lock may be operated only by the resident keeper, who should, if possible, be given notice of arrival (Torksey 202). The lock may be used at nearly all states of tide. Although the village is some way to the north, there are plenty of services available at the lock, including a grocery/chandlery, a garage and a pub. There is a good restaurant in the village. A great number of pleasure boats are moored above the lock. Leaving Torksey the canal twists slightly before settling down to a series of long, wide, dead straight reaches flanked by high banks. This sets the pattern for the course of the navigation all the way to Boston, which is 44 miles but only 2 locks from Torksey. The long straight reaches make the navigation somewhat unexciting, as the banks prevent boatmen from seeing much of the countryside; but the canal is quiet and pleasant, and the green banks harbour plenty of wild life, while cattle browse by the water. At Hardwick there used to be a ferry across the canal. At the end of a very long straight a busy main road joins, and the canal completely loses its privacy. They curve together towards Saxilby, passing a garage and an AA telephone box.

Torksey
Lincs. PO, tel. Once a Roman port, but now a small riverside village quite separate from the thriving settlement centred on the lock. The main feature is the ruined castle, whose gaping Tudor façade is best seen from the Trent. The 17thC pub houses a restaurant. A short distance north of the railway is the site of Torksey Pottery, now completely vanished. It was established in 1802 by William Billingsley, a noted porcelain decorator who previously had worked at Pinxton. Although an excellent decorator, Billingsley was not a sound business man, and the pottery closed down after 3 years. Examples of his work can be seen in Lincoln's Usher Art Gallery.

Kettlethorpe
Lincs. A secluded village not easily accessible from the canal. The church and the 14thC gate of the Hall face each other across the little green. The Hall itself is predominantly Victorian, although it contains an 18thC dining room. *Open irregularly.*

BOATYARDS

BWB Torksey Yard at Torksey Lock. (Torksey 202) R S W

PUBS

White Swan Torksey. Near the lock. Also a caravan and camping site.

Hume Arms Torksey. An attractive old pub with 2 bars, situated 300yds from the junction of the Fossdyke and Trent Navigations.

Carpenters Arms Fenton.

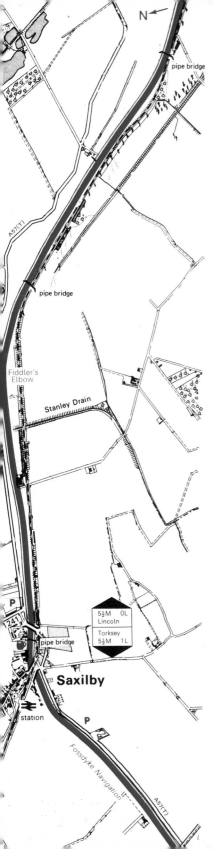

Saxilby

The main road clings to the canal all the way
into Saxilby, where it disappears behind
houses. It seems strange that the railway bridge
in Saxilby is the first one since Torksey, 5½
miles away to the north west. Emerging from
the railway bridge one finds the main street of
this attractive village laid out right beside the
navigation. The canal is below the level of the
street, but there are plenty of excellent
moorings, and 2 pubs are just across the road.
Unfortunately the railway makes quite a lot of
noise. Leaving Saxilby, the canal is rejoined by
the busy main road, the A57, which runs right
beside it again for 1½ miles. As the road finally
moves away, the Gainsborough–Lincoln
railway line moves in to take its place on the
other bank, although separated from the canal
for much of the way by a low hedge. After a few
industrial works on the way out of Saxilby, the
canal is entirely in countryside, green and flat.
For most of this stretch, the towers of the
mighty Lincoln Cathedral are clearly visible in
the distance. As usual the canal's course
consists mainly of a series of dead straight
reaches broken up by occasional corners.

Saxilby
*Lincs. PO, tel, stores, garage, bank, station, fish
& chips.* The presence of the Fossdyke canal
has clearly determined much of the layout of
the village, although the siting of the church
over ½ mile to the north has obviously
provided another focal point, and as a result
Saxilby extends between the two. All the
buildings in the main street face the waterway,
which is a welcome change for canal veterans,
and a line of cherry trees completes the scene.
The church is pretty, and has a generous
Perpendicular clerestory. Inside the church are
the alabaster figures of a knight and his lady;
they date from the 14thC, but are badly
defaced.

PUBS
- **Sun** Saxilby. Canalside. Fish & chips
nearby.
- **Ship** Saxilby. Canalside, near the Sun.
- **Anglers Hotel** Saxilby.
- **Bridge Hotel** Saxilby. Near the canal.

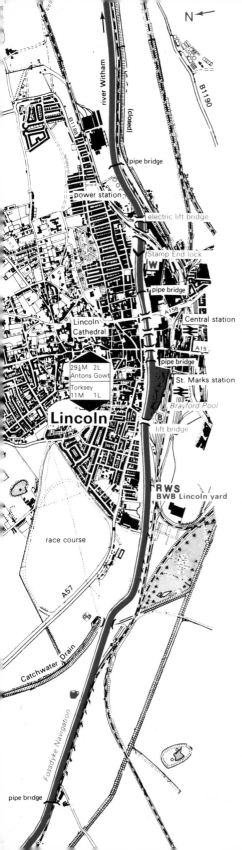

Lincoln

This is in parts a fascinating stretch of
waterway. The approach of Lincoln is marked
by the magnificent towers of the cathedral on
the hill. Passing the remarkable isolated Pye
Wipe pub on the canal bank, the Fossdyke
bends briefly as it reaches Lincoln Racecourse,
which is edged by trees. Then a long line of
moored pleasure boats leads to a lift bridge
operated by British Rail. This bridge is
normally left open at night and at weekends – at
other times, just hoot. Beyond this bridge, the
navigation widens out dramatically into the vast
expanse of water known as Brayford Pool.
There is a boatyard here and boat clubs.
Boatmen should resist the temptation to cruise
all over this lake, since much of it is heavily
silted: it is advisable to keep to the north side.
Continuing straight through the pool, boatmen
will see the River Witham flowing in as an
unnavigable stream at the south corner, and
from here onwards (eastward) the Fossdyke
Navigation is replaced by the Witham
Navigation. Leaving Brayford Pool, one passes
under the new concrete bridge; here the
channel becomes extremely narrow and goes
straight through the heart of old Lincoln,
passing through the famous and well-named
'Glory Hole', an ancient half-timbered building
astride the navigation. Lincoln High Street
runs over the heavily vaulted bridge that carries
this house. East of the Glory Hole the
navigation continues its narrow course along a
pleasantly landscaped stretch – definitely one of
the best lengths of urban canal in England.
Soon the channel widens out, passing the old
flour mills that once used barges for shipping
the grain. Further on are Stamp End Lock and
sluices: the lock keeper lives across the road,
and will come to operate the lock and its swing
foot bridge. The top gate has no paddles, for it
is simply raised *à la guillotine* into a steel
framework to let the water rush in and the boats
pass underneath. Beyond the next railway
bridge is another, larger bridge with a
headroom of about 5ft. An operator should be
summoned by sounding your horn. One moves
out into uncluttered, flat landscape and
wonders at the difference between the
Fossdyke Canal and the River Witham. To the
west is Lincoln Cathedral, standing proudly on
the hill above the town.

Navigational note
Water levels on the River Witham can change
rapidly – leave some slack in your lines when
mooring, and use the anchor as an added
precaution.

Lincoln
All services. Lincoln is a very fine city, with a
vast amount for the visitor to see. Once the
Celtic settlement of Lindon, it became Lindum
Colonia, a Roman town; and many Roman
remains have been discovered. Plenty of these
traces can be seen around the town. The old
part of Lincoln is of course grouped around the
cathedral, which sits on a hill to the north of the
river, overawing the city and the surrounding
countryside for miles. There are some splendid
rows of houses in the Close and just outside it,
where the steep and narrow cobbled streets
have remained unchanged for centuries, and
motor traffic can hardly penetrate.
Lincoln Cathedral This very splendid building
dominates the city and should certainly be seen
by visitors to Lincoln. The original Norman
cathedral was begun in about 1074, but a fire
and an earth tremor in the next century made 2
extensive restorations necessary. The present
triple-towered building is the result of
rebuilding in Early English style begun in 1192
after the second disaster, although the
magnificent central tower (271ft high) was not
finished until 1311. The vast interior contains
an abundance of fine stone monuments and
wood carvings, and in the Cathedral Treasury is
one of the original copies of the Magna Carta.
Lincoln Castle Built as a stronghold for
William the Conqueror in 1068, it stands on the
crest of the hill close to the cathedral. Over 6
acres of lawns and trees are enclosed by the
thick walls, the 2 towers and the Cobb Hall – a

14thC addition. The Observatory Tower and the old keep were built on separate mounds on the south side of the castle. The keep is now a mere shell, but the Observatory Tower is in good repair and there is an excellent view of the surrounding area from the top. Cobb Hall, a lower battlemented tower, was built in the north east corner of the castle and was a place of imprisonment and execution.

Brayford Pool This great sheet of water separates old Lincoln from the railway tracks of industrial Victorian Lincoln. It joins the Fossdyke Canal to the River Witham Navigation, and provides the navigator with a welcome relief from the long straight stretches of navigation on either side of Lincoln.

BOATYARDS

BWB Lincoln Yard Fosse Bank South, Lincoln. (20148). R̄S̄W̄

Ⓑ **Lincoln Marina, James Kendall & Co** Brayford Pool, Lincoln. (26896). R̄W̄D̄ Gas, chandlery, slipway, moorings, storage, boat and engine sales. Telephone. Licensed bar. *Open all year.*

BOAT TRIPS

Spitfire Narrowboat Cruises (Saundby 729). Trips from Salter Gate (behind the ABC cinema).

PUBS

🍺✕ **Green Dragon** Broadgate, Lincoln. By main road bridge 300yds east of the Glory Hole. Medieval pub beside River Witham.
🍺 **Royal William IV** North east corner of Brayford Pool. Old pub.
🍺✕ **Pye Wipe Inn** Canalside, 2 miles west of Lincoln. Very isolated pub, with moorings. Terrace overlooking the Fossdyke.

Lincoln Cathedral.

Washingborough

Leaving Lincoln, the River Witham heads due
east in a series of straight wide reaches. The
landscape is similar to that seen from the
Fossdyke, but the river follows the bottom of a
wide valley. Right beside the navigation is a
railway line which accompanies the river for
most of the way to Boston, but is now open only
as far as Bardney. There are no passenger
trains, but closed riverside stations along the
way remind the traveller of the former service.
To the west, the towers of Lincoln Cathedral
are visible from the river for about 10 miles out
of Lincoln. Overhead, RAF transport planes
approach the landing strip at Waddington
airfield, 5 miles south of Lincoln. There are
several villages on the hills overlooking the
Witham; to the south is Washingborough, all
trees and chimneys, while opposite is the little
stone church and hall of Greetwell. Further east
is the unappealing sprawl of Cherry
Willingham, and then Fiskerton. At the end of
this section is the old Five Mile House station:
this is, predictably, exactly 5 miles from
Lincoln Cathedral. The former ferry service
has been replaced by a steel footbridge.

Fiskerton
Lincs. PO, tel, stores, garage. The name of this
village comes from 'fisher's town', for in the old
days it was a fishing village. Once, fishing boats
could sail right up to Fiskerton Church on the
tide. Later, the fens here were drained and the
river diverted into its present straight course.
Since then Fiskerton has stood back from the
river. However when the river breached its
banks in 1962, the water once again reached the
church. The village is full of new housing. The
church is curious, having the only round tower
in Lincolnshire. Near the church lives a
blacksmith; apparently the base of his petrol
pump is just 5ft above sea level.

Washingborough
Lincs. PO, tel, stores, garage. A pretty village on
the south side of the Witham valley. There are
some attractive stone terraced cottages and
many trees. This has clearly become a smart
commuter village.

PUBS
🍺 **Carpenter's Arms** Fiskerton.
🍺 **Five Mile House** Fiskerton, (in the village,
not on the river).
Several pubs in Washingborough.

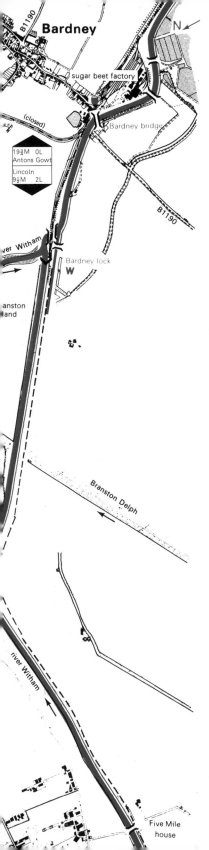

Branston Island

Leaving Five Mile House, where,
paradoxically, no house stands, the river
continues eastwards for nearly 2 miles through
the unchanging flat and empty landscape. Then
it turns south east and maintains this general
course right through to Boston. There is a small
pumping station at the point where the old
course of the river branches off round a loop to
the north, forming a large island known as
Branston Island. Meanwhile the navigation
runs in a straight line to Bardney Lock, the
only lock between Lincoln and Boston. Below
the lock, the old course of the river flows in
again from the north, the railway crosses and a
river-sized drain enters from the north west.
(Boats heading *upstream* at this point should be
sure to pass under the railway bridge and turn
immediately left.) The village of Bardney is
near the next bridge; pubs and fish or chips are
close here, but access is poor with no form of
wharf or jetty at which to land. The big
industrial buildings here are the famous
sugar-beet factory works.

Bardney
*Lincs. PO, tel, stores, garage, banks
(intermittently).* A small village to the east of the
river, on a slight rise. Bardney is attractive,
with a mellow 15thC church and a pleasant
village green. The parish almshouses by the
green were built in 1712. There are the remains
of a Cistercian abbey to the north of the village.
Bardney has become well known recently as the
scene of music festivals; in fact the site is to the
south east of the village, towards Southrey.
Bardney station is closed but the sugar-beet
factory keeps the line open for goods between
here and Lincoln. Downstream, the line is now
closed.

PUBS
- **Railway** Bardney, by the old station.
Telephone outside, and fish & chips nearby.
- **Jolly Sailor** Bardney. Near the railway.
- **Nags Head** Bardney. In the village centre.
Food.
- **Angel Hotel** Bardney.
- **Tyrwhitt Arms** Short Ferry, between
Bardney and Fiskerton. Snacks, caravan site.
Access for boats by sailing north from Bardney
Lock up the old course of the Witham.

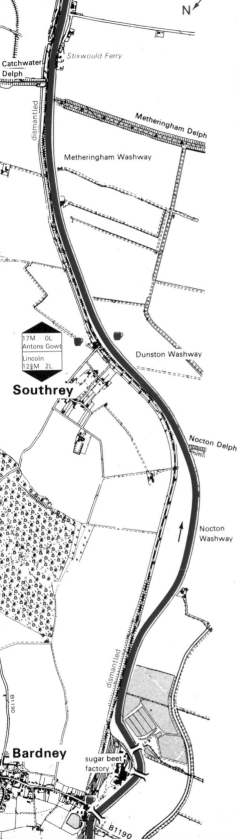

Southrey

Two bridges over the river connect the Bardney sugar-beet works with its associated settling ponds. The big ungainly buildings of the factory continue to dominate the flat landscape for several miles. The river flows between high banks to Southrey, passing the drain (or field dyke) called Nocton Delph. At Southrey there are 2 pubs facing each other across the water, connected by a small ferry. There are occasional farms on the south bank; the closed railway continues to hug the other side of the navigation to Stixwould. There is an ancient wooden ferry there, now no longer used.

Southrey
Lincs. PO, tel, stores. A small village of little intrinsic interest, but with reasonable river access. The little wooden church, with its belfry, was built by the villagers in 1898. A mile to the north, in undulating countryside, are the ruins of Tupholme Abbey, founded in 1160.

PUBS
🍺 **Copper Hood** Southrey. On north (Lindsey) side of river.
🍺 **White Horse** Across the river from the Copper Hood, on the Kesteven side.

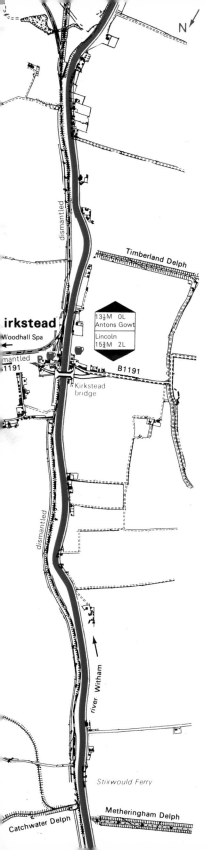

Kirkstead Bridge

The river continues on its straight course through the quiet flat Lincolnshire countryside. At Kirkstead there is a large new bridge – virtually a viaduct – built in 1968 to replace an older, low-level bridge. Unfortunately there is no proper place to moor. South of Kirkstead, the river is flanked on one side by the old railway line and on the other by a minor road linking many old farms and cottages along the river bank.

Kirkstead Abbey ¾ mile east of Kirkstead Bridge is a solitary finger of masonry about 30ft high. This is all that remains of the enormous Cistercian monastery known as Kirkstead Abbey, founded in 1139. The trained eye can recognise the former fishponds attached to the monastery ground.

Woodhall Spa
Lincs. EC Wed. PO, tel, stores, garage, bank, cinema. A curious resort town in the woods a mile north east of Kirkstead Bridge. The town grew up in Victorian times after waters rich in mineral salts were discovered in 1824. It has the characteristic atmosphere of most English Spa towns. There is a very popular 'Kinema' tucked away in the woods; also the town boasts Lincolnshire's only championship golf course.

St Leonard's Church, Kirkstead
Originally an extramural chapel of the abbey, the church was built in the mid 13thC, and survives largely intact. It contains a 13thC wooden screen, one of the oldest in the country, and an effigy of a knight of the same period. The church is just a few hundred yds north east of the bridge.

PUBS

Kings Arms Kirkstead. On the west bank of the river.
Railway Hotel Kirkstead. On east bank near the station.

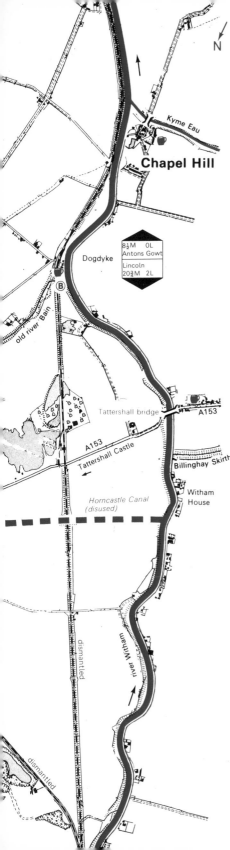

Dogdyke

The river continues southward on a winding course, providing a pleasant contrast to the former straight navigation. The old railway line runs in a straight line over to the east. Along the Kesteven bank are a number of farm cottages served by a minor road. The old junction with the Horncastle Canal can be seen as a slight dent in the east bank. At the 3-arched Tattershall Bridge there is a pub and a grocer's shop, but no moorings. A mile from Tattershall Bridge is Dogdyke beyond the old steam pump, an attractive place where there is a boatyard, a restaurant and another riverside pub. Coningsby airfield is nearby: one end of the runway is near the river, so navigators may find aircraft screaming over them at a height of perhaps 100ft. This can be disconcerting on an otherwise quiet summer's afternoon. South of Dogdyke there is a small landing stage on the west bank; this marks a caravan site with facilities useful to those on boats (shop, shower, gas, water etc). Beyond it are the houses of Chapel Hill, where the Kyme Eau or Sleaford Navigation joins. If you pass through the flood protection gates you will find it navigable for two miles to Kyme Lock, which is currently being repaired. Restoration of the whole 12½ miles to Sleaford is planned – meanwhile the towpath is in good condition throughout. Beyond Chapel Hill, the river becomes straight and wide once again, with piling to protect and strengthen the bank on one side and reeds on the other. Boston Stump, the tower of the church, can be seen from here. It is 9 miles away.

Chapel Hill
Lincs. PO, tel, stores, garage. A pleasantly compact tiny village at the entrance of Kyme Eau into the Witham.

Dogdyke
Lincs. Tel. A curious riverside settlement with a pub and boatyard on one side and a restaurant opposite. The ferry still works. Pleasure boats moor where the River Bain joins the navigation. The old railway station is now occupied by a residential caravan site. A nearby signpost indicates 2½ miles to New York and 12 miles to Boston. One is reminded that the names of 2 settlements in the New World originated here.

Tattershall Castle 1 mile north east of Tattershall Bridge. Only the keep remains of this superb building. The castle was rebuilt in brick in the 15thC for Ralph Cromwell, Treasurer of England 1434–35. Stone was used only for some windows and door frames. Best approach is along the derelict Horncastle Canal, which used at one time to feed the moat at Tattershall Castle. *Open daily.*

The Horncastle Canal This navigation, 10 miles long, was built 1792–1802 to serve the small country town of Horncastle. It left the River Witham ½ mile upstream of Tattershall Bridge, but now an embankment has been built over the junction in the cause of flood prevention, so those travelling on the river must look carefully to discover any trace of the junction. The remains of the first lock are about 300yds from the river. Nearer Horncastle parts of the canal are still in water, and the town basin survives. It was abandoned in 1885.

BOATYARDS

Ⓑ **The Old Mill** Dogdyke. (Coningsby 42124). Ⓦ Hire craft, moorings.

PUBS & RESTAURANTS

🍺 **Crown** Chapel Hill
🍺 **Packet Inn** Dodgyke. Riverside.
✕🍷 **Captain's Table** Dogdyke. (Coningsby 42434). Riverside restaurant. Mooring.
🍺 **Royal Oak** Tattershall Bridge. Shop nearby.

Round House Farm

The river continues south east in familiar straight, wide reaches with occasional bends of a few degrees that do little to break the monotony. The navigation is accompanied by the disused railway line on one side and high grassy banks on the other. Cattle graze on the banks. All around, but hidden from those in boats by the high bank, is a flat fenland landscape.

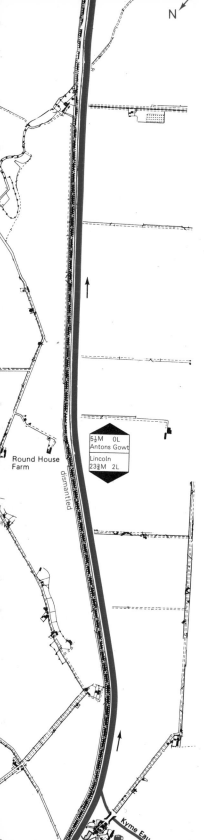

N

Round House
Farm

dismantled

5½M   0L
Antons Gowt

Lincoln
23¾M   2L

Kyme Eau

Langrick

At Langrick the river is crossed by a big iron
girder bridge as it curves round to head due east
for 2 miles. At the end of this reach is Anton's
Gowt; there is a lock and its cottage here, for
this is the entrance into the great network of
waterways known as the Witham Navigable
Drains, and navigators with time to spare can
easily continue through to Boston by this
alternative route and will, as a reward, find
good moorings in the *centre* of Boston. At
Anton's Gowt there is a sailing club near the
lock. The river turns here on its final course to
Boston and the sea.

Witham Navigable Drains This remarkable
network of waterways north of Boston exists to
drain and irrigate the flat and highly vulnerable
tract of fenland. The network is a vital part of
the local economy and of the defence of the area
against the encroachment of the North Sea.
Fortunately most of them happen to be
navigable for much of the time, and navigators
can spend many fascinating days exploring the
system. However, one should always remember
that navigation is not the top priority of the
drainage authority: sometimes a navigator is
brought up sharply by a low bridge, often in a
place where the channel is no wider than 30ft
for several miles. Anton's Gowt Lock is the
only entrance to these waterways. The best
(widest) course is to head east from here, along
Frith Bank Drain for 2 miles, to the great
junction of waterways at Cowbridge Lock.
From here one may go north towards the
Lincolnshire Wolds, or south into Boston along
the Maud Foster Drain. (But note that there is
no longer a connection with the tidal Witham
this way).
Langrick
Lincs. Stores, garage. This tiny settlement grew
to serve the ferry crossing, replaced by an iron
bridge in 1907. There is an old jetty facing
Witham Lodge, an attractive house where the
ferry used to be. The pub is nearby. The late
Georgian brick church was built in 1828.

PUBS

Malcolm Arms Anton's Gowt, on north side
of Frith Bank Drain.
Ferry Boat Inn Langrick, on north side of
river. Snacks, lunches and evening meals.

Boston

The River Witham now completes its journey
to Boston, aiming straight for Boston Stump,
the tower of St Botolph's Church. A low black
iron railway bridge crosses at the Boston Grand
Sluice, which marks the end of the non-tidal
Witham. Boats should keep away from the
powerful 'draw' of the sluices on the south west
side of this structure (the lock is at the north
east end of it). The river here is a very attractive
scene, and a fitting end of the trip from
Torksey. On either side of the river is a line of
town houses; these are particularly elegant on
the north bank. There are 2 boat clubs: Boston
Sailing Club and Boston Motor Yacht Club,
also a rowing club, a boatyard and a riverside
pub. There are good moorings here. The centre
of Boston is a short walk away.

Navigational note

At Boston Grand Sluice the River Witham
becomes tidal, leading down through Boston
past the docks and into the Wash. It is most
inadvisable to venture down the tideway unless
you have a suitable, sea-going boat and are
familiar with the currents and shallows in the
Wash. The Grand Sluice is of course a sea lock,
with gates facing both ways, but what is
particularly interesting about it is that, unlike
most tidal locks, the sea gates (referred to
locally as 'doors') here are actually used at every
tide. In other words the North Sea at high
water is always above the level of the non-tidal
Witham, and the sea gates close automatically
twice a day to keep out the tide. This makes
locking through the Grand Sluice somewhat
complicated as far as times are concerned. It is
not possible to lock up into the tide, since there
is only 1 pair of outward facing gates, but on
the other hand the tidal river practically dries
out at low water. The best time to lock through
is in fact 2 to 3 hours either side of high water.
The lock will take boats up to 50ft long by 30ft
wide. A lock keeper is on duty in the nearby
office: his telephone number is Boston 64864.

Boston

Lincs. EC Thur. MD Wed. An immensely
attractive town at the mouth of the Witham,
Boston has been an important seaport for over
800 years. There are many splendid buildings
in the town, but of course the most conspicuous
among them is the famous Boston Stump – the
272ft tower of the parish church. There are 2
large market places, virtually contiguous. This
area is the scene of much revelry in the spring,
when the May fair takes place. Under a charter
of Elizabeth I dated 1573 the fair is held from
3–10 May.

St Botolph's Church

beside the Witham. This
enormous building is a magnificent example of
late Decorated architecture, and reflects the
prosperity of Boston following the rise of its
wool trade in the 13thC. The thriving guilds
paid for the church, into which were built their
respective chapels. Inside, the church is
immensely spacious, the tall roof carried by
slender quatrefoil columns. There are plenty of
interesting things to look at here. The main
south door is a remarkable piece of dovetailing,
the pulpit is an elaborate Jacobean affair and
the choir stalls are an excellent example of
14thC carving. There are some good brasses
and other monuments. The 272ft tower may be
ascended, at a small charge; with hundreds of
steps up a claustrophobic narrow turret, this
can be heavy going, but one may walk right
around a balcony near the top and of course the
view over the fenland is unbeatable – on a clear
day Lincoln, 32 miles away, is visible. The
church is much loved by the inhabitants of
Boston, Massachusetts, who have largely
financed its structural repairs this century.

The Guildhall

South Street. An ancient and
fascinating building, now a museum illustrating
Boston's history. It contains the cells that in
1607 held William Brewster and his friends
after their unsuccessful attempt to leave the
country. They were tried in the courtroom
above. On the ground floor of this dark but
historic building is the original kitchen. The
roasting spit is self-propelled; the heat rising
from the fire drives simple fans connected to a
chain that operates the turning gear. This
remarkably useful device is over 500 years old.
Open Mon–Sat (not Sat afternoon in winter).

Fydell House next to the Guildhall. A superb town house built in 1726 by William Fydell, a successful wine merchant who was 3 times Mayor of Boston. The building was saved from demolition in 1935 by the pioneering Boston Preservation Trust, who have fully restored this and many other venerable buildings hereabouts. Fydell House is now partly financed and used by Nottingham University as a college for Americans (Pilgrim College). *Open daily until sunset.*

Blackfriars Spain Lane, next to the Guildhall. This was once part of a 13thC Dominican friary, and much of the old stone structure remains. But the building has now been skilfully converted by the Boston Preservation Trust into Boston's only theatre. It backs onto Spain Court, a charming little square which is being renovated at the moment.

BOATYARDS

Ⓑ **Boston Marina** Witham Bank, Boston. (64420). Ⓡ Ⓦ Ⓓ Gas, chandlery, slipway, mooring, engine sales and repairs, toilets.

PUBS

🍺 **Witham Tavern** Boston. Riverside, above the Grand Sluice.

🍺 **Barge** Boston, near the Grand Sluice. Plenty of pubs and restaurants in the town.

The Grand Sluice at Boston, separating the tidal River Witham (foreground) from the non-tidal Witham.

LANCASTER

Maximum dimensions

Preston to Tewitfield
Length: 75'
Beam: 14'
Headroom: 7' 6"
Glasson Branch
Length: 70'
Beam: 14'
Headroom: 8'

Mileage

PRESTON to
Garstang: 16¼
Junction with Glasson Branch: 24
Lancaster: 29¼
Carnforth: 37¼
CANAL TERMINUS: 41¼

No locks

Glasson Branch: 2¾ miles, 6 locks

The city of Lancaster has always been slightly unfortunate in being situated a little too far up the Lune estuary to allow easy navigation. By the late 18thC industrial developments in north west England created a great demand for better access from Lancaster to Preston, Manchester and the busy manufacturing areas near the River Mersey. A link such as a canal would enable much needed coal to be brought up from the pits around Wigan, while farm produce from the fertile plains of north Lancashire could be sent back to feed the teeming town workers to the south.

After various proposals had been aired, including suggestions for a ship canal up the Lune estuary and a canal along the coast, a smaller canal was promoted to run from Kendal to Westhoughton (a few miles east of Wigan). This was authorised as the Lancaster Canal by Parliament, and construction began in 1792, after a survey by John Rennie, the company's engineer. He designed the new navigation as a 'broad' canal, with locks 72ft long by 14ft wide, to take barges with a 50-ton carrying capacity. The water supply for the canal was – and still is – drawn from a reservoir at Killington (between Sedburgh and Kendal).

The route chosen included only 8 locks (at Tewitfield), but several aqueducts, the most important being across the River Lune at Lancaster. It was intended that the Ribble should be crossed at Preston by locking down to the river and up the other side, but this plan was constantly shelved because of lack of capital. By 1799 the canal was open from Tewitfield to Preston (including the great Lune Aqueduct), and from Clayton to Chorley. There remained a 5-mile gap between the 2 sections, which became known as the North and South Ends respectively. The gap was closed in 1803 by a horse tramway from Walton Summit to Preston, which was carried over the River Ribble by a wooden trestle bridge. This tramway was intended only as a cheap, temporary solution to the gap, but it was never replaced by a proper canal line, so the North End was doomed to be separated for ever from the rest of the country's inland waterways. (The tramway was closed in 1857.)

On the South End, the Lancaster Canal Company agreed with the Leeds & Liverpool Canal Company to extend the former's line past Chorley to Wigan (they never continued it to Westhoughton). The L & L then shared the Lancaster Canal for 10 miles – for a substantial consideration. Meanwhile the North End was extended from Tewitfield to Kendal and opened in 1819. The branch down to Glasson Dock, near Lancaster, was opened in 1826 as the canal's only direct outlet to the sea.

There are several unusual aspects about the Lancaster Canal and its history. One is that the 75-mile long main line was constructed with only 8 locks, at Tewitfield. (There are of course also 6 locks on the Glasson branch.) This was naturally a great benefit to traders and helped to counteract the disadvantage imposed by the tramway at Preston. One may also notice that the towpath is on the same side all the way along the canal, except for a short stretch in Lancaster. This fostered the growth in the 1820s of an express passenger service along the canal. Using special 'fly-boats', a constant change of horses at special staging posts, and precedence over all other craft, this service lived up to its name, averaging up to 10mph along the run from Preston to Kendal.

Another interesting aspect of the Lancaster Canal was the extraordinary but canny interest the company took in the new railway companies, alternately leasing whole lines and then being leased by railways. Eventually, in 1885, the Canal Company sold out altogether to the London & North Western Railway – except for the South End, which was already leased in perpetuity to the Leeds & Liverpool Canal Company.

Since the 1930s the canal has been progressively shortened from the Kendal end; and in 1968, after Tewitfield locks had been disused for several years, the canal north of Tewitfield was closed so that the M6 motorway could be driven across the canal. In Preston the canal has been shortened by over half a mile.

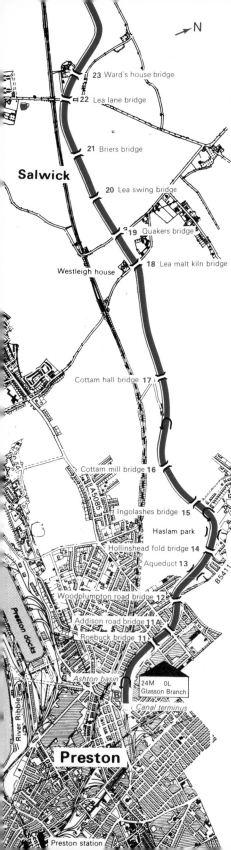

Preston

The canal in Preston, shortened many years ago
by over ½ mile, now starts in the middle of
nowhere, on an embankment by the old Ashton
Basin where there is a boatyard. (There is not
much left of the original line, although pubs in
Preston like the Lamb & Packet recall the days
when passenger 'fly boats' or 'packet boats'
used to leave Preston to do the trip to Kendal in
8 hours – a remarkable speed.) From Ashton
Basin, the canal runs through dull urban areas
for a short while. There is nothing to see and no
pubs or shops nearby except at bridge 11,
where there is a butcher. However, the
attractive Haslam Park appears at bridge 12 and
while housing estates line the offside bank for a
mile, the towpath side of the canal is effectively
already in the countryside. Soon Preston is left
behind and the canal runs through flat and
featureless but always green, open, agricultural
countryside; the first of many sheep and cows
are seen grazing along here. Passing Westleigh
House and several farms, one begins to see the
large industrial works at Salwick where fuel
elements are made for atomic power stations.
Farm eggs may be bought at bridge 18.

Salwick
Lancs. PO, tel, stores, station. A village scattered
over a large area. The school, post office,
telephone and pub are just ¼ mile south of
bridge 22: the station is ¼ mile south west of
bridge 25.

Preston
Lancs. MD Mon, Wed, Sat. All services. A large
industrial town which prospered as a cotton
manufacturing centre. The teetotal movement
was founded in Preston in 1834, and Joseph
Livesey's Temperance Hotel (the world's first)
used to stand at the corner of Church Street and
North Road. The Market Place is dominated by
the huge classical building of the Harris Public
Library and Museum. There are many
churches whose tall spires are a distinctive
feature of the town. Attempts to redevelop the
centre of the town have resulted in a good new
shopping precinct and a large modern bus
station housed in a remarkably long multistorey car park. With the end of commercial
use, the huge basin of Preston Dock is now to
be developed as a marina complex, with the
turbine steamer 'Manxman' as the centrepiece.
Harris Museum & Art Gallery Market
Square. The museum has a specialised
collection of the Devis family of painters in
addition to exhibits illustrating 18thC and
19thC art, including ceramics, porcelain, glass,
toys, stamps and costume. *Closed Sun.*
Information centre Town Hall, Harris Street.
(Preston 54881).

BOATYARDS

(B) **Omissa Marina** 52 Waterloo Road,
Ashton-on-Ribble, Preston. (729210). At
Ashton basin. R S W Chandlery, slipway up to
40ft, moorings, winter storage. Boat & motor
sales & repairs, agents for all major firms.
Closed Sun & Thur.

PUBS

Smith's Arms Salwick. ¼ mile south of
bridge 22.

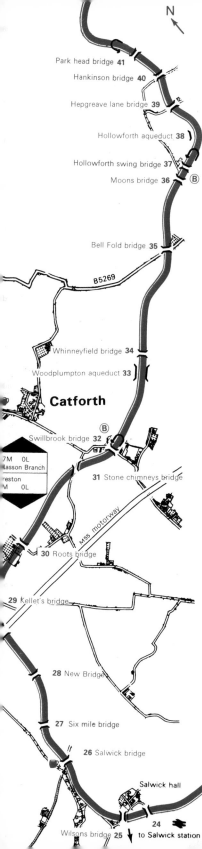

Catforth

The canal now reaches Salwick Wharf, where
the moorings are administered by the Duchy
of Lancaster. On one side of the wharf is the
moated Salwick Hall; on the other side is Salwick station, on the Preston–
Blackpool line, and a disused windmill
beyond. Here the canal turns north
into a wooded cutting, passing a canalside pub
– unfortunately a rare sight on this canal. At
Kellet's Bridge the navigation turns sharply
east to Catforth (*PO, tel, stores*). All along this
section the countryside is soft, open pasture
land dotted with dairy farms, entirely peaceful
and untouched by busy roads. At Swillbrook
Bridge there is one of the few boatyards on this
canal: the proprietor's house was the old canal
cottage with stables for the towing horses.

The Fylde
A large flat area of northwest Lancashire (west
of the canal) which is the 'market garden' of the
many industrial towns in Lancs. There used to
be a wonderful array of windmills covering the
land, but nearly all of these are gone now.

BOATYARDS
ⓑ **Preston Hire Cruisers** At bridge 36. Moons
Bridge Wharf. Hollowforth Lane, Wood
Plumpton, near Preston. (690627). R W D Gas,
hire craft, mooring.
ⓑ **Adventure Cruisers** Jolly Roger Boating
Haven, Catforth, nr Preston. (Catforth
690232). At bridge 32. R W Boat hire, slipway,
gas, boat repairs, mooring, chandlery, toilets,
winter storage, tel. Day boat hire & gift shop.
Closed Thur in winter.

PUBS
🍺 **Running Pump** Catforth.
🍺 **Bay Horse** Catforth.
🍺 **Clifton Arms** Salwick. Canalside.

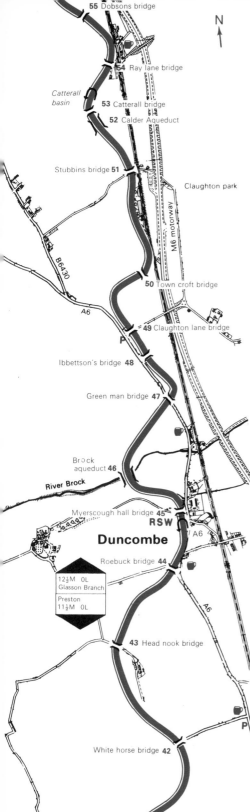

Duncombe

Starting at White Horse Bridge (¼ mile to the east of which is a pub, garage, post office and telephone kiosk), the canal sweeps round to enter the village of Duncombe on a minor embankment: the A6 joins the canal here and continues to dog it for many miles, as does the main railway line to Scotland, and the M6. When these rival transport routes keep their distance the canal is again delightfully quiet, still passing peaceful green farmland, while the foothills of the Pennines begin to converge from the east. Just south of Stubbins Bridge can be seen the canal cottage and stable which was one of the places where towing horses were exchanged for fresh animals to pull the express passenger boats between Preston and Kendal. Near the former Garstang and Catterall station is Catterall basin; both are now disused.

Claughton Hall ¼ mile east of the canal. This hall was originally an Elizabethan mansion built next to the village church for the Croft family, but in 1932–5 the whole house, except for one wing, was dismantled and reassembled on top of the moor north of the village. It was quite a remarkable undertaking and still stands there in defiant isolation.
Duncombe (or **Bilsborrow**)
Lancs. PO, tel, stores, garage. A village straggling along the A6, which must have been very noisy before the M6 was built. The church is set apart, up on a hill: there are 2 pubs very close to the canal.

PUBS
Kenlis Arms Garstang. 50yds east of bridge 54.
Green Man Duncombe. South of bridge 47.
White Bull Duncombe. Canalside.
Roebuck Duncombe. 30yds from canal.
White Horse ¼ mile east of bridge 42 on A6.

Garstang

The canal moves away from the hills and the remains of Greenhalgh Castle, crossing the River Wyre on a fine stone aqueduct and passing the attractive town of Garstang; Garstang Basin is a popular mooring for pleasure boats. There is a restaurant and museum in the restored wharf buildings here. The canal then winds through countryside that is as green and pleasant as ever but which is now overlooked by the steep slopes of the Pennines. Enthusiastic walkers up the hills will be rewarded with splendid views over Cockerham Sands and the Fylde.

Winmarleigh Hall ½ mile west of bridges 68 and 70. A red brick hall built in 1871 for Lord Winmarleigh. It was largely rebuilt after a fire in 1927. It is now an agricultural college.
Garstang
Lancs. PO, tel, stores, bank, garage. A friendly place, touching the canal, which retains the feeling of a small market town. Just near the canal is the 18thC church of St Thomas surrounded by a tidy churchyard. Opposite the cobbled market place is an interesting little town hall with its diminutive bell-tower. The Town Hall, built in 1680 to acknowledge its promotion by the King to borough status, was rebuilt in 1939. There used to be a dozen ale houses in the town; but the present 6 seem quite enough.
Greenhalgh Castle Just north of the canal on a grassy knoll are the modest ruins of Greenhalgh Castle. It was built in 1490 by the Earl of Derby, who placed Richard III's crown on Henry Tudor's head after the victory at Bosworth Field. In the 17thC it was destroyed by the Roundheads during the Civil War when the Royalists made a final stand there. Ask at the adjacent farm to visit the ruins.
St Helen's Church 1½ miles south west of the canal at Churchtown, west of the A6. A magnificent parish church known as the 'Cathedral of the Fylde', in an attractive setting of a shady churchyard near the River Wyre. Parts of the building date from c1300 and inside are 15thC arches on Norman pillars with the Creed written on them. The massive beams in the roof are from the 4 oaks that Henry IV granted to Churchtown when forests were the property of the monarch.

PUBS

🍺 **Eagle & Child** High Street, Garstang.
🍺 **Farmer's Arms** Church Street, Garstang.
🍺 **King's Arms** High Street, Garstang.
🍺✕ **Royal Oak Hotel** Market Place, Garstang.
🍺 **Wheatsheaf** Park Hall Road, Garstang.

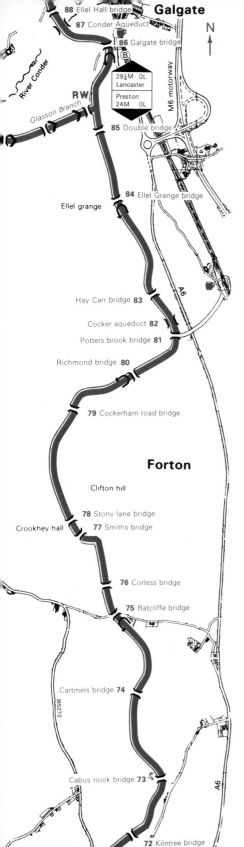

Galgate

Continuing northwards through quiet, modest
and unspoilt pasture land, the canal passes
countryside that is empty of villages but full of
farms and houses dotted about the landscape.
The absence of any locks certainly makes this
an ideal waterway for restful cruising, while the
wildlife and the generously proportioned
stone-arched bridges always supply interest
along the way. Near Forton, a sharp S-bend
carries the canal between Clifton Hill and
Crookhey Hall, while from Potters Brook
Bridge a lane across the A6 leads to a post
office, telephone and hotel beside what used to
be Bay Horse station. Just north of Potters
Brook is the Ellel Grange estate with its
remarkable spired church, ornamental canal
bridge and the Grange itself, shrouded by tall
trees; unfortunately the estate is private.
Double Bridge is worth a closer look; beyond
the rocky cutting that it spans is the junction
with the Glasson Branch, and round the corner
is Galgate and a large boatyard and mooring
site.

Galgate
Lancs. PO, tel, stores, garage. An unassuming
village on the A6 but dominated by the main
railway to Scotland, which strides through the
place on a high embankment and an impressive
viaduct. The back of the village up the hill is
quiet; by the church of St John are the
buildings of what is apparently the oldest
surviving silk spinning mill in England (built in
1792).

Ellel Grange
On the banks of the canal. A very fine Italianate
villa built for a merchant in 1857–9. It is a large
mansion with 2 broad towers that compete in
vain with the graceful spire of the charming
little church of St Mary that stands in the
grounds of the house. Both are private.

BOATYARDS
Ⓑ **Ladyline (Nor' West Marina)** Canal Wharf,
Galgate, nr Lancaster. (Lancaster 751368).
Ⓡ Ⓦ Gas, chandlery, slipway, moorings, winter
storage. Boat & engine sales & repairs.

PUBS
🍺 **Plough** Galgate. Near bridge 86. Lunches.
🍺 **Bay Horse Hotel** ¼ mile north east of
bridge 81, across the A6.

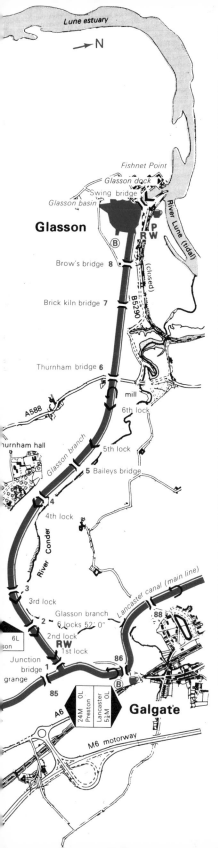

Glasson

Between Ellel Grange and Galgate the Glasson
Branch leads off down to the west to connect
the Lancaster Canal with the Lune estuary via
Glasson Dock. The branch was finished only in
1826, long after the main line of the canal was
completed, and provided the canal with its only
direct link with the sea. There are 6 wide locks
whose bottom gates feature the same excellent
type of sliding paddles as one sees on the Leeds
& Liverpool Canal. The top gates are all kept
padlocked for security reasons: boatmen should
ensure that they have the requisite key on board
(available from BWB staff) and are asked to
lock the gates after use, and also to leave the
locks **empty** after use, even when going up the
locks. The arm falls through the Conder valley,
a pleasant, quiet stretch of countryside whose
proximity to the sea is betrayed by the many
seagulls cruising around. The spire in the trees
on the south bank belongs to Thurnham
church; Thurnham Mill is beside the bottom
lock, and its mill race shows that it still takes
water from the canal. After the bottom lock,
the canal runs in a straight line through saltings
and marshland to Glasson Basin, where there is
a large boatyard, mainly for seagoing yachts,
and BWB moorings.

Navigational notes
1. The entrance lock from Glasson Dock up
into Glasson Basin will take boats up to 95ft
long, 26ft wide and 12ft draught. Anyone
wishing to use the lock or take up a mooring in
the basin should contact the BWB lock keeper
at Galgate 751566.
2. The locks on the Glasson Branch will take
boats up to 72ft long, 14ft wide and 5ft
draught.
3. Crew or owners wishing to leave via the
entrance lock should give the lock keeper 24hrs
notice. The lock is in operation 1hr before high
water.
4. In case of emergency, when the Glasson lock
keeper is not available, telephone Lancaster
32712.

Glasson
Lancs. PO, tel, stores, garage. A fascinating tiny
port that is still busy with trade from coastal
and continental vessels. The canal no longer
contributes to this trade and the huge basin is
only occupied by an assortment of pleasure
boats using its excellent sheltered mooring. In
the tidal dock, however, there are usually
plenty of coasters that discharge into lorries,
since the old railway line from Lancaster has
now been dismantled.
Thurnham Hall On south west bank of canal.
This ancient family home of the Daltons is a
battlemented 16thC mansion that was given a
new façade and beautiful chapel in the 19thC.

BOATYARDS

Ⓑ **Glasson Basin Yacht Co** Glasson Dock,
near Lancaster (Galgate 751491). Ⓡ Ⓢ Ⓦ Boat
hire, slipway to 70ft; gas, drydock, boat
building & repairs, mooring, chandlery,
showers, winter storage, 55 ton crane,
telephone, toilets. Charter for sea.
Ⓑ **Ladyline (Nor' West Marina)** Canal Wharf,
Galgate, near Lancaster (Galgate 751368). At
bridge 86. (See preceding page for details).

PUBS

🍺 **Caribou Hotel** Glasson Dock.
🍺 **Dalton Arms** Glasson Dock.
🍺 **Victoria Hotel** Glasson Dock.

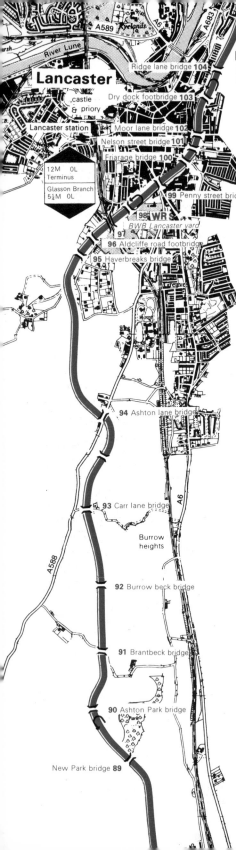

Lancaster

The canal continues northwards through beautiful undulating green countryside, then passes through an unusually long wooded cutting which ends in the outskirts of Lancaster. Going underneath the main line railway, one can see the 2-storey building where the old packet boats used to be refitted, being hauled out of the water from pulleys on the beams of the upper floor. The BWB maintenance yard is nearby, at the bridge where the towpath changes sides. Past the bridge are the Aldcliffe basins and wharves which were once the headquarters of the canal company. Opposite are some canal stables which have been tastefully converted into a place for punting, eating and drinking. At bridge 101 the towpath returns to the left side of the canal, where it stays for the rest of the journey northwards. The navigation now leaves Lancaster, on the side of the hill that overlooks the Lune estuary.

Lancaster
Lancs. EC Wed. MD Sat. All services. The name Lancaster is derived from a combination of Lune (after the river) and Latin 'castrum' meaning camp, which refers to the Roman fortress that once stood on this site. Today the quay, once a great shipping port handling more cargo than Liverpool, is only a quiet backwater with a pleasant walk provided by the tree-lined quayside promenade. A large new university was opened at Bailrigg, south of the town, in 1964. The Boat Regatta takes place annually in May and the Agricultural show in Aug.
Lancaster Castle A handsome but forbidding building on the site of Roman fortifications; mainly 13thC and 14thC construction, except for the Norman keep, which is surmounted by a beacon tower known as John of Gaunt's Chair. The Shire Hall contains an impressive display of over 600 heraldic shields. Most of the castle has reverted to its earlier function as a prison. *Various escorted tours. Closed during the winter, and while Assizes, Quarter Sessions or County Courts are sitting.*
Priory Church of St Mary Vicarage Lane, by the Castle. Attractive 15thC church in late Perpendicular style though the original Saxon western doorway still remains and the belfry was added in 1754. Elaborately carved choir stall c1340 and fine Jacobean pulpit.
Town Hall Dalton Square. A very impressive building of classical design, with a grand marble staircase and domed council chamber. It was the generous gift of Lord Ashton to Lancaster city in 1909. It is open to visitors, who are shown the magnificent entrance hall, the council chamber and concert hall, as well as the historic charters. To arrange a visit contact the Town Clerk.
Lancaster Museum Old Town Hall, Market Square. Prehistoric, Roman and medieval exhibits; pottery and porcelain, firearms and topographical paintings. *Open weekdays.*
Ashton Memorial Williamson Park, Quernmore Road. The 'Taj Mahal' of the north. Yet another generous gift from Lord Ashton to the city as a memorial to his family. In the centre of a beautiful park, containing a palm-house and ornamental lake, the memorial is a vast structure consisting of 2 domed chambers, 1 on top of the other. It was designed in neo-classical style by J. Belcher and constructed of Portland stone in 1907–9.
Information Centre Nelson Street. (Lancaster 32878).

BOATYARDS

BWB Lancaster Yard At bridge 98 (Lancaster 32712). $\boxed{R}\boxed{S}\boxed{W}$

BOAT TRIPS

'Lady Fiona' is a canal motor barge converted and licensed to carry 100 passengers. *Trips Easter–Nov, last 3¹/₂hrs* leave from opposite The Stables near bridge 98. Licensed bar on board. Only party bookings accepted, will run any day of the week. Enquiries to Poulton-le-Fylde 899684.

The Stables On the towpath east of bridge 98. Punts for hire; snacks and drinks served from the former canal stables.

PUBS

Large number of pubs, hotels, etc, in Lancaster: none on the canal bank but:
🍺 **The Wagon & Horses** is on the quayside.

A typical stone bridge on the Lancaster Canal. *Derek Pratt*

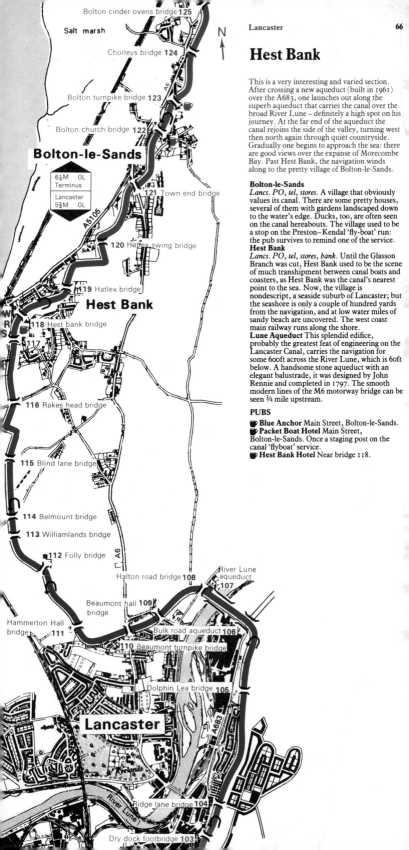

Bolton cinder ovens bridge **125**

Salt marsh

N

Chorleys bridge **124**

Bolton turnpike bridge **123**

Bolton church bridge **122**

Bolton-le-Sands

6¼M 0L
Terminus

Lancaster
5¾M 0L

121 Town end bridge

120 Hatley swing bridge

119 Hatlex bridge

Hest Bank

118 Hest bank bridge

117

WRS

116 Rakes head bridge

115 Blind lane bridge

114 Belmount bridge

113 Williamlands bridge

112 Folly bridge

Halton road bridge **108**

River Lune aqueduct **107**

Beaumont hall **109** bridge

Hammerton Hall bridge **111**

Bulk road aqueduct **106**

110 Beaumont turnpike bridge

Dolphin Lea bridge **105**

Lancaster

Ridge lane bridge **104**

River Lune

Dry dock footbridge **103**

Hest Bank

This is a very interesting and varied section.
After crossing a new aqueduct (built in 1961)
over the A683, one launches out along the
superb aqueduct that carries the canal over the
broad River Lune – definitely a high spot on his
journey. At the far end of the aqueduct the
canal rejoins the side of the valley, turning west
then north again through quiet countryside.
Gradually one begins to approach the sea: there
are good views over the expanse of Morecombe
Bay. Past Hest Bank, the navigation winds
along to the pretty village of Bolton-le-Sands.

Bolton-le-Sands
Lancs. PO, tel, stores. A village that obviously
values its canal. There are some pretty houses,
several of them with gardens landscaped down
to the water's edge. Ducks, too, are often seen
on the canal hereabouts. The village used to be
a stop on the Preston–Kendal 'fly-boat' run:
the pub survives to remind one of the service.
Hest Bank
Lancs. PO, tel, stores, bank. Until the Glasson
Branch was cut, Hest Bank used to be the scene
of much transhipment between canal boats and
coasters, as Hest Bank was the canal's nearest
point to the sea. Now, the village is
nondescript, a seaside suburb of Lancaster; but
the seashore is only a couple of hundred yards
from the navigation, and at low water miles of
sandy beach are uncovered. The west coast
main railway runs along the shore.
Lune Aqueduct This splendid edifice,
probably the greatest feat of engineering on the
Lancaster Canal, carries the navigation for
some 600ft across the River Lune, which is 60ft
below. A handsome stone aqueduct with an
elegant balustrade, it was designed by John
Rennie and completed in 1797. The smooth
modern lines of the M6 motorway bridge can be
seen ¾ mile upstream.

PUBS

🍺 **Blue Anchor** Main Street, Bolton-le-Sands.
🍺 **Packet Boat Hotel** Main Street,
Bolton-le-Sands. Once a staging post on the
canal 'flyboat' service.
🍺 **Hest Bank Hotel** Near bridge 118.

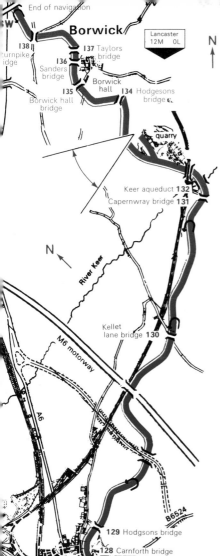

End of navigation

Borwick

138 ·· ·SW

·urnpike
·idge

137 Taylors
bridge

Lancaster
12M 0L

N

136
Sanders
bridge

Borwick
hall

135   134 Hodgsons
Borwick hall   bridge
bridge

quarry

Keer aqueduct 132
Capernwray bridge 131

N

River Keer

Kellet
lane bridge 130

M6 motorway

A6

B6524

129 Hodgsons bridge
128 Carnforth bridge

Carnforth
station

0L
·ninus
·caster 0L

PWR
wharf
B

Carnforth

A6

127 Thwaite end bridge

126 Barkers bridge

125 Bolton cinder ovens
bridge

124 Chorleys
bridge

Carnforth

The A6 now runs beside and below the canal
into Carnforth. One may catch occasional
glimpses westward of the distant shores around
Morecombe Bay, then the canal passes
Carnforth, mostly in a cutting. A few small
abandoned quarries are scattered between the
canal and the M6. After passing under the
motorway spur road, the canal finds itself
diverted along a new channel for several
hundred yards before going under the main line
of the M6: this diversion was presumably
cheaper to build than a long, finely angled skew
bridge over the navigation. Beyond the
motorway lies peaceful green countryside
backed, unmistakably, by the foothills of the
Lake District. At Capernwray the canal crosses
the River Keer on a minor aqueduct; the
nearby railway, which goes to Leeds, crosses
the Keer on an impressive viaduct, framing a
tiny old derelict watermill. Past the railway
bridge is a short branch to a worked-out
quarry, then the canal winds round the hillside
to end abruptly just beyond Borwick. The
abandoned Tewitfield locks are just beyond the
terminus. It is possible to walk from Tewitfield
to the original terminus at Kendal (and get a
bus back). Boats can safely be left at the BWB's
terminus moorings (facilities available, and a
winding hole).

Borwick
Lancs. Tel. A small, old and attractive village,
spread around a green. Overlooking the canal is
Borwick Hall, a large and sombre Elizabethan
manor house, built around a high 15thC tower.
Extensive gardens.
Warton
Lancs. PO, tel, stores. About 2 miles west of
Borwick. Ancestors of George Washington
lived in this village and their family crest
containing the famed Stars and Stripes is to
be seen on the 15thC tower of the church of
St Oswald.
Carnforth
Lancs. PO, tel, stores, garage, bank, station. Not
particularly attractive but of interest as an
important railway junction. One may catch
trains not only north–south but east over the
beautiful green hills to Skipton and Leeds, west
to Barrow and right round the coast to Carlisle.
Carnforth was the last town in the country to
lose its regular British Rail steam locomotive
service in 1968. Since then a company of steam
engine enthusiasts and volunteers have
privately set up the 'Steamtown' museum – a
depot with 5 miles of track along which
preserved engines steam on certain weekends.
The collection of motive power includes the
'Flying Scotsman'. At Carnforth Wharf are
some useful facilities: BWB moorings, slipway,
dustbins and fresh water. A petrol station is
nearby.

BOATYARDS

Nu-Way Cruisers Carnforth Wharf.
(Carnforth 4457). R S W P D Pump-out, boat
hire, slipway, gas, mooring, toilets, winter
storage. Day boat hire.

PUBS

 Longlands Hotel Tewitfield. 100yds north
east of canal terminus. Bar food.
✗ **Carnforth Hotel** Market Street,
Carnforth.
✗ **County** Lancaster Road, Carnforth.

Present day commercial carrying on the Leeds & Liverpool Canal. *David Perrott*

LEEDS & LIVERPOOL

Maximum dimensions

Liverpool to Wigan, and Leigh Branch
Length: 72'
Beam: 14' 3"
Headroom: 8' 6"
Wigan to Leeds
Length: 60'
Beam: 14' 3"
Headroom: 8'
Rufford Branch
Length: 62'
Beam: 14'
Headroom: 8'

Mileage

LIVERPOOL. Canal terminus to Burscough,
junction with Rufford Branch: 24½
Wigan, junction with Leigh Branch: 35
Johnson's Hill Locks: 47¼
Blackburn, Top lock: 56
Burnley: 72½
Skipton: 98
Bingley five rise: 110¾
Apperley Bridge: 118
LEEDS, River Lock: 127

Locks: 91

Leigh Branch: 7¼ miles, 2 locks
Rufford Branch: 7¼ miles, 8 locks

With a length of 127 miles excluding branches, the Leeds & Liverpool Canal is easily the longest single canal in Britain built by a single company. It is hardly surprising that its construction costs amounted to £1·2 millions, and that it took well over 40 years before the main line was completed.

The canal has its beginnings in the River Douglas, a little river made navigable by 1740 – well before the canal age – all the way from Wigan to Parbold, Tarleton and the Ribble estuary. The navigation provided a useful outlet for coal from the Wigan area.

After a few years the idea of purely artificial canals as traffic routes became popular among businessmen, and several ambitious trans-Pennine schemes were mooted; 1 of these was for a canal from Liverpool to Leeds, where it would connect with the head of the Aire & Calder Navigation.

After much predictable argument between the promoters in Yorkshire and those in Lancashire about the actual route of the proposed canal, the Leeds & Liverpool Canal was authorised in 1770, and construction began at once, with John Longbotham as engineer. The first (lock-free) section from Bingley to Skipton was opened within 3 years; by 1777 2 long sections were open from the Aire & Calder at Leeds to Gargrave (incorporating many of the dramatic new staircase locks) and from Wigan to Liverpool. The River Douglas navigation had been embarrassingly close to the new canal's line, so the L & L had bought it out at an early stage to gain control of its valuable water supply. It was replaced by a proper canal branch to Rufford and Tarleton, where it joined the (tidal) River Douglas.

Construction was halted at this stage while trade flowed on to the separate lengths of navigation and the company summoned the resources to continue work on the canal. In 1790 a new money-raising Act of Parliament gave fresh impetus to the scheme for completing the difficult middle half of the canal. Work began again, with Robert Whitworth as the company's engineer; but after 1792 and the outbreak of war with France, the nation's purse strings grew steadily tighter while after the boom year of 1794 investment in canals declined steadily. The canal company did not do badly to finish the whole of the main line from Leeds to Liverpool by 1816, under a convenient arrangement with the Lancaster Canal Company, the finished L & L line actually *shared* the channel of the Lancaster Canal for 10 miles). This stretch is from Wigan to Top Lock to Johnson's Hill Bottom Lock. The Lancaster used then to branch off up what later became the Walton Summit Branch.

In 1820 a branch was opened to join the Bridgewater Canal at Leigh. A short branch (the Springs Branch) was also made to rock quarries at Skipton and an important 3-mile long canal from Shipley to Bradford. The cut down into the Liverpool Docks was made in 1846.

The prosperity of the company after 1820 was not, at first, greatly affected by the early advent of railways in that part of the country. The scale of the navigation (the locks were built – and remain – as barge locks 62ft by 14ft, allowing big payloads to be carried in each barge along the canal) no doubt contributed to the high dividends paid to shareholders for several years. Water supply was, however, a thorny problem from the very beginning, and in spite of the building of many reservoirs along the summit level, the canal had to be closed for months on end during many dry summers. Although through traffic has never been a very significant proportion of the trade on the canal, this lack of reliability tended, not surprisingly, to drive carriers' custom away to the railways. Use of the navigation for freight has declined throughout this century; the hard winter of 1962/63 finished off many traders. Today there is no large scale commercial traffic at all, although the occasional independent carrier may be seen at the eastern end.

Liverpool

The first ¼ mile of this canal has been filled in, so the navigation begins now at bridge 'A'. It runs north from the city centre for about 6 miles, parallel and close to Liverpool Docks, before turning east to Aintree, Wigan and the Pennines. Liverpool is not an attractive place from the canal, which is completely shut off from the town by rows and rows of factories with their backs turned to the canal. For much of the way, substantial electricity pylons span the navigation. Access at the bridges to or from the canal is very difficult, because the towpath is officially closed to walkers, but naturally it is often alive with small boys fishing, playing and dropping or throwing things into the canal. The water, however, is surprisingly clear.

Navigational notes
1 Just north of the terminus is the Stanley Dock Branch. This useful connection from the canal down into Liverpool Docks and the River Mersey is nowadays the main *raison d'etre* of the west end of the Leeds & Liverpool Canal. There are 4 locks on the branch: they can be opened only by the resident BWB lock keeper *in working hours from Mon–Fri*. Any person wishing to use these locks should give *24hrs notice* to the lock keeper (tel 051-207-2449) or to the BWB Liverpool Section Inspector at Burscough 893160. Below the locks, one enters immediately the Stanley Dock: this belongs to the Mersey Docks & Harbour Company, whose permission should be sought before one enters the Dock. (Telephone 051-200 2177). The MD & HC are unlikely to refuse such a request, but do not like pleasure boats to tie up in the Dock. Navigators are encouraged to move straight on to the big lock down into the tidal River Mersey. (The lock is operated *24hrs a day*.)
2 Those navigating the Leeds & Liverpool will need, as well as a windlass, a BWB anti-vandal key and a sanitary station key.

Liverpool
Merseyside. All services. EC Wed. In the first century it was 'lifrugpool', a settlement next to a muddy creek; now it is Britain's second largest port (after London) with a population of ½ million. Famous worldwide as the place where the Beatles began their march to fame, (in the 'Cavern' club, now demolished), and equally well known for the exploits of Liverpool Football Club who are successful in both the UK and Europe, attracting a fanatical and generally good-natured following. There is much to be seen in this ancient port – for example the Anglican Cathedral, begun in 1904 and finished in 1978, is the largest in the world; the Roman Catholic Cathedral is a striking conical structure topped with a lantern tower and illuminated with stained glass by John Piper and Patrick Reyntiens. The Walker Art Gallery has a collection of paintings second only to those in London, and includes the original of Yeames popular work 'And when did you last see your father' among works by Reubens, Holbein, Stubbs (born in Ormond Street), Turner and Reynolds. Gladstone, Prime Minister during the reign of Queen Victoria, was born in Rodney Street in one of a row of superb Georgian houses. Down by the Mersey is the Royal Liver Building and Cunard offices, a reminder of the days when the great transatlantic liners used to berth here. Beneath the river are the Queensway Tunnel (opened in 1934, and at 2 miles then the world's longest underwater tunnel) and the Kingsway Tunnel (opened in 1971). On the pierhead is a memorial to the engineers lost on the 'Titanic', which sunk in 1912.
Information Centre Near Lime Street station (051-709 3631).

PUBS
There are many to be found here.

Litherland

North of Litherland the conurbation thins out
and wastelands and suburbs appear, while the
canal turns east to Aintree. Soon the first of
many swing bridges is encountered; for the first
few miles these bridges have to be padlocked to
combat vandalism, so progress through them is
necessarily slow. All navigators should ensure
that they have the requisite key before reaching
these bridges. (Keys obtainable from the BWB
section offices at Burscough, Wigan, Burnley
and Apperley Bridge.)

PUBS
🍺 **Tailor's Arms** Canalside, at bridge 4A.

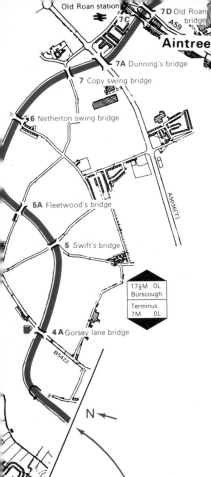

Old Roan station

7D Old Roan bridge
A59
7C

Aintree

7A Dunning's bridge

7 Copy swing bridge

6 Netherton swing bridge

A5036(T)

5A Fleetwood's bridge

5 Swift's bridge

17½M 0L
Burscough

Terminus
7M 0L

4A Gorsey lane bridge
B5422

N ←

N ↑

4

Litherland

A5036(T)

2J Litherland bridge

Seaforth and
Litherland Station
2H

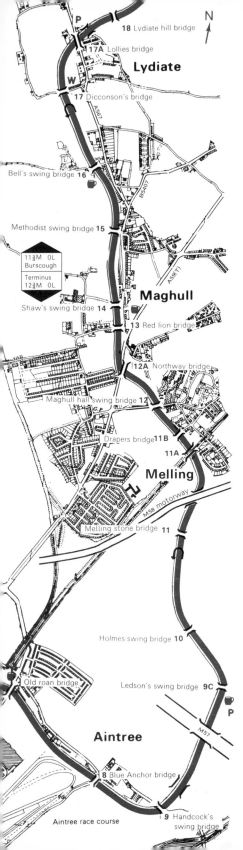

Maghull

Aintree marks the limit of the Liverpool
outskirts. The great feature here is of course the
Aintree Race Course: the famous Grand
National steeplechase is run every year on a
spring Saturday. Much of the course lies right
beside the canal, but would-be spectators from
the canal will have to stand upon their boat's
cabin top to see over the fence surrounding the
course. At the east end of the racecourse is
another swing bridge; this carries a busy main
road and traffic lights are installed, but boat
crews operate the bridge themselves. Here the
canal turns north again, and as the little church
tower at Melling comes into view the navigation
emerges at long last into open countryside,
although Maghull soon looms up to interrupt
this with a series of swing bridges.

Navigational note
Those heading towards Liverpool should
remember that all the usual city problems with
vandals will become apparent beyond bridge
11. There is a winding hole here for those who
wish to turn around.

Maghull
Merseyside. EC Wed. All services. A small town
astride the canal, convenient for supplies. Since
the last war it has greatly expanded, but still
maintains its former village atmosphere.
St Andrew's Church Damfield Lane. Just
north of bridge 12A. Though separated from
the rest of the town by a dual carriageway, it is
well worth a visit: it has a cosy setting among
trees that seem to compete with the tower for
height. It was built in the late 19thC but its
style is in imitation of that of the 13thC to
accord with the tiny 700-year-old chapel known
as Old St Andrew's in its grounds. The chapel
is a charming little building, said to be the
oldest church in the Merseyside area.
Melling
Merseyside. PO, tel. The sight of this little
village is like a breath of fresh air to anyone
coming along the canal from Liverpool,
although southbound travellers probably find it
unremarkable. The village stands on an isolated
hillock at a safe distance from the big city. The
church is a landmark in the area; it was built in
the 15thC with rock from an adjacent quarry.

PUBS
Scotch Pipers Lydiate. North of bridge
17A.
Running Horses Maghull. Canalside, at
bridge 16.
Hare & Hounds Maghull. Near bridge 14.
Bootle Arms Melling.
Horse & Jockey Near bridge 9C.
Old Roan Aintree. Near Old Roan bridge
7D.

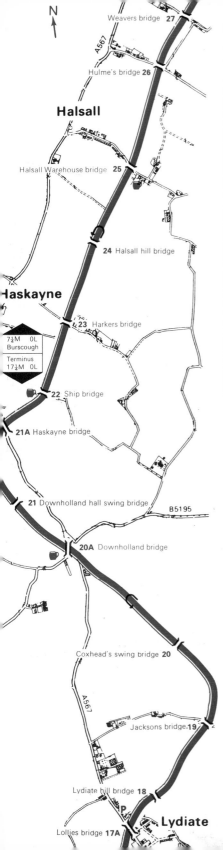

Halsall

The canal now enters continuous open countryside, which soon establishes itself as extremely flat and intensively cultivated lowlands: indeed it is more akin to Cambridgeshire or Lincolnshire than to the rest of Lancashire. However it is pleasant enough and the canal forms one of its more important features – a view which is borne out by the large number of people usually to be seen walking and boating upon it, as well as the hundreds of anglers enjoying their sport in this well stocked length of canal. As if in compensation for the unexciting landscape, the traveller is offered a truly astonishing number of pubs on or near the canal all the way from Lydiate to Wigan.

Halsall
Lancs. PO, tel, garage. There is a handsome tall 14th–15thC church here (St Cuthbert's), with a fine spire. The choir vestry, erected in 1592, was formerly a grammar school. There is an interesting pair of pulpits/lecterns. One of them is generously illuminated by a solitary overhead window; the other, more sheltered, gives the occupant the unfortunate air of being behind bars . . .

Haskayne
Lancs. PO, tel, stores. There are just 2 pretty houses here: the post office and the old thatched cottage opposite. No sign of a church.

PUBS
🍺 **Saracen's Head** Halsall. Canalside, at Halsall Warehouse Bridge.
🍺 **Ship** Haskayne. Canalside, at Ship Bridge. A well-known canal pub with a garden.
🍺 **King's Arms** Haskayne. 100yds north of bridge 21A.
🍺 **Scarisbrick Arms** Canalside, at Downholland Bridge.

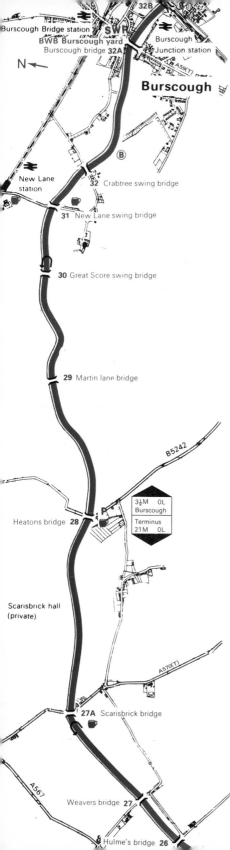

Burscough

One moves now past a massive caravan site on one side and attractive woods containing the private Scarisbrick Hall on the other; then out again into the open flat lands. The Southport–Manchester line converges from the north west; it runs near the canal all the way into Wigan, and has some wonderfully remote stations. A flurry of swing bridges brings the canal into Burscough: just beyond is the junction with the Rufford Branch.

Burscough
Lancs. PO, tel, stores, garage, bank, station. Formerly a canal village and a staging post on the one-time Wigan–Liverpool 'packet boat' run, this place attaches more significance nowadays to the benefits of road and rail transport. It still boasts 2 stations (one is on the Preston–Liverpool line) and suffers from heavy through traffic. A very convenient place for taking on victuals.

BOATYARDS

Ⓑ **Latham Marina** The Workshop, Crabtree Lane, Burscough. (894782). Pump-out, slipway, boat and engine repairs, salvage works, toilets.
BWB Burscough Yard (Burscough 893160). Ⓡ Ⓢ Ⓦ Drydock.

PUBS

🍺 **Royal** Burscough.
🍺 **Railway** At New Lane station.
🍺 **Latham Slipway** Canalside at bridge 32. Food Ⓡ Ⓢ Ⓦ Mooring.
🍺 **Farmer's Arms** Canalside, by swing bridge 31.
🍺 **Heatons Bridge Inn** Canalside at bridge 28.
🍺✕ **Red Lion** Near Scarisbrick Bridge.

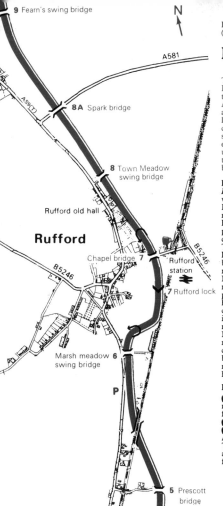

9 Fearn's swing bridge

A581

8A Spark bridge

8 Town Meadow
swing bridge

Rufford old hall

Rufford

B5246

Chapel bridge **7**

Rufford
station

7 Rufford lock

Marsh meadow **6**
swing bridge

P

5 Prescott
bridge

Chicken lock **6**   **4** Baldwins
bridge

Germans lock **5**   **3** German's bridge

Rufford branch

Burscough

4 Moss lock

Burscough Bridge
Station

2A

32A Burscough bridge

BWB Burscough yard

3 Runnel Brow lock

SWR   **2** Runnel Brow
bridge

32B   Latham locks

2   7¼M 8L
1   Tarleton

1 Junction bridge

Burscough
Junction Station

Leeds & Liverpool
(main line)

Glovers swing bridge **33**

24¾M 0L
Terminus
Wigan 10¾M 6L

A5209

Rufford

The Rufford Branch leaves the Leeds &
Liverpool main line just east of Burscough,
through an imposing arched bridge dated 1816.
A little canal settlement surrounds the top lock
and the roomy drydock for barges here. The
locks come thick and fast to begin with, as the
canal falls through the very fertile and gently
sloping farm lands towards the distant Ribble
estuary. The country is generally quiet, flat and
unspectacular but agreeable. A line of trees and
the spire of Rufford church are followed by the
beautiful Rufford Old Hall, on the west bank.

Rufford
Lancs. PO, tel, stores, garage, station. Main road
village noted for its Hall. The church is a small
Italianate Victorian building containing many
monuments to the Heskeths who owned
Rufford Hall for many centuries; obviously a
prolific family judging by one large sculpture
depicting a brood of 11 children, dated c1458.
The family now resides in Northamptonshire.
Rufford Old Hall *NT property* On the west
bank of the canal. A medieval timber framed
mansion with Jacobean extensions given to the
National Trust in 1936. The interior is
magnificently decorated and furnished in
period style, especially the great hall with its
hammer-beam roof and 15thC intricately
carved movable screen – one of the few still
intact in England. The Hall also houses a folk
museum. *Open afternoons Apr–Oct (closed Fri)*.
Note: although the Hall is beside the canal, one
may **not** enter the grounds direct from the
canal. Navigators should therefore tie up near
bridge 7, then walk up to the village and turn
right at the main road. The entrance is a few
hundred yards along the wall on the right.

PUBS
New Fermor Arms Near Rufford station. A
new building has replaced the old, which was
famous for its tilt. Real ale and food.
Hesketh Arms Rufford.
Ship Burscough. Near second lock down.
An old canal pub formerly known as the 'Blood
Tub' – black puddings were once made here,
and a bucket of pig's blood could be exchanged
for a pint of beer.

continued
page 77

Tarleton

At Sollom there used to be a lock, but now it is
no more. This is where the canal turns into the
old course of the River Douglas, and it twists
and turns as though to prove it. The towpath
has been ploughed up from here onwards. The
'new' course of the Douglas (which was once
navigable from the sea right up to Wigan)
comes alongside the canal at the busy road
bridge near Bank Hall, a house hidden by trees.
From here it is only a short distance to the final
swing bridge and Tarleton Lock, where the
canal connects with the tidal River Douglas –
which in turn flows into the River Ribble near
Preston.

Navigational notes
1. Vessels wishing to enter or leave the Rufford
Branch via Tarleton Lock can only do so at
high water. The Douglas is then a relatively
easy navigation, and since the removal of the
old railway swing bridge a mile downstream,
there has remained only one limitation on
headroom from Tarleton to the open sea. This
is a pipe bridge not far north of Tarleton Lock:
the clearance at normal high water is about
20ft. The boatyard at the lock may help callers
with advice regarding tide times, etc.
2. Navigators entering the Rufford Branch
canal from the sea should remember that they
will need a padlock key – as well as a windlass –
to open the locks up the branch. Arrangements
can be made with the BWB Burscough Yard
(Burscough 893160) to have such a key left with
James Mayor's boatyard.

Tarleton
Lancs. PO, tel, stores, garage, bank. A large
village luckily avoided by the A59 road. There
are some useful shops and a good take-away
food shop.

BOATYARDS
ⓑ **James Mayor** The Boatyard, Tarleton,
Preston. (Hesketh Bank 2250). Ⓡ Ⓦ Ⓓ At
Tarleton Lock. Caters for canal craft and
sea-going boats. Gas chandlery, 5 slipways up
to 90ft, 3 ton crane, moorings. Boat & motor
sales & motor repairs. Steel & wood boats built
& fitted out. Telephone, showers, toilets.
Extremely helpful people.

Pubs
🍺 **Tarleton Hotel** In Tarleton village.
🍺 **Ram's Head** Tarleton. ½ mile west of
bridge 11. Bed and breakfast.

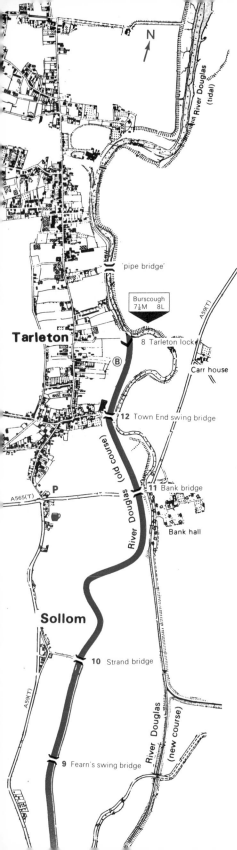

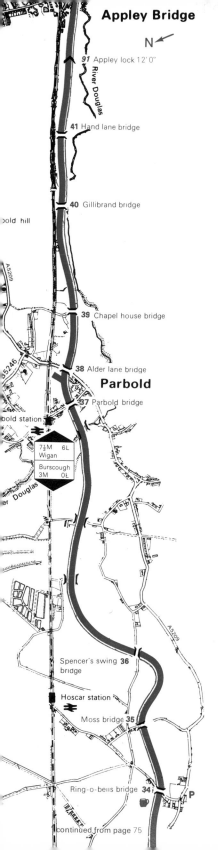

Appley Bridge

N ←

91 Appley lock 12′ 0″

River Douglas

41 Hand lane bridge

40 Gillibrand bridge

bold hill

A5209

39 Chapel house bridge

A55246

38 Alder lane bridge

Parbold

37 Parbold bridge

bold station

7¼M 6L
Wigan
Burscough
3M   0L

er Douglas

A5209

Spencer's swing **36**
bridge

Hoscar station

Moss bridge **35**

Ring-o-bells bridge **34** P

continued from page 75

Parbold

East of the junction with the Rufford Branch,
the canal meanders through the flat countryside
to the village of Parbold with its ancient sail-less
windmill. Here the scenery changes completely
as the canal crosses the River Douglas and then
joins the Douglas valley. This is a very pretty,
narrow wooded valley which the canal shares
with the railway: there are several convenient
stations along the line. Appley Lock is reached:
there was once a duplicate lock to save water, 1
being used as a navigable sidepond to the other
for boats passing in opposite directions. The
present lock is extremely deep. **As with all
subsequent locks, the gates should be closed
and the paddles lowered and padlocked after
use to combat vandalism and wastage of
water.**

Parbold
Lancs. PO, tel, stores, garage, station. A large
village climbing up from the west end of the
Douglas valley. Parbold is prettiest near the
canal bridge, where the big brick tower of the
old windmill is complemented by an equally
attractive pub. Unfortunately the rest of the
village is being engulfed by acres of new
housing. Local landmarks are the tall spires of
Parbold's 2 churches, and Ashurst's Beacon
high on a hill to the south. The latter was built
in 1798 by Sir William Ashurst in anticipation
of an invasion by the French. (The beacon was
intended as a local warning sign.)
The Douglas Navigation
The little River Douglas, or Asland, was made
navigable in the first half of the 17thC, well
before the great spate of canal construction. It
provided the Wigan coalfield with a useful
outlet to the tidal River Ribble, from which the
cargoes could be shipped over to Preston or
along the coast. When the Leeds & Liverpool
Canal was built to share the Douglas valley, the
old river navigation became superfluous. It was
bought up by the new company, who
constructed their own branch to the Ribble
estuary (the Rufford Branch). Between Parbold
and Gathurst it is possible to find many traces
of the old navigation, including several locks.

PUBS
🍺 **Windmill** Parbold. Near bridge 37.
🍺✕ **Ring O' Bells** Canalside, at bridge 34. Bar
food and restaurant.

Douglas Valley

The canal now goes through Appley Bridge and runs up the beautifully rural Douglas Valley, with the river on one side and the Wigan–Southport railway on the other. Passing 3 consecutive swing bridges, one soon reaches Dean Locks, a pleasant spot in spite of the high motorway viaduct nearby. This used to be a very busy place, for in addition to the duplicated canal locks there used to be a lock down into the River Douglas Navigation, when this was navigable before the Rufford Branch was built. Just east of the locks is a pleasant canalside pub, then the valley widens out to reveal the chimneys and factories of Wigan. Hell Meadow (sometimes mistaken for 'Ell Meadow') and Pagefield Locks lead the canal up through the now drab scenery towards the centre of Wigan. For those wishing to stop in the town, the best place to leave a boat is further on, at the boatyard by the BWB Repair Yard at Wigan Bottom Lock (no 87). The BWB Wigan Area Engineer's office is here.

Appley Bridge
Lancs. PO, tel, stores, station. A canalside hamlet dominated by large mills and works, the place is nevertheless attractively situated in the wooded Douglas valley.

PUBS
🍺 **Crooke Hall Inn** Crooke. Near bridge 47. Garden, mooring.
🍺 **Navigation** Gathurst. Canalside, at bridge 46.
🍺 **Railway** Appley Bridge by the canal.

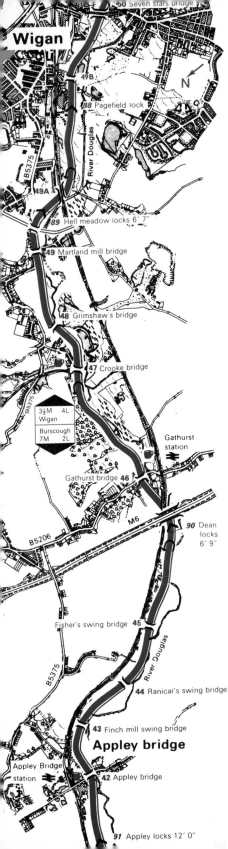

Abram

The Leigh Branch leaves the main line of the
Leeds & Liverpool Canal in Wigan, between
the big power station and the 22nd lock. The
famous 'Wigan Pier', a coal staithe, is by bridge
51 and has been rebuilt. It was made fun of by
George Formby snr, and written about by
George Orwell in 'The Road to Wigan Pier', in
1937. The area around the pier is being
handsomely restored. Descending through 2
locks, it enters the lock-free level that extends
all the way along the Bridgewater Canal to
Preston Brook and Runcorn, over 40 miles
away. The branch passes through empty, flat
wasteland that is gradually being landscaped.
Most of the way, the canal is on an
embankment, well above the level of the
surrounding landscape; this is a relatively new
situation and is due to severe mining
subsidence in the area. (The canal has had to be
built up – appropriately with pit waste – while
the land on either side has sunk.)

Trencherfield Mill Engine By Bridge 51.
Probably the largest working mill engine in
Britain, installed when the mill was built in
1907. Manufactured by J & E Wood of Bolton
it is a horizontal four cylinder triple expansion
engine with a 26½ ft diameter flywheel. *Open
and in steam 10.00–17.00 Sat, Sun & B. Hols.*
Admission charge.

BOATYARDS

BWB Wigan Yard at Wigan Bottom Lock.
(Wigan 42239). R S W and toilet opposite at
lock 86.
Ⓑ **Wayfarer Narrow Boats** Mayors Boatyard,
Swan Meadow Road, Wigan. (41890).
R S W D Pump-out, gas, narrow boat hire,
repairs, chandlery, short term mooring.
Slipway & drydock close by.

PUBS

🍺 **Red Lion** Canalside, at Dover Bridge 4.
There used to be 2 locks nearby: they were
removed years ago, becoming unnecessary as
the level of the land changed.
🍺✕ **The Orwell** Large pub and restaurant in a
warehouse opposite bridge 51. This is a very
handsome building, and the conversion has
been well done – the pub is spacious,
comfortable and restrained. Tetleys real ale and
bar meals (*lunchtime and evenings*) are available.
Outside drinking on canalside verandah. Plenty
of moorings close by.

The Leeds & Liverpool Canal in Wigan. The hump in the towpath to the right is Wigan Pier; Trencherfield Mill stands in the background with the new Orwell pub on the left. *David Perrott*

Leigh

The Leigh Branch continues eastwards through
a no-man's land. There is just one working
coalmine left along here now: Bickershaw
Colliery. Near this big colliery is Plank Lane
swing bridge (actually a lift bridge) which is
mechanically operated. Navigators should
knock at the adjacent house in *daytime only
(08.00–20.00 summer, 17.00 winter)* to ask the
resident bridge keeper to operate the bridge,
which carries a busy road. Past the bridge, tall
cotton mills mark the entrance into Leigh,
where the canal suddenly becomes the
Bridgewater Canal (without the customary stop
lock), giving access to Manchester and the
Trent & Mersey via Preston Brook. This
navigation is owned by the Manchester Ship
Canal Company: boats licensed by the BWB
may use the Bridgewater without further
charge for up to 7 days.

Leigh
Gt Manchester. EC Wed. All services. An
archetypal mill town centred around its old
market place and parish church. Most of the
town buildings are the result of a large
redevelopment scheme, which provided
housing estates and a new market; even the
medieval church of St Mary was largely rebuilt
between 1869 and 1873. Standing prominently
in the Market Place, it is a forbidding,
battlemented structure – an unlikely setting for
the unusual ceremony taking place there every
Maundy Thursday, when 40 poor people step
over the grave of Henry Travice to qualify for
his bequest of 5 shillings each. Mr Travice
made out this bequest in 1626.

PUBS
Eagle & Hawk Chapel Street, Leigh. Food.
Railway Twist Lane, Leigh.
Packet Inn By Plank Lane swing bridge.
Britannia Plank Lane, by the bridge.

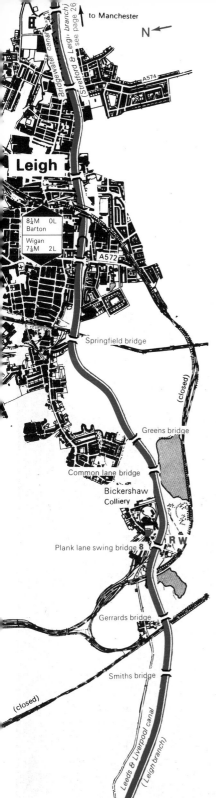

to Manchester

Bridgewater canal

(Stretford & Leigh branch) see page 26

A574

Leigh

| 8¼M | 0L |
| Barton |
| Wigan |
| 7½M | 2L |

A572

Springfield bridge

(closed)

Greens bridge

Common lane bridge

Bickershaw
Colliery

Plank lane swing bridge 8

R W

Gerrards bridge

Smiths bridge

(closed)

Leeds & Liverpool canal (Leigh branch)

Dover bridge 4

Wigan Locks

Leaving the junction with the Leigh Branch, the main line of the canal passes the large Wigan Power Station – no longer served by the canal – and starts immediately on the Wigan flight of 21 locks. It is a long and arduous climb to the top by boat, for these wide, deep locks raise the canal level by over 200ft. For the faint-hearted, there are shops and pubs near bridges 53 and 54. Up at the top lock, however, are 2 canal pubs – a comforting sight. Here is a T-junction as the canal meets what used to be the southern end of the Lancaster Canal (see the history section) on its disjointed way to Johnson's Hill Locks, Walton Summit and Preston. In the middle of the housing estate behind the Kirkless Hall is a fish and chip shop, *open for lunch and supper most days except Sun.* Turning left, the traveller is soon aware of the great height he has climbed as the navigation winds along a hill. It soon enters the woods that precede Haigh Hall and Park.

Navigational notes
1 The locks between Wigan and Leeds are 60ft long, and therefore cannot accommodate a full length narrow boat.
2 The locks are heavy to work, and the paddle gear varies from great levers on the ground paddles to ratchet gear worked from precarious platforms on the gates. The top gate paddles are *very fierce* – always open the ground paddles first when filling a lock, and wait until the water level reaches the bottom of the gates before slowly opening the gate paddles.
3 You will require a BWB anti-vandal key.

Wigan
Gt Manchester EC Wed. MD Fri. All services. A large, heavily industrialised town whose skyline is now a mixture of industrial chimneys and towering concrete blocks of offices and flats. There is a good and extensive covered market. The old market place in the centre of the town has some attractive black-and-white-timbered houses above the shops. It has long been the butt of many jokes referring to Wigan Pier – not a Victorian structure devoted to amusement at sea, but a coal staithe! George Formby snr started the confusion, which lasted for years.
All Saints Church A very large and impressive parish church surrounded by beautiful rose gardens. Parts of the original medieval structure remain but it was largely rebuilt in 1845–50, still following the rather ornate design of the former church. There are several very fine stained glass windows and numerous monuments and effigies.
Powell Museum Station Road. Exhibits include geology, coins and the history of local industrial development. *Open weekdays.*

BOATYARDS
BWB Wigan Yard At Wigan Bottom Lock. (Wigan 42239). R S W and toilet opposite at lock 86.
ⓑ **Wayfarer Narrow Boats** Mayors Boatyard, Swan Meadow Road, Wigan. (41890). R S W D Pump-out, gas, narrow boat hire, repairs, chandlery, short-term mooring. Slipway & drydock close by.

PUBS
🍺 **Crown** West of bridge 59A. Burtonwood real ale.
🍺 **Kirkless Hall** Canalside, near Wigan Top Lock. Distinctive black and white building housing spacious and comfortable bars. Burtonwood real ale and good bar meals.
🍺 **Commercial Inn** Canalside, at bridge 57. Sturdy Tetleys pub.
🍺 **Imperial** Just east of bridge 54. A basic Tetleys real ale pub, well placed on the flight. Payphone here.
🍺 **Shepherds Arms** Tetleys pub at bridge 53.

The Toll House Museum, part of The Weavers Triangle, Burnley. *David Perrott*

Adlington

The canal continues to run as a 9-mile lock-free
pound – known as the 'Lancaster Pool' – along
the side of the valley from which the industries
surrounding Wigan can be viewed in the
distance. It enjoys a pleasant and quiet isolation
in this lightly wooded area. Already the
navigation is well over 300ft above the sea, and
the bleak hills up to the east give a hint of the
Pennines that are soon to be crossed. The
conspicuous tower east of Adlington stands on a
hill that is over 1500ft high. Points of interest
on this stretch include Arley Hall, a large and
elegant moated house that is now the club
house of the local golf club, and the nearby
skewed aqueduct over a closed railway track.

Navigational note
For those heading east, Adlington is the last
pump-out station until Skipton (bridge 178).

Adlington
Gt Manchester. PO, tel, stores, garage, station. A
small industrialised town very useful for pubs
and supplies – the local licensed store east of
bridge 69 is open late most evenings.
Haigh Hall On east bank of the canal. The
pre-Tudor mansion was rebuilt by its owner,
the 23rd Earl of Crawford, between 1830 and
1849. The reconstruction was designed and
directed by the Earl, and all the stone, timber
and iron used on the job came from the estate.
The Hall is now owned by Wigan Corporation,
who allow the citizens to use it for private
wedding receptions, etc. There is little to see in
the house and it is not normally open to the
public. The park and grounds around the hall
are *open daily all year*, and contain much that
caters for the family: there are children's
amusements, glasshouses, a nature trail and a
golf course.

BOATYARDS

ⓑ **L & L Cruisers** Rawlinson Lane, Heath
Charnock, Nr Chorley. (Adlington 480825).
Ⓡ Ⓢ Ⓦ Ⓓ Pump-out, boat hire, slipway, gas,
boat building & repair, toilets. 12 person trip
boat/day boat.
ⓑ **White Bear Marine and Leisure** Park Road,
Adlington. (481054). Ⓡ Ⓢ Ⓦ Gas, chandlery
and gifts, slipway, mooring, overnight
mooring, winter storage, boat and engine
repairs, showers, toilets, refreshments and
picnic area. Boat sales and watersports
equipment for sale and hire – also watersports
tuition.

PUBS

🍺 **White Bear** Adlington. Matthew Brown
beers.
🍺 **Clayton Arms** Adlington. Matthew Brown
beers, bar food.
🍺 **Bridge** Adlington. Canalside, at bridge 69.
Greenall Whitley real ale.
🍺 **Crawford Arms** Canalside, at Red Rock
Bridge. Greenall Whitley real ale. Live music
some evenings.

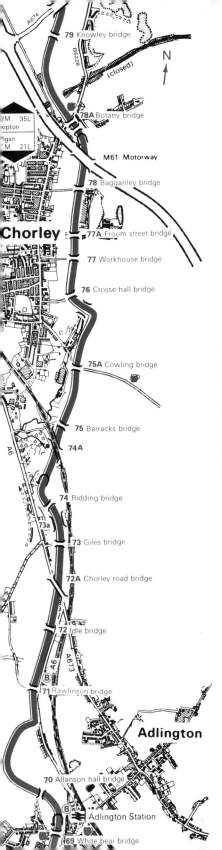

Chorley

This is an initially attractive section as the canal wanders northwards from Adlington. Hemmed in for much of the way by woodlands, the canal is undisturbed by the railway and main roads that for a while follow it closely. Soon the greenery gives way to views of Chorley's rows of rooftops across the valley. The canal crosses this valley, but shuns the town: it passes instead some large and resplendent outlying textile mills. The M61 motorway zooms up from Manchester around the mills and over the navigation before disappearing in the direction of Preston in a flurry of flyovers, feeder roads and roundabouts.

Chorley
Lancs. EC Wed. MD Tue, Fri, Sat. All services.
On the west bank of the canal, a busy town based on the manufacture of textiles and spare parts for commercial and public service vehicles. (Leyland, where the vehicles are built, is just a few miles away, to the north west.) Chorley has avoided too much industrial grimness by maintaining its market-town traditions and by extensive new housing development. Sir Henry Tate, the founder of the Tate Gallery in London, was born in Chorley in 1819 and began his career here as a grocer's assistant.
St Laurence's Church Church Brow. Surrounded by trees in the centre of the town, parts of the church date back to the 14thC. The bones that are enshrined in a recess in the chancel are believed to have belonged to St Laurence.
Astley Hall At the north west end of the town just over a mile from Botany Bridge. Set in a large parkland beside a lake, the appearance of this Elizabethan mansion is very striking, for in the 17thC the existing timberframing was replaced by a new façade that is lacking in symmetry. The interior is very fine with splendid ceilings, furnishings, tapestries and pottery. *Open afternoons.*

PUBS

Railway Chorley, Canalside, at Botany Bridge 78A. Whitbread beers, bar food, garden.
Skinner's Arms Chorley. 150yds uphill from bridge 75A.

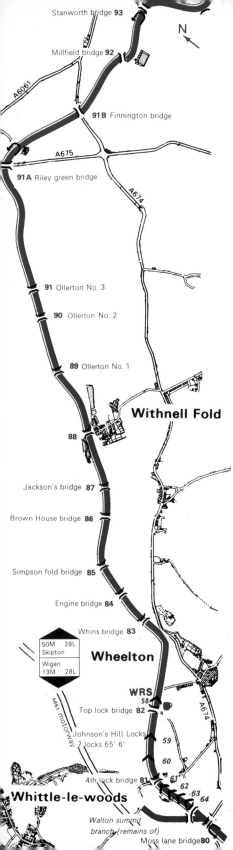

Withnell Fold

This is a most delightful stretch of waterway.
The junction with the old Walton Summit
Branch features a canal cottage and the bottom
lock in the Johnson's Hill flight. A short but
energetic spell of windlass-wielding is required
here, for the 7 locks are very close together. It is
rewarding work, for the steep countryside
yields good views, and the locks are tidily
maintained and painted. Near the middle lock
is an old toll house, a post office, telephone and
store; at the top lock is a pub and, usually, a
medley of boats (there is a boat club here). The
canal now changes course to north east and
flows along a beautifully secluded and often
wooded valley at a height of over 350ft above
sea level. Even the old mills at Withnell Fold,
which once brought a glimpse of industry, are
now gone.

Withnell Fold
Lancs. A remarkable village well worth a short
visit. It is a small estate village, built to house
workers at the canalside paper mills which are
now demolished. They used to export banknote
paper to all over the world until 'rationalisation'
transferred their work elsewhere.
Symmetrically grouped around 3 sides of a
spacious square, the terraced cottages present
an intimately united front which is almost
unnerving to the casual visitor – especially as on
the fourth side of the square is an old set of
wooden stocks.
Wheelton
Lancs. PO, tel, stores, garage. There are steep
terraces and cobbled streets in this village
which has been recently bypassed and has thus
rid itself of much road traffic.
The Walton Summit Branch
The short branch leading off to the north from
Johnson's Hill Locks used to be part of the
Lancaster Canal, which was originally
projected to run south from Preston past Wigan
to the Bridgewater Canal. But the Lancaster
Canal Company was very short of money, and,
after arranging with the Leeds & Liverpool
Company to share a common course between
Johnson's Hill Locks and Wigan Top Lock, was
daunted by the prospect of constructing a large
and necessarily expensive aqueduct over the
River Ribble in Preston. A 'temporary'
tramroad was therefore built to connect the 2
lengths of canal between Preston and Walton
Summit about 3 miles north of Johnson's Hill.
The tramway, which opened in 1803, featured a
short tunnel and a light trestle bridge over the
Ribble. Through traffic now began to use the
canal, and one may imagine the busy scenes at
either end of the tramway as cargoes were
trans-shipped from boats into wagons and back
into boats at the far end. The tramroad,
although designed only as a short-term
measure, was never replaced by a canal; indeed
the whole line was closed by 1880. Most of the
canal branch has recently been severed by the
building of a motorway, although plenty of it
still remains in an unnavigable state.

PUBS
● Royal Oak Riley Green. ¼ mile north west
of bridge 91A. Sandwiches daily.
● Top Lock Canalside, at Johnson's Hill Top
Lock. Good bar food and Matthew Brown beer
in this comfortable pub. Moor below the top
lock – there is no room above.

N

103B Paradise bridge
103A Enam bridge
103 Cicely bridge
102A Audley bridge
Cathedral
Blackburn station
Brewery bridge 102
Grimshaw park bridge 101
Blackburn
52 Top lock
Highfield road bridge 100
53
54
Hall st. bridge 99A
Blackburn
6 locks
54' 8½"
55
RSW
Bolton road bridge 99
56
Nova Scotia wharf
57 Bottom lock
98A
Hollin bank bridge 98
Ewood aqueduct
Whiteley bridge 97
Mill Hill Station
Moorgate fold bridge 96B
96A Kings bridge
96 Bower house fold bridge
Witton park
95 Cherry Tree bridge
Cherry Tree station
94 Livesey hall bridge
P
93B Feniscowle's bridge
A6062
dismantled
River Darwen
Stanworth bridge 93
Millfield bridge 92

42½M 26L
Skipton

Wigan
20½M 30L

A674

B6447

A6447

Blackburn

The canal now curls round a steep and thickly wooded valley, crossing it on a high embankment before entering the outskirts of Blackburn. Close to bridge 94 there is a useful shop. It seems to take a long time to get through this large town, as there is a flight of 6 locks here, raising the canal's level to a height of over 400ft above sea level. However one can get an excellent view of local bowls matches from the embankment between bridges 97 and 98. The safest place to moor (although space is limited) in Blackburn is just above lock 56: shops and pubs are close at hand, and the lock keeper lives here. He keeps a tidy flight – indeed most of the passage through the city is now pleasant – there is little rubbish or graffiti, and the views are excellent. A good towpath exists throughout. Of particular interest to those on the canal are the fine old canopied wharves of the defunct BWB Blackburn depot – although clearly its days are numbered. The aroma of the Thwaites brewery is refreshing.

Blackburn
Lancs. EC Thur. All services. Few of the Pennine towns which sprang up with the Industrial Revolution can be described as beautiful for aesthetic feelings were rarely consulted in the rush to raise mills and cram houses round them. In an attempt to rectify this, Blackburn has taken drastic steps in recent years to construct a new city centre, which includes multistorey blocks of flats, a large shopping precinct and a vast covered market. Nevertheless the most impressive features of the town are still the old cotton mills.
Blackburn Cathedral Dating from 1820–6, the parish church was raised to cathedral status in 1926. Extensive renovations have been made inside. Very striking 13ft sculpture of 'Christ the Worker' in aluminium and black iron by John Hayward. Large churchyard.
Lewis Textile Museum Exchange Street. A series of period rooms demonstrating the development of the textile industry from the 18thC onwards by means of full-size working models, including Hargreaves' 'Spinning Jenny'. *Closed Sun.*
Museum & Art Gallery Library Street. Exhibits include natural history, pottery, early manuscripts and a large collection of English, Greek and Roman coins. In the art gallery are over 1200 beautiful Japanese prints, as well as English water colours of the 18thC–20thC. *Closed Sun.*
Witton Park At the western end of the town, north of Cherry Tree station. Nearly 500 acres of magnificent parkland, including the beautiful landmark, Billinge Hill. Splendid abundance of rhododendrons and azaleas. *Open daily to the public.*
Information Centre Near the Town Hall (55201).

PUBS
🍺 **Packet House Inn** Near bridge 103A.
🍺 **Infirmary** Blackburn. By lock 56. Thwaites real ale, good bar food, children welcome in this down to earth pub.
🍺 **Horse Load Inn** At Bolton Road Bridge. Very basic friendly local serving Thwaites real ale.
🍺 **Navigation** Blackburn. Canalside, at bridge 96A. Thwaites real ale.
🍺 **Moorgate Arms** West of bridge 96A.
🍺 **Barge Inn** Blackburn. Near the canal. New pub with canal theme serving Thwaites real ale.

Rishton

Clayton-le-Moors

114B Whalley road bridge
114A Enfield changeline bridge
114AA Enfield Green bridge
Rileys
114 swing bridge

Church

35M 26L
Skipton
Wigan
28M 30L

113A Peel Bank bridge
Church swing bridge **113**

Dunkenhalgh park

urban development
Simpson's bridge **111D**

Church Kirk changeline bridge **112**

Burys bridge No 2   **111B**
Burys bridge No 1   **111A**
Fox hill bank bridge   **111**

New Barn bridge **109**
aqueduct

P

Tottleworth bridge
108

108 A Rishton bridge

Aspen bridge **110**

Rishton

107A Norden bridge

Rishton station

107 Cut bridge

106 Side Beet bridge

power station

Whitebirk bridge **104 B**   **P**

Gorse bridge **104A**

104 Sour milk hall bridge

Blackburn

Paradise bridge **103B**

Blackburn Station
Enam bridge **103A**

The canal leaves Blackburn and embarks upon a course of twists and turns that emphasise the hilliness of the countryside. The scenery varies all the time between heavy industrial development (and its effects) and – just around a corner – green fields, farms and distant views of wild moorlands. The contrast repeats itself time and again, but the moorlands always seem to remain tantalisingly out of reach. However, anyone prepared to take a short but energetic walk away from the canal will find remote and beautiful countryside remarkably close. The new Calder valley motorway (M65) follows the line of the canal to Burnley, making many new crossings and requiring re-routing of the navigation in 2 places. It is pleasing to see the care taken with such items as stone walling, which makes the new aqueduct by bridge 109 a positive asset to the canal. Of less recent vintage, but of equal interest, is the fine wharf building with a large central arch at Simpson's bridge. Beyond Church, the first of 4 swing bridges appears: they are the only ones between Wigan and Gargrave.

Church
Lancs. EC Wed. PO, tel, stores, garage, bank.
An industrial community which was originally based on calico printing, established on the canal bank by the family of the famous Sir Robert Peel. The rows of terraced houses are characteristic of so many of the towns in this industrial area. The parish church of St James is right on the banks of the canal; only the tower and font remain from the original 15thC building.
Dunkenhalgh Hall Clayton-le-Moors. Standing in 16 acres of gardens and woodland, it is a beautiful Elizabethan mansion, extensively altered in the 19thC. Its name is said to be derived from a Scottish raider named Duncan, who chose to settle there. The Hall is now used as an hotel.
Rishton
Lancs. EC Wed. PO, tel, stores, garage, bank, station. A small grey town that grew up around the cotton mills in the 19thC by courtesy of the Petre family of the Dunkenhalgh Estate, who used to be lords of the manor and are still local landowners.

PUBS
Hare and Hounds 250 yds east of bridge 114A. Shops and fish & chips nearby.
Old England for Ever Church Street, Clayton-le-Moors. Matthew Brown real ale in tiled bar.
Wellington Barnes Square, Clayton-le-Moors.
Both the above are about 250yds west of bridge 114B.
Roebuck Rishton. Near bridge 108A.

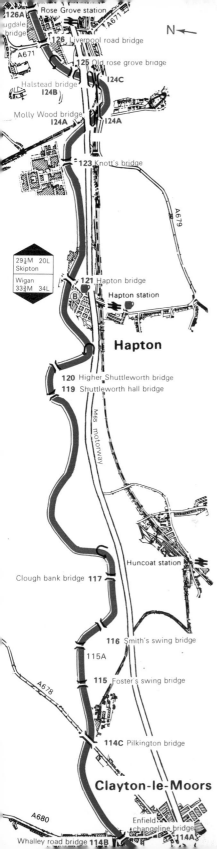

Hapton

The navigation continues to wind eastwards along the side of what turns out to be the Calder valley with the new motorway under construction to the south. High ground rises on each side of the valley, and in the distance the summit of Pendle Hill (1831ft high) can be clearly seen when it is not obscured by cloud. This is an attractive length of canal, unspoilt by industry and greatly enhanced by the ever-changing views from the side of the hill along which the canal is cut, although the new motorway is uncomfortably close throughout, and power station cooling towers are ever present. Soon the distant mass of dwellings is recognisable as the suburbs of Burnley.

Navigational note
You will require a BWB sanitary station key to operate Foster's swing bridge 115.

Hapton
Lancs. PO, tel, stores, station. A small and unmistakably northern town, with its regular streets of terraced houses.

BOATYARDS
Ⓑ **Hapton Boatyard** (Padiham 73178). Ⓓ Gas, repairs, moorings, slipway.

PUBS
🍺 **Bridge** Hapton. By bridge 121. Thwaites real ale, lunchtime bar snacks.
🍺 **Railway** Hapton. Along the road from the Bridge.

Burnley

The canal now wanders through the suburbs into Gannow Tunnel (559yds long), then round the hillside into Burnley. This is an industrial stretch where the canal was once a main artery for the town and its industries. The area around bridge 130 known as the Weavers' Triangle has been recognised to be of great interest – fine warehouses, tall chimneys and loading bays flank the canal here. There is a museum in the Toll House, and a steam mill engine is being restored. The huge Burnley Embankment carries the navigation across part of the town – called 'the straight mile' it is ¾ mile long, but no less dramatic for that fact. 60ft high, it incorporates an aqueduct over a main road. The whole area of the embankment has been tidied up and the towpath opened and improved: access is now good and this, together with the BWB yard, makes a good mooring site. Shops are within easy reach.

Burnley
Lancs. All services. A large industrial northern town, which has worked hard to improve its appearance. It was once the world centre for cotton weaving. The excellent shopping centre is only 10 minutes walk from Finsley Gate Bridge, and if you feel like a swim, a sauna or a solarium, the Thompson Recreation Centre is even closer. Fish & chips are two minutes walk south west of the bridge.
The Weavers' Triangle The area between bridges 129B and 130B is one of the best preserved 19thC industrial districts in the country – there are weaving sheds with 'north light' roofs, engine houses, spinning mills and well-preserved terraces of 19thC houses. An explanatory leaflet and town trail guide are available from: the Tourist Information Centre or the Toll House Museum of local history and the cotton industry, which is also the information centre for the Weavers' Triangle. *Open 14.00–16.00 Wed & Sun, & 1st Sat of month Apr–Oct.*
Townley Hall On the southern outskirts of Burnley, 1¼ miles south east of the BWB yard. Set in extensive parklands with a golf course and play area, the grandiose, battlemented house dating from the 14thC was the home of the Townley family until 1902. It is now an art gallery and museum with the rooms lavishly furnished in period style. *Closed Sat & Sun morning.*
Information Centre Burnley 25011, ext 236.

BOATYARDS

BWB Burnley Yard Finsley Gate. (Burnley 28680). R W S Toilet, slipway, moorings. Telephone kiosk outside.

BOAT TRIPS

Trips along Burnley Embankment and through Gannow Tunnel. Ring Burnley 20444 for details.

PUBS

🍺 **The Stork** North of bridge 129B. Tetleys ales.
🍺 **Mitre Hotel** By bridge 129B. Bass.
🍺 **Sparrowhawk** Church Street, Burnley.
🍺 **Gannow Wharf** Canalside at bridge 127A. Bass and bar snacks. Plenty of pubs in Burnley.

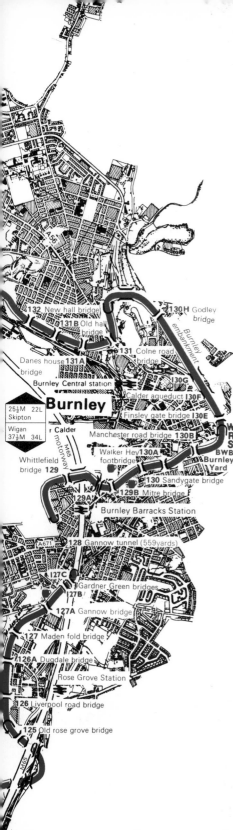

132 New hall bridge
131B Old hall bridge
130H Godley bridge
131 Colne road bridge
Danes house 131A bridge
Burnley embankment
Burnley Central station
130G
Calder aqueduct 130F
Burnley
25½M 22L Skipton
Wigan 37½M 34L
Finsley gate bridge 130E
r Calder
Manchester road bridge 130B
W R S BWB Burnley Yard
Whittlefield bridge 129
Walker Hey 130A footbridge
M65 motorway
130 Sandygate bridge
129A
129B Mitre bridge
Burnley Barracks Station
128 Gannow tunnel (559yards)
127C
Gardner Green bridges
127B
127A Gannow bridge
127 Maden fold bridge
126A Dugdale bridge
Rose Grove Station
26 Liverpool road bridge
125 Old rose grove bridge
A56
A671
M65

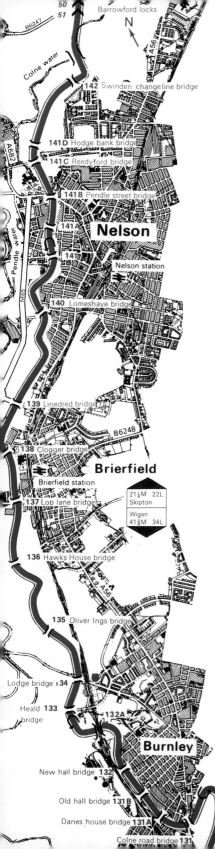

Brierfield

Here again the canal negotiates a landscape
which alternates between open country, towns
and semi-towns, with the massive distant bulk
of Pendle Hill in the background. Cobbled
streets of terraced houses run down to the
canal, and old wharves lie disused and
overgrown. The navigation winds as it follows
the hillside; but this ceases at Nelson, where it
crosses the valley on a minor aqueduct and
begins to climb the pretty Barrowford Locks
having finally seen off the new motorway.

Nelson
Lancs. EC Tue. MD Wed, Fri, Sat. All services.
Nelson is a conglomerate of a number of small
villages that combined in the 19thC to form one
industrial town. The centre has been
redeveloped with a large covered shopping
precinct. One of Nelson's more valuable assets
is the easy access to the beautiful moors and
Forest of Pendle, behind which looms Pendle
Hill.
Brierfield
*Lancs. PO, tel, stores, garage, bank, station,
cinema.* A small industrial town merging into
Burnley at one end and into Nelson at the
other. The parish church of St Luke in Colne
Road is a Victorian building with an unusually
designed clock tower culminating in a steep
pyramid roof.

PUBS
Leeds & Liverpool Brierfield. Up the hill
from bridge 137.
Reedly Hallows Hotel 50 yds east of bridge
134.

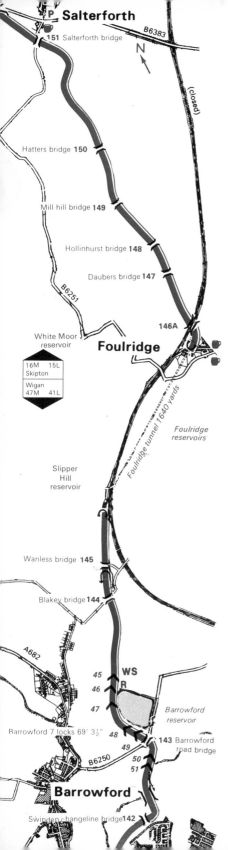

Foulridge

This is a refreshing stretch, in which the canal shakes off for good the succession of industrial towns that dog it through much of Lancashire. It rises through the 7 Barrowford Locks, passing Barrowford reservoir (in which the summit level's surplus water is stored), and at the beautifully kept top lock reaches the summit level of the whole canal. Soon one begins to notice the various feeder streams continuously pouring vital water supplies into the navigation. Meanwhile, distant mountainous country frames beautiful old stone farms nearer at hand. Soon everything is blotted out as one enters Foulridge Tunnel; at the other end, by the railway bridge, is an old wharf where one can tie up to visit the village. Meanwhile the navigation continues northward through this very fine countryside to Salterforth, crossing over the little 'Country Brook' between bridges 149 (milk and eggs for sale) and 150.

Salterforth
Lancs. PO, tel, stores. A small village of narrow streets and terraced houses in an upland setting.

Foulridge
Lancs. PO, tel, stores. Attractive around the green, where alleys festooned with washing lines give the place a homely air. In the surrounding countryside are scattered the reservoirs that feed the summit level of the canal.

Foulridge Tunnel
1640yds long, with no towpath, this tunnel is, not surprisingly, barred to unapproved boats. The hole in the hill sprang to fame in 1912 when a cow fell into the canal near the tunnel mouth and for some reason decided to struggle through to the other end of the tunnel. The gallant but weary swimmer was revived with alcohol at the Foulridge end. Photographs in the Hole in the Wall pub recall the incident. The tunnel roof drips liberally.

BOAT TRIPS

Foulridge Leisure Cruises 56 Hibson Rd, Nelson (694978). 'Marton Emperor' available for private hire for parties of up to 50 people.

PUBS

🍺 **Anchor** Salterforth. Canalside, at bridge 151. A traditional pub serving Bass Charrington real ale, where a second building was built on top of the first – hence where you now drink was once the bedrooms. The cellar has stalactites. Good moorings.
🍺 **Hole in the Wall** Foulridge. 250yds east of tunnel, north end. Here is recorded the famous cow in the canal incident. Stones real ale is served, and there is a room where children can sit. Steeles stores close by gives genial service and stocks splendid pies – savoury or sweet.
🍺 **New Inn** Foulridge. Carry on past the Hole in the Wall and cross the main road. Thwaites real ale, bar food (*not Sun or Mon Oct–Mar*). Children may eat here. Spotlessly clean.

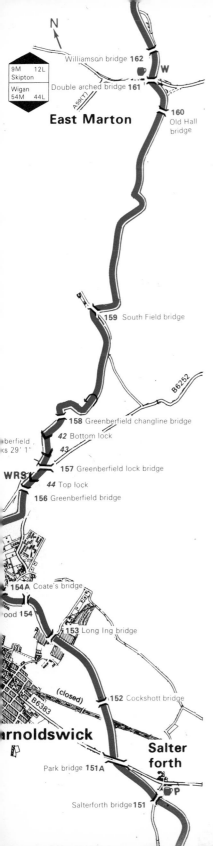

Barnoldswick

This is one of the most remote sections of the whole canal and probably the most beautiful. There is also much canal interest, for just south of bridge 153 was the junction, now disappeared, of the Rain Hall Rock Branch, essentially a linear quarry where the limestone was loaded directly from the rock face onto the boats. Walk up the road from the bridge (east) and turn right at the top where it will come into view, straddled by a tall 3-arched viaduct. A mile further along one rounds a corner and is confronted by Greenberfield Top Lock, which introduces the beginning of the long descent towards Leeds. (The feeder from the distant Winterburn reservoir enters the canal at the top lock.) The 3 locks here were built in 1820 to replace the original flight (the old dry bed of the earlier route can be seen on the towpath side) and are set in beautiful uplands; and for the next few miles the canal winds through scenery that is composed of countless individual hillocks, some topped by clumps of trees. Beyond are distant mountains. Around East Marton, after skirting the isolated church, the surroundings change briefly: the navigation enters a cutting, passes under a double-arched main road bridge and enters a sheltered fold housing a farm, a pub and some moorings. But a steep wooded cutting leads the canal out of this pastoral interlude and back into the rugged moorlands.

Pennine Way The Pennine Way is a walking route covering over 250 miles of Pennine highland from Edale in the south to Kirk Yetholm in the north. Because of the nature of the route much of the Way is rough, hard walking, but it gives a superb view from the mountains. At East Marton the Pennine Way shares the canal towpath for a short distance – you will notice that the stones here abound with fossils.

Barnoldswick
Lancs. EC Tue. PO, tel, stores, garage, bank. Set back from the canal, the mainstay of this town's existence is the Rolls Royce factory, where experimental work is done on aero engines. The centre of the town is compact and dominated by the new Holy Trinity Church completed in 1960.

BOATYARDS

ⓑ **J & J Crook** Barnoldswick (~~Bradford 728718~~). By bridge 152. Boat building and repairs, moorings. 0282-815883

PUBS

Cross Keys East Marton. (Earby 843485). By bridge 161. Large and handsome pub with a comfortable polished wood interior. Theakston, Thwaites and Websters real ales, bar snacks and more substantial meals in the candlelit dining room. Next door is the Cottage Stores – it does not look like a shop and can be easily missed. Telephone kiosk close by. Plenty of pubs in Barnoldswick.

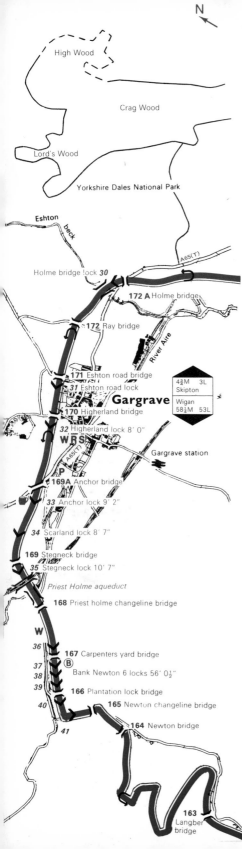

Gargrave

This is another outstanding stretch, in which the navigation continues to snake extravagantly around the splendid green and humpy hills that fill the landscape. The 6 Bank Newton Locks in their wooded setting lower the canal into upper Airedale, yielding excellent views across the valley to the hills and moors beyond. The River Aire flows in from the north, accompanied by the railway line to Skipton and Leeds from Morecambe, Settle and distant Carlisle. The canal crosses the river by a substantial stone aqueduct. Meanwhile, yet more locks take the canal round Gargrave, between the village and the hills; the beauty of the area may be judged by the fact that the Yorkshire Dales National Park borders the navigation along here. There is a BWB launching slipway at Higherland Lock.

Gargrave
N. Yorks. PO, tel, stores, garage, bank, station.
A very attractive and much-visited village. Holding an enviable position near the head of Airedale between the canal and the river, this place is the ideal centre for boat crews to explore the surrounding countryside. The River Aire cuts Gargrave in two, and the bridge over it forms the centre of the village. There is a charming station, and some pretty stone cottages along the green. The church is mostly Victorian, except for the tower, which was built in 1521. Excellent home bakery.
Yorkshire Dales National Park Some of England's finest walking country is contained in this area of fine views, deep valleys, open moorland and rugged hills. Designated as a National Park in 1954 the Dales, covering 680 sq miles, are hardly scarred by habitation.

BOATYARDS

Ⓑ **Yorkshire Dales Hire Cruisers** (Inland Marine Leisure) Bank Newton, Skipton, (Gargrave 492). An immaculate hire craft base with services sometimes available. *Closed Sun.*

PUBS

🍺 **Mason's Arms** Gargrave. Opposite the church. Attractive old pub.
🍺 **Old Swan** Gargrave.
🍺✕ **Anchor** Gargrave. By Anchor Lock. A large, smart pub/hotel/restaurant with comfortable low ceilinged bars where you can choose from Theakston, Tetley or Youngers real ales. Bar food or restaurant meals. In the large garden there is a superb children's play park.

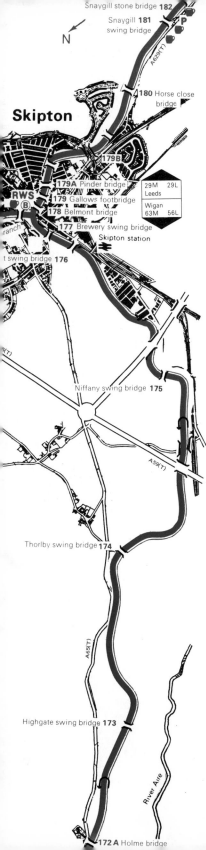

Skipton

The canal now turns south east and proceeds down Airedale, a valley which contains it from here right through to Leeds. Upper Airedale is a flat, wide valley defined by tall steep hills. The countryside is open, unploughed and very inviting to walkers, especially with the moorlands stretching away over the top of the hills. In this robust landscape the navigation hugs the hillsides just above the valley floor, enjoying a lock-free pound that is 17 miles long – although the navigator's relief at the absence of locks may be tempered by the abundance of swing bridges (174, 175, 176 and 177 require an anti-vandal key). Entering Skipton, which is usually bristling with pleasure boats, the navigator will see the Springs Branch, a little arm that leads off past the town centre and soon finds itself in what is virtually a ravine, overlooked by the castle more than 100ft above. Boats longer than 35ft will have difficulty in turning round along the branch. At the junction is a boatyard: next door is a restored canal warehouse.

Navigational note
For those heading west, Skipton is the last pump-out station until Adlington (bridge 71).

Skipton
N. Yorks. EC Tue. MD Mon, Thur, Sat. All services (including cinema) and excellent shops.
Skipton is probably the most handsome town along the whole Leeds & Liverpool Canal. It is an excellent place for visiting from the canal, for one can moor snugly and safely about 1 minute's walk away from the centre. It still maintains its importance as a market town, which is referred to in its name: Saxon 'Scip-tun' means sheep-town. The wide High Street is very attractive, lined with mostly Georgian houses, and headed at the northern end by the splendid castle and the well-kept graveyard of the parish church. There is an interesting watermill beside the Springs Branch: this is often opened to visitors on *summer Sunday afternoons.*
Church of the Holy Trinity Standing opposite the castle, it is a long battlemented church, encircled by large lawns and flourishing gardens. It is in Perpendicular style dating from the 14thC, though it was greatly renovated after suffering serious damage during the Civil War. It has a fine oak roof and a beautifully carved Jacobean font cover.
Skipton Castle A magnificent Norman castle, with 17thC additions, that dominates Skipton High Street. After a 3-year siege during the Civil War, Cromwell's men allowed the restoration of the castle, but ensured that the building could never again be used as a stronghold. The 6 massive round towers have survived from the 14thC and other notable features are the 50ft long banqueting hall, a kitchen with roasting and baking hearths, a dungeon and the 'Shell Room', the walls of which are decorated with sea shells. *Open daily (Closed Sun morning). Admission charge.*
The Springs Branch A short (770yds) but very unusual branch that leaves the Leeds & Liverpool Canal, passes the centre of Skipton and soon finds itself in what is virtually a ravine, overlooked by the Castle that towers 100ft above. The branch is navigable, and makes an interesting diversion by boat or foot. (The towpath continues past the arm, into Skipton Woods.) It was built by the Earl of Thanet, the owner of Skipton Castle, to carry limestone away from his nearby quarry. It was extended 240yds in 1797 from the watermill bridge through the deep rock cutting, and chutes were constructed at the new terminus to drop the rock into the boats from the horse tramway that was laid from the quarry to the castle. The quarry still flourishes, but the canal and tramway have not been used since 1946. Trains and lorries have replaced them. The Springs Branch acted for many years as a feeder to the Leeds & Liverpool Canal, taking water from Eller Beck, which runs beside it. It is now a picturesque backwater and an excellent place to moor if your boat is less than 35ft long or you are confident that you can reverse out, as turning is restricted.

Skipton Woods Fine woods leading up the little narrow valley from the Springs Branch. For access, just keep on walking up the towpath of the branch.

BOATYARDS

ⓑ **Pennine Cruisers** The Boat Shop, 19 Coach Street, Skipton. (2061). At junction with Springs Branch W̄ D̄ Pump-out, narrow boat hire, gas, chandlery. Drydock, boat building & repairs, extensive boat sales, 24hr emergency service.

TRIP BOAT

Pennine Boat Trips Skipton (60829). Trips and party hire in 'Cobbydale'.

PUBS

⬤╳ **Bay Horse** Canalside, at bridge 182. Tetley real ale.

⬤ **Copper Beech** Close to bridge 181. Large pub with pond in the garden. Food.

⬤ **Alcove Inn** Not far from bridge 181. Tetley real ale.

⬤ **Rose & Crown** Coach St, Skipton. By the junction with the Springs Branch. Tetley real ale served in this town centre pub.

⬤ **Royal Shepherd** Canal St, Skipton. Whitbread, Castle Eden and Chester real ale available in this lively pub overlooking the Springs Branch.

╳♥ **Waterfront** Skipton. Restaurant and disco at junction of Springs Branch.

⬤ **Hole in the Wall** High Street, Skipton.

⬤ **New Ship** Canalside, up the Springs Branch; and 25 other pubs and hotels in the town.

The Springs Branch, Skipton. *David Perrott*

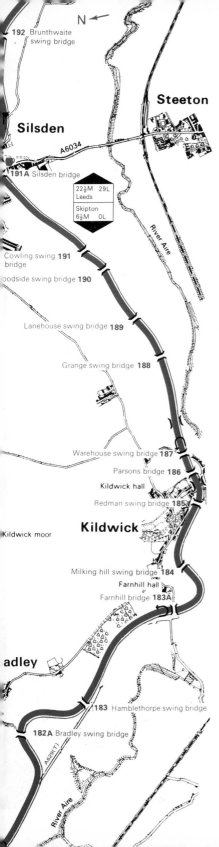

Kildwick

The canal continues along the hillside down the valley of the River Aire, with the main road just beside and below the navigation. Excellent views are offered up and down this splendid valley and the surrounding countryside. The village of Bradley has an attractive waterfront – the *PO stores* are situated beyond the imposing mill building. There is a fine wooded stretch north of Kildwick; then one curves sharply round the outcrop on which crouches Farnhill Hall, a mellow stone building. The intriguing village of Kildwick has some well restored canalside buildings now used as private residences. There are good moorings here prior to quieter country: the main road and the railway cut the valley corner while the canal takes the longer route round to Silsden and beyond. This stretch of the navigation is liberally punctuated with swing bridges many, thankfully, not requiring an anti-vandal key.

Silsden
W. Yorks. EC Tue. PO, tel, stores, garage, bank.
A well-contained, stone-built industrial town spreading uphill from the canal. In addition to its proximity to the Yorkshire Dales National Park, it offers plenty of shops near the canal. The canalside warehouses are attractive; there is also an old corn mill dated 1677.

Kildwick
W. Yorks. PO, tel, stores. An interesting and unusual village spilling down the hillside. The streets are extremely steep; one of them goes under the canal through a narrow skewed aqueduct.

BOATYARDS

ⓑ **Black Prince Narrowboats** The Wharf, Silsden, near Keighley. (Steeton 53675). Ⓡ Ⓦ Ⓓ Pump-out, narrow boat hire, canal shop, slipway, gas, toilets, winter storage. *Closed Sun.*

ⓑ **Snaygill Boats** Skipton Road, Bradley, near Keighley. (Skipton 5150). At bridge 182. Ⓡ Ⓢ Ⓦ Ⓓ Pump-out, boat hire, gas, drydock, boat & engine repairs, canal shop, mooring, toilets, showers. *Closed Tue in summer, Sat & Sun in winter.*

PUBS

🍺 **Bridge** Silsden. Canalside. Courage beers.
🍺 **The Grouse** Silsden. ¼ mile north of bridge 191A.
🍺 **Kings Arms** Silsden. ⅓ mile north of bridge 191A.
🍺 **White Lion** Kildwick. Near the canal. Tetley real ale.

Keighley

Here the canal continues south east along the
side of the green hills that overlook Airedale.
The hills are very steep and beautifully wooded
in places. The distant rows of chimneys,
factories and terraced houses across the valley
comprise Keighley; most of its industrial and
suburban tentacles are quickly passed by the
canal, although the constant succession of little
swing bridges intermittently impedes a boat's
progress. Some of these bridges can be rather
stiff to operate.

East Riddlesden Hall
NT property. Just south of swing bridge 197A.
A 17thC stone manor house complete with tithe
barn. Fine collection of furniture, paintings
and armour. Fishing is permitted in the ponds
in the grounds. *Open Mon afternoons. Closed
Dec.*
Keighley
*W. Yorks. EC Tue. MD Wed, Fri, Sat. All
services.* Compared with some other industrial
centres in the area, Keighley is a clean and
pleasant town. It boasts a large new shopping
centre, much modern housing and some
handsome older stone terraces. The oldest part
is around the parish church of St Andrew, a
large perpendicular building whose main
attraction is its shady churchyard.
Cliffe Castle Spring Gardens Lane. Once the
home of the Butterfield family, it has been
completely restored and now houses the
museum and art gallery. Local exhibits
illustrate the archaeology, natural history and
industrial history of the area. There are
reconstructed craft workshops and a textile
room. Picturesque grounds where band
concerts are held. *Closed Sun morning.*
Keighley & Worth Valley Railway Privately
preserved by volunteers of the Keighley &
Worth Valley Railway Preservation Society, the
line runs for 5 miles from the British Rail
station at Keighley up to Haworth, the home of
the Brontë family, and Oxenhope, British
Railways closed the line in 1961, but the
Society eventually succeeded in reopening
it in 1968 with a regular service of steam
trains. In the mornings, the service is operated
by diesel railbuses but in the afternoons
magnificent steam engines puff their way along
the track. In the goods yard at Haworth the
Society has a splendid collection of steam
engines and carriages, mostly ancient. The line
was made famous by the film 'The Railway
Children'.

PUBS

🍺 **Marquis of Granby** At swing bridge 197A.
Wilsons real ale. *PO and stores* the other side of
the bridge.
Plenty of pubs in Keighley.

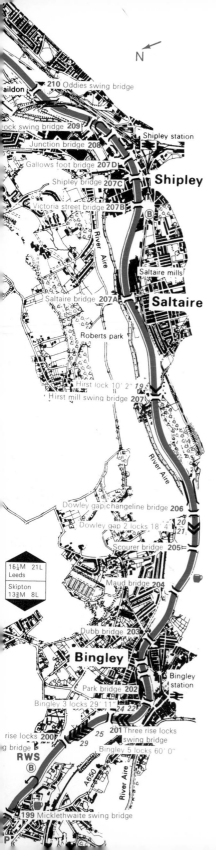

N

210 Oddies swing bridge

aildon

ock swing bridge 209

Junction bridge 208

Shipley station

Gallows foot bridge 207D

Shipley 207C

Shipley

Victoria street bridge 207B

Saltaire mills

Saltaire bridge 207A

Saltaire

River Aire

Roberts park

Hirst lock 10' 2" 19.?

Hirst mill swing bridge 207

River Aire

Dowley gap changeline bridge 206

Dowley gap 2 locks 18' 4"
20
21

Scourer bridge 205

16¾M   21L
Leeds

Skipton
13¾M   8L

Maud bridge 204

Dubb bridge 203

Bingley

Park bridge 202

Bingley
station

Bingley 3 locks 29' 11"
24 22?

201 Three rise locks
swing bridge

rise locks 200

25

29

g bridge

RWS

Bingley 5 locks 60' 0"

A650

River Aire

199 Micklethwaite swing bridge

Bingley and Shipley

The impressive Bingley 5-rise staircase locks
(see below) mark the end of the long level
pound from Gargrave, and from here to Leeds
there are no more views of a sweeping,
uncluttered river valley. Just a few hundred
yards south of the 5 locks are the 3-rise staircase
locks, which bring one steeply down into
Bingley. The canal bisects this town but one
can see little of the place from the water.
Leaving Bingley, trees lead to Dowley Gap and
the 2 staircase locks. At the foot of the locks the
towpath changes sides and the navigation
crosses the River Aire via a stone aqueduct.
Woods escort the canal along to the single Hirst
Lock; from here one moves past the big mills at
Saltaire and right through Shipley.

Baildon
W. Yorks. EC Tue. All services. 1½ miles north
of Shipley. A very old industrial town huddled
on a hilltop on the edge of Baildon Moor.
Stretching from Baildon to Bingley is The
Glen, a wooded valley that curves below the
heights of the moor. A splendid scenic tramway
carrying 2 tramcars connects the coach road to
the higher parts of Baildon Moor. (In summer a
frequent service operates, but in winter it is
arranged only to suit the needs of residents at
the upper level.)
Shipley
W. Yorks. EC Wed. MD Fri, Sat. All services. A
dark stone town built on a generous scale and
based on textile and engineering industries.
There are powerful-looking mills to be seen, as
well as the town hall and a suitably
battlemented Salvation Army citadel. Shipley is
lucky enough to be on the edge of Baildon
Moor and Shipley Glen. The 3-mile long
Bradford Canal used to join the Leeds &
Liverpool in Shipley, by bridge 208, but this
has all been filled in for years.
Saltaire
W. Yorks. An estate village that owes its
existence to the Utopian dream of Sir Titus
Salt, a wealthy Victorian mill owner. He was so
appalled by the working and living conditions
of his workers in Bradford that he decided to
build the ideal industrial settlement. This he
did in 1850 on the banks of the canal and the
River Aire – hence the name Saltaire. He
provided every amenity including high
standard housing, but no pub – for he was a
great opponent of strong drink. The village has
changed little since those days; everything is
carefully laid out and the terraced houses are
attractive in an orderly sort of way. (And there
is still no pub!) There is an Italianate church
near the canal, and a large park beside the river.
(Rowing boats can be hired here in the summer.)
Bingley
W. Yorks. EC Tue. MD Fri. All services. An
industrial town now known nationally as a
centre for thermal underwear. Standing at the
south east end of it amidst several old cottages
is the massive parish church of Holy Trinity,
with its massive spire conspicuous from the
canal.
Bingley 5-rise locks A very famous and
impressive feature of the canal system built in
1774 in 'staircase' formation, ie they are
all joined together rather than being separated
by pounds of 'neutral' water. The top gates of
the lowest lock are the bottom gates of the
lock above, and so on. This means it is not
possible to empty a lock unless the one below is
itself empty. The rapid elevation thus resulting
is quite daunting. The locks are *open*
08.00–18.30 and may be used only under the
supervision of the lock keeper, who lives in the
interesting house at the top of the flight. The
BWB Sanitary Station is housed in a handsome
old stable, where towing horses were once
rested.

BOATYARDS
Ⓑ **Apollo Canal Carriers** Wharf Street,
Shipley. (Bradford 595914). Ⓡ Ⓦ (emergency
Ⓓ Pump-out. 46-seater passenger boat and
50-seater cruising restaurant. Temporary
mooring by arrangement.
Ⓑ **Hainsworths Boatyard** Bingley (Bradford
565925). 200 yards above the 5-rise. Ⓓ Gas,
chandlery, boat sales and repairs, mooring,
slipway.

PUBS

🍺 **Shoulder of Mutton** Otley Road, Charlestown. ¼ mile east of bridge 210.
🍺 **Sun** Market Place, Shipley. 250yds south of bridge 207C.
🍺 **Fisherman** Canalside, above Dowley Gap locks.

🍺 **Brown Cow** Ireland Bridge, Bingley. ¼ mile west of bridge 202.
🍺 **Ferrands Arms** Queen Street, Bingley. 250yds south of bridge 202.
Plenty of pubs in Bingley and Shipley.
🍺 **Royal** 200yds down the hill from Micklethwaite swing bridge. Tetley real ale.

Ascending the Five-Rise, Bingley. *David Perrott*

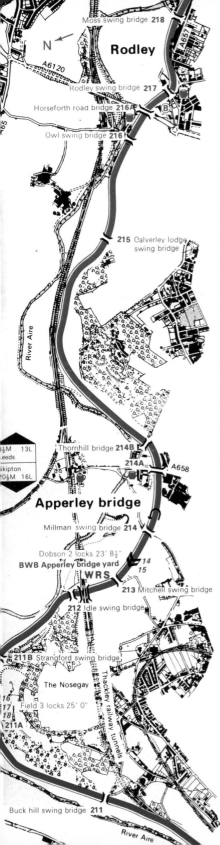

Apperley Bridge

This section sees the end of the wide open moorlands that frame the scenery further upstream: from now on, industry and houses begin to feature more as one approaches the outskirts of Leeds. The navigation, however, is thankfully sequestered from these intrusions into the landscape. Leaving Shipley, the adjacent railway cuts through a 500ft high hill in 2 mile-long tunnels. The canal goes all the way round this delightfully wooded hill, tenaciously following the Aire valley. Halfway round the long curve are Field Locks: there is an extensive but inconspicuous sewage works nearby, which boasts its own railway system. Beyond the main railway bridge is a BWB maintenance yard at the head of Dobson's Locks. The BWB facilities here for boats are housed in former canal stables. Temporarily traversing a built up area, the navigation emerges yet again onto a wooded hillside overlooking the still rural and charming valley that contains the River Aire.

Rodley
W. Yorks. PO, tel, stores. A useful village on the canal bank. There are 2 pubs, several shops and a launderette, as well as good temporary moorings.

BOATYARDS

Ⓑ **Rodley Boat Centre** Canal Wharf, Canal Road, Rodley, Leeds. (576132). By bridge 216A. ⓇⓈ🆆Ⓓ Pump-out, boat hire, slipway, gas, mooring, chandlery, winter storage, trip boat for charter. Marine engineering and outboard repairs. *Closed Tue afternoons.*
BWB Apperley Bridge Dobson Locks. (Bradford 611303). ⓇⓈⓌ

PUBS

🍺 **Owl** Rodley.
🍺 **Rodley Barge** Canalside, near swing bridge 217.
🍺 **Railway** Near canal, by bridge 216.
🍺✕ **George & Dragon** Apperley Bridge. 200yds north east of bridge 214A. Restaurant lunches *Mon–Fri.* PO, tel, stores, garage nearby.
🍺✕ **Stansfield Arms** Apperley Bridge. Just over the River Aire from the George & Dragon. *No food on Sun.*

Leeds

This is a section full of contrasts; and it probably represents the most pleasant way of entering the city of Leeds. Although the area becomes more and more built up as one travels eastward, the canal remains unaffected by it, maintaining its privileged position on the wooded south side of the narrowing Aire valley. Leaving the ruined Kirkstall Abbey on the other side of the river, the navigation passes the Mackeson brewery and borders for a while the steeply sloping edges of an extensive park. Kirkstall Power Station is reached, with its own private canal 'lay-by': until the mid 1960s, scores of barges every week used to come up to fuel this establishment, now both dock and power station are unused. There are 6 locks in the last mile down to Leeds and the junction with the Aire and Calder navigations at River Lock which, along with the preceding two locks, looks spruce and smart, due to recent landscaping and refurbishment. A good place to moor a boat in Leeds is just above Office Lock or above River Lock; an arm leaves this short pound to disappear into the dark under City station – it once served the river wharves, but is now closed off and soon to be infilled. The route of the Aire and Calder is shown on page 160 *at reduced scale*.

Leeds
W. Yorks. EC Wed. MD Tue, Fri, Sat. All services. A vast industrial city whose mass of factory chimneys is the price it has paid for prosperity. Its major industry is the clothing and textile trade. Large areas of the city centre have now been developed. Headingly, the home of Yorkshire cricket, is a famous test match venue.
City Art Gallery The Headrow. Large collection of Old Masters: French 19thC paintings, English water colours and fine modern sculpture by Moore and Hepworth. *Open daily and Sun afternoons.*
City Museum Calveley Street. Despite losing valuable exhibits when the museum was bombed in the last war, it still contains a very fine collection illustrating the natural history and archaeology of many parts of the world. *Open daily and Sun afternoons.*
Kirkstall Abbey The large elegant ruins of a Cistercian abbey founded in the 12thC. The remaining walls narrowly escaped demolition in the late 19thC, but are now carefully preserved surrounded by a small, attractive park.
Abbey House Museum. Just near the abbey is the splendid folk museum illustrating the life and work of the people of Yorkshire during the last 300 years. As well as exhibiting toys, costumes and pottery, it houses 3 streets of fully furnished 19thC shops, cottages and workshops, including those of a saddler, chemist, tanner and blacksmith. *Open daily and Sun afternoons.*
Information centre Central Library. (Leeds 462067).

PUBS
🍺 **Ancestor** Just south of bridge 223.
🍺 **Bridge** 100yds east of bridge 222.
🍺 **Abbey** 50yds downhill from bridge 221.
There is a large selection of pubs in Leeds, with a narrow choice of beer.

MACCLESFIELD

Maximum dimensions

Length: 70′
Beam: 7′
Headroom: 7′

Mileage

HARDINGS WOOD JUNCTION (Trent &
Mersey Canal) to
Congleton Wharf: 5¾
Bosley top lock: 11½
Macclesfield: 17
Bollington: 20
MARPLE JUNCTION (Peak Forest Canal):
27¾

Locks: 13

Ever since the Trent & Mersey Canal had been completed in 1777, there had existed a demand for an alternative canal link between the Midlands and Manchester, and a more direct line through the manufacturing town of Macclesfield was an obvious choice of route.

However, it was not until 1825 that Thomas Telford was asked by promoters of the canal to survey a line linking the Peak Forest Canal and the Trent & Mersey Canal. The 28-mile line he suggested was the canal that was built, from Marple to just north of Kidsgrove, but Telford did not supervise the construction. (He left to go and build the Birmingham & Liverpool Junction Canal.) William Crosley was the canal's engineer. It is interesting to note that the Macclesfield Canal (which opened in 1831) was built so long after the peak period of canal construction that it was actually envisaged by some of its promoters as the route for a possible railway track.

The canal, which runs along the side of a tall ridge of hills west of the Pennines, bears the distinctive mark of Telford's engineering. Like his Birmingham & Liverpool Junction Canal (ie the Shropshire Union from Autherley to Nantwich), the Macclesfield is a 'cut and fill' canal, following as straight a course as possible, and featuring many tremendous cuttings and embankments. Apart from the stop lock at Hall Green whose 1ft rise was insisted upon as a water preservation measure by the Trent & Mersey Canal Company – to whose Hall Green Branch the Macclesfield Canal connected at the stop lock – all the locks are grouped into the flight of 12 at Bosley. The canal is fed from nearby reservoirs, at Bosley and Sutton.

In spite of intense competition from neighbouring railways and the Trent & Mersey Canal, the Macclesfield carried a good trade for many years. Much of this was coal, and cotton from the big mills established along its northern reaches.

This was not greatly affected by the surrender in 1846 to what was to become the Great Central Railway Company. (The Peak Forest and Ashton Canals were also bought by that railway.) The railway company ran the 3 canals efficiently, but as narrow canals they were all bound to decline sooner rather than later.

The Macclesfield Canal today is an extremely interesting cruising waterway, and forms part of the popular 100-mile 'Cheshire Ring' canal circuit.

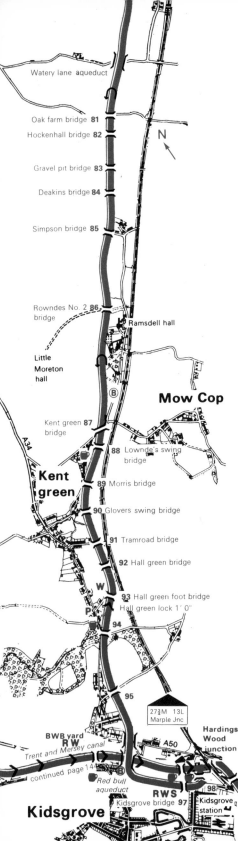

Watery lane aqueduct

Oak farm bridge **81**

Hockenhall bridge **82**

Gravel pit bridge **83**

Deakins bridge **84**

Simpson bridge **85**

N

Rowndes No. 2 **86**
bridge

Ramsdell hall

Little
Moreton
hall

Ⓑ

Mow Cop

Kent green **87**
bridge

88 Lowndes swing
bridge

**Kent
green**

89 Morris bridge

90 Glovers swing bridge

91 Tramroad bridge

92 Hall green bridge

W

93 Hall green foot bridge
Hall green lock 1' 0"

P

94

95

27¾M 13L
Marple Jnc

BWB yard
R W
Trent and Mersey canal

A50

Hardings
Wood
junction

continued page 144

Red bull
aqueduct

R W S

Kidsgrove bridge **97**

98

Kidsgrove
station

Kidsgrove

Kent Green

The junction of the Macclesfield with the Trent & Mersey Canal is a curious one, for the former leaves the Trent & Mersey on the south side, then crosses it on Red Bull Aqueduct after the T & M has fallen through 2 locks. After passing through the stop lock in the cutting at Hall Green, one comes out into the open countryside at Kent Green. To the east, Mow Cop crowns the tall ridge of hills that stretches parallel to the navigation for miles to come. The canal wanders past the front lawn of the mansion that is Ramsdell Hall. Beyond this point, the canal loses itself in the countryside for several miles. A telephone box is near bridge 85.

Little Moreton Hall
NT property. ¾ mile west of canal. (Walk north west from bridge 86, along the footpath on the left side of the hedge.) This fabulous moated house is an outstanding example of black-and-white-timbered architecture. It was built between 1559 and 1580, with carved gables and ornate windows and has scarcely changed since. It contains a fine collection of oak furniture and pewter. *Open afternoons (except Tue) Mar–Oct.*

Mow Cop
NT property. A hill nearly 1100ft above sea level, which gives a magnificent view across the Cheshire Plain, across Stoke and into Wales. (This looks particularly good at night.) On top of the hill is Mow Cop Castle, an imitation ruin built in 1750. It was on this spot that the Primitive Methodists held their first meeting in 1807 which lasted 14 hours.

Kent Green
Ches. PO, tel, stores. The main interest of this place is in its pubs, especially the little one on the canal by swing bridge 88.

BOATYARDS

Ⓑ **Dyecraft** Station Road, Kent Green, Scholar Green, Stoke-on-Trent. (Kidsgrove 5700). Ⓦ Ⓓ Pump-out (*Mon–Fri*), gas, chandlery. Hire narrow boats. Slipway, moorings. *Open Mon–Sat, Mar–Oct.*

Ⓑ **David Piper** Red Bull Basin, Church Lawton, Stoke-on-Trent. (Kidsgrove 4754). By Red Bull Aqueduct. Pump-out, gas, slipway up to 60ft, winter storage. Boat & engine sales & serving. Steel boats built & fitted out.

PUBS

🍺 **Bird in Hand** Kent Green. A superbly old-fashioned canalside pub: the unembarrassed landlord fetches real ale up from the cellar in a jug. Canal talk is the usual entertainment.

🍺 **Rising Sun** Kent Green. Near the canal.

🍺 **Three Horseshoes** Kent Green. Near canal.

🍺✕ **Bleeding Wolf** Hall Green. Near bridge 94. Food, except at weekends. PO, tel, stores nearby.

🍺 **Canal Tavern** Canalside, at Hardings Wood.

🍺 **Blue Bell** Canalside, at Hardings Wood Junction. Real ale.

🍺 **Red Bull** By lock 43 on the T & M. Snacks.

Congleton

The canal continues north east. On one side,
the land falls away gradually; to the east, the
ever-present range of substantial hills reminds
one that the Pennine Chain lies just beyond.
Passing a golf course, one arrives at the
embanked wharf that overlooks Congleton:
there is an aqueduct over the road that runs
down into the town and then a beautifully
symmetrical 'roving' bridge (76). Past
Congleton railway station, the canal is carried
by a high embankment – a common feature of
the Macclesfield – across a narrow valley,
affording a good view westward of the tall and
elegant railway viaduct crossing the same
valley. Meanwhile the looming fell known as
The Cloud (over 1000ft high and with remains
of ancient earthworks) is given a wide berth as
the navigation continues on its lonely lock-free
course through this very fine landscape. Fish
& chips may be found near bridge 68.

Congleton
Ches. EC Wed. MD Tue, Sat. All services. A
compact, busy market town hemmed in by
hills. The Victorian Town Hall in the High
Street, looks like a cross between a 17thC
Dutch guildhall and St Mark's, Venice.
Astbury
Ches. PO, tel, stores. About 1 mile north west of
bridges 79 and 80. A pretty village set back
from the A34. Tudor and 18thC houses are set
around the green. The church is amazing: its
roomy interior and wide aisles are
complemented externally by generous
battlements along the roof and a spired tower
standing quite separate from the body of the
church.

PUBS
● ✗ **Bull's Head Hotel** Congleton. Restaurant.
● **Robin Hood** ¼ mile south west of bridge 61.
● **Railway** Near Congleton station. Food.
● **Wharf** Near Congleton Wharf. Snacks:
children welcome lunchtime and early evening.
● ✗ **Lion & Swan Hotel** Congleton.
Restaurant.
● **Egerton Arms** Astbury.

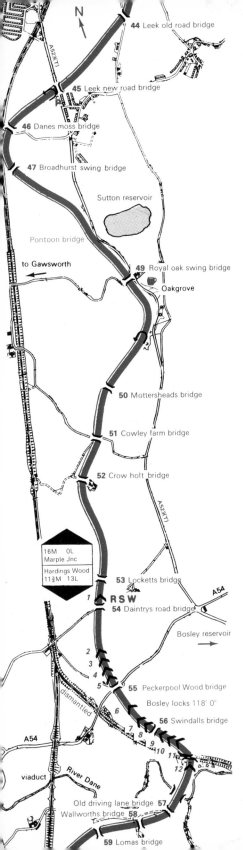

Bosley Locks

Scenically, this is another impressive stretch. The massive hills to the right still dominate as the canal crosses the River Dane on an embankment and arrives at the foot of Bosley Locks. These are in a really delightful setting which is semi-wooded and semi-pastoral, all the time overlooked by The Cloud from the south. Beyond the locks, the hills/mountains (some are over 1200ft high) spill right down to the canal near Oakgrove. The navigation follows the contour of the land as it begins to swing round the hills containing Macclesfield, which is now clearly visible to the north.

Navigational note
Royal Oak Swing Bridge (49) is very heavy work – despatch at least 2 of your strongest crew.

Sutton Reservoir
Close to the canal north of bridge 49, this reservoir holds up to 94 million gallons of water. There is a private sailing club: and the public are welcome to ramble and picnic here.

Oakgrove
A delightful spot incorporating a very stiff and heavy swing bridge over the canal, a nearby pub and a superb backcloth of tall, green hills which are ideal for energetic walks. The lane west of the bridge leads to Gawsworth. Sutton reservoir is just north.

Gawsworth
Ches. 2 miles west of Oakgrove. A refreshingly unspoilt village with several small lakes and a lovely 13thC church, approached by a long avenue of elm trees. Facing the church is the old rectory, a half-timbered house built by Rector Baguley in 1470. Close to the church is Gawsworth Hall, a beautiful 16thC black-and-white manor house. The park encloses a medieval jousting ground. *Open Wed, Sat, Sun & G. Fri afternoons, Mar–Oct.*

Maggoty's Wood In this pleasant wood just outside the village is the grave of the eccentric fiddler and playwright, Maggoty Johnson. After being totally rejected by London critics he returned to Gawsworth where he died in 1773, having ordered that he should be buried far from the vulgar gentry who did not appreciate his genius.

Bosley Locks
Effectively the only locks on all the 27 miles of the Macclesfield Canal, these 12 splendid stone locks are relatively deep, raising the canal level by fully 118ft to well over 500ft above the sea. Each lock has a pair of mitre top gates instead of only a single one – indeed Bosley Locks are very rare among narrow locks in this respect. They are a good example of Telford's practice of grouping locks together in flights; here are 12 in 1 mile.

Bosley Reservoir
1 mile east of Bosley locks, along the A54. A canal reservoir with a wide variety of land and water birds, which holds 402 million gallons of water. An excellent rambling and picnic area. The fishing rights are exercised by an angling club.

PUBS

Fool's Nook Oakgrove. Horsebrasses and light meals.

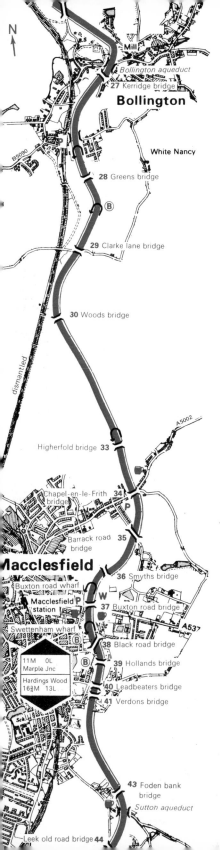

N

Mill

Bollington aqueduct

27 Kerridge bridge

Bollington

White Nancy

B5090

28 Greens bridge

B

29 Clarke lane bridge

30 Woods bridge

dismantled

A5002

Higherfold bridge 33

Chapel-en-le-Frith bridge 34

P

Barrack road bridge 35

Macclesfield

36 Smyths bridge

Buxton road wharf

Macclesfield station   P   W

37 Buxton road bridge

Swettenham wharf   B

A537

38 Black road bridge

39 Hollands bridge

11M   0L
Marple Jnc

Hardings Wood
16¾M   13L

40 Leadbeaters bridge

41 Verdons bridge

43 Foden bank bridge

Sutton aqueduct

Leek old road bridge 44

Macclesfield

Leaving the green and hilly countryside, the navigation enters the outskirts of Macclesfield. A very wide stretch overshadowed by a vast, empty flour mill marks the site of the headquarters of the original Macclesfield Canal Company. The town centre itself is down the hill: the best place to moor is at the wharf north of bridge 37. Meanwhile the canal continues northwards near a closed railway to Bollington. A 60ft-high embankment and 2 aqueducts carry the navigation over the valley to the huge Clarence textile mill – one of several mills in the area which have closed in recent years owing to retrenchment and rationalisation in the major textile companies.

Bollington
Ches. EC Wed. PO, tel, stores, garage, bank.
One gets a good view of this stone-built town from the huge canal embankment that cuts across it. Hills crowd round the town, which is only a mile from the boundary of the Peak District National Park. The white tower on the ridge south of the town is called White Nancy. One popular story is that it was built to commemorate the battle of Waterloo by a member of the Gaskell family and took its name from one of the ladies of the family called Nancy.

Macclesfield
Ches. EC Wed. MD Tue, Fri, Sat. All services.
An interesting combination of a thriving silk manufacturing town and an old market town with its cobbled streets and its picturesque medieval Market Place. There are several interesting classical buildings, making the most of the local stone. In the 18thC it was one of the leading silk producing centres and is still important for its textile and pharmaceutical industries. An interesting feature of the town is the Unitarian Chapel in King Edward Street, approached through a narrow passage and guarded by a lovely wrought-iron gate: it is dated 1689 and is 'for William and Mary's subjects dissenting from the Church of England'.

St Michael's Church Market Place. Very little remains of the original structure founded in 1278 by Queen Eleanor but it still contains many fine monuments.

Museum & Art Gallery West Park. It was built, equipped and presented to the town in 1898 by the Brocklehurst family, the largest silk manufacturers in Macclesfield. It contains exhibits of local interest, as well as sketches by Landseer, Egyptian craftswork and a stuffed giant panda. *Open daily (Closed Sun morning).*

Note: those negotiating the Cheshire Ring in an anti-clockwise direction should remember the next pump-out station is at Preston Brook.

BOATYARDS

Ⓑ **Kerridge Dry Dock** Between bridges 28 and 29. (Bollington 74287).

Ⓑ **Peak Forest Cruisers** The Wharf, Buxton Road, Macclesfield. (24172). Ⓡ Ⓢ Ⓦ Ⓓ Pump-out, hire cruisers, day trip boat. Chandlery, moorings, winter storage, boat & engine repairs, grocery, toilets.

Ⓑ **Macclesfield Marina** Swettenham Wharf, Brook Street, Macclesfield. (20042). Ⓡ Ⓢ Ⓦ Ⓓ Slipway, gas, boatbuilding & repairs, mooring, chandlery, toilets, provisions, winter storage. *Closed Wed.*

PUBS

Macclesfield and Bollington have been described as one of the 7 wonders of the real ale drinkers' waterways, with 86 such pubs within striking distance of the canal. For those who cannot manage even a short walk back:

🍺 **George & Dragon** Near bridge 34.

🍺 **Puss in Boots** Bridge 37.

🍺 **Bridgewater Arms** Bridge 37. Good sign.

🍺✕🍽 **Ellesmere Hotel** Buxton Road, Macclesfield. Macclesfield 23791. 200 yds from Macclesfield mooring. Hotel with restaurant. Bar snacks too. *Open LD Mon-Sun.*

One of the beautifully situated Bosley Locks. Macclesfield Canal. *David Perrott*

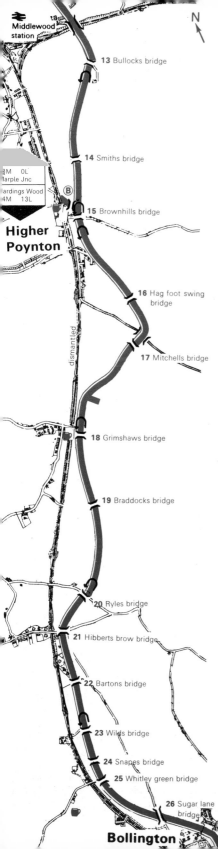

Higher Poynton

This lonely stretch is typical of the Macclesfield Canal and in its beautifully quiet, rural isolation it is representative of much of the charm that most canals possess. Winding northwards along the summit level at over 500ft above the sea, the navigation generally follows the contours of this upland country, but crosses several valleys on embankments with fine aqueducts. There are few centres of population, only the odd pub here or there, and the countryside is entirely unspoilt. Around Higher Poynton (*PO, tel, stores, garage*) the canal becomes very deep, and in places wide: this is the result of ancient subsidence from a coalmine, which necessitated the continual raising of the canal banks and bridges (to hold the water in the sinking canal). Be sure to adhere to the main channel here, or you will run aground. An old branch near bridge 15 used to lead to the mine; now it is a mooring site. A mile north of here, one crosses yet another massive embankment and a tall aqueduct (over a railway) on the way into High Lane.

Lyme Park
NT property. 2 miles east of Higher Poynton. Pedestrian entrance at West Parkgate, ¼ mile south east of bridge 17. (Vehicular access from Disley, on the Peak Forest Canal.) In the centre of an extensive park containing deer, is a magnificent Elizabethan house that belonged to the Legh family from the 14thC until 1947 when it was handed over to the nation in payment of death duties. It has a fine interior containing many works of art and 4 Chippendale chairs claimed to be covered with material from a cloak worn by King Charles I at his execution. *House open afternoons, except Mon, gardens open daily.*

Adlington Hall
2 miles west of bridge 21. An attractive manor house with a mixture of architectural styles: a Georgian south front and an Elizabethan black-and-white-timbered wing. The banqueting hall contains a 17thC Bernard Smith organ. Pleasant gardens. *Open summer Sun & B. Hols, also Sat in Jul & Aug.*

BOATYARDS
Ⓑ **Constellation Cruises** Lyme Road, Higher Poynton, Stockport (Poynton 873471). Near bridge 15 Ⓦ Ⓓ Boat hire, slipway, gas, boat & engine repairs, mooring, chandlery, toilets.

PUBS
🍺 **Boars Head** Higher Poynton. Down the hill from bridge 15.
🍺 **Miner's Arms** Near bridge 18.
🍺 **Windmill** 250yds west of bridge 25.

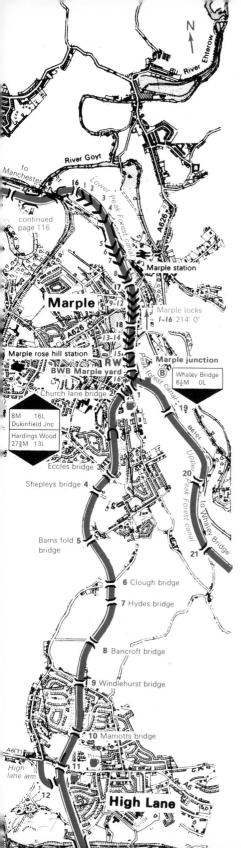

Marple Junction

The canal proceeds northwards in a cutting through High Lane, passing the junction with the short High Lane Arm – now used as a club mooring site. Beyond the town is a derelict mill, then open country intervenes, offering views westward of Stockport and the southern outskirts of Manchester. Yet another mill appears: it heralds Marple, a busy boating centre much enjoyed by the citizens of Manchester. The area of the junction with the Peak Forest Canal is delightful: an old turnover bridge, mellow wharf buildings and the nearby flight of Marple Locks are framed by the distant mountainous country across the Goyt valley. The canal here is 500ft above sea level – the highest usable pound on the English canal system. There is a useful general store by bridge 3.

Marple
Gt Manchester. All services. A typical residential town, serving as a dormitory base for Stockport and Manchester. Elements of the old village can still be seen, buried among the suburbia, but much the most attractive part is by the canal. The rugged Ludworth Moor is not far away, where 'Robin Hood's Picking Rods' still stand, the supposed remains of a Celtic Druid's temple.

Marple Locks
The flight of deep, narrow locks is superbly sited, at the top flanked by terraced houses and a play park; midway fine gardens and restored stone cottages back on, and towards the bottom the passage is tree-lined. Half-way there is a superb canal warehouse, restored and used as offices. The friendly lock keeper lives by lock 9. The top lock is the second deepest narrow lock in the country.

High Lane
Gt Manchester. PO, tel, stores, garage, station. More a spread than a village; useful for supplies. High Lane is effectively at the south-east corner of the Manchester conurbation, and is quite indistinguishable from its neighbours. The very long Disley railway tunnel passes deep underneath the place.

BOATYARDS

BWB Marple Yard Marple Junction. (061-427 1079). R S W Toilet.

BOAT TRIPS

Top Lock Marine 5 Lime Kiln Lane, Marple. (061-427 5712). 12-seater restaurant boat for private charter, and 12-seater trip boat operating 1hr cruises. Also private mooring marina and emergency engine repairs.

PUBS

🍺✕ **Ring O'Bells** Marple. By bridge 2. Robinson's real ale, good food and excellent children's menu. Telephone kiosk outside.
🍺 **Bull's Head** High Lane. Near bridge 11.
🍺 **Dog & Partridge** 200yds from bridge 11. Food.

PEAK FOREST AND ASHTON

Maximum dimensions:

Length: 70'
Beam: 7'
Headroom: 6'

Mileages

ASHTON CANAL
Duckinfield Junction to
Ducie Street Junction: 6

Locks: 18

PEAK FOREST CANAL
Whaley Bridge to
Marple Junction: 6½
Dunkinfield Junction: 14½

Locks: 16

THE ASHTON CANAL

This navigation was authorised in 1792 and opened shortly afterwards, as an isolated narrow canal from the centre of Manchester to Ashton-under-Lyne. It is short, at only 6½ miles, but several substantial branches were built, with a total length twice that of the main line.

From the beginning, the Ashton was a strong rival of the Rochdale Canal – with which it connects in Manchester. The 2 canals were constructed simultaneously, partly to tap the big coal producing area around Oldham (north east of Manchester): in addition the Ashton opened a new trade route from Manchester to the textile mills of Ashton, while the Rochdale served as a broad canal link over the Pennines between the Mersey and the rivers of Yorkshire. Before long, the Ashton Canal was joined by the Peak Forest and Huddersfield Canals: both provided useful trade and the latter provided a secondary through route across the Pennines. And in 1831 completion of the narrow Macclesfield Canal gave the Ashton the added bonus of becoming part of a through route from Manchester to the Potteries.

The 1830s saw the peak of the Ashton Canal's prosperity. After this it was seriously threatened by railway competition, and the canal company sold out to the forerunner of the Great Central Railway Company in 1846. This company continued successfully to maintain and operate the canal for many years, but traffic declined in the present century and the branches began to decay.

By 1962 it was unnavigable – however a determined effort by the Peak Forest Canal Society, the IWA, local councils and the BWB resulted in its reopening in 1974.

THE PEAK FOREST CANAL

This canal runs from the Ashton Canal at Ashton through Marple to Whaley Bridge and Buxworth. Its name is misleading, for Peak Forest is only a small village 2½ miles east of Doveholes, and the canal never went to Peak Forest. Its history is similar to and tied up with its neighbour the Ashton Canal; authorised by Act of Parliament in 1794, it was aimed at providing an outlet for the great limestone deposits at Doveholes, a few miles south east of Whaley Bridge. However, since Doveholes is over 1000ft above sea level, the canal was terminated in a basin at Buxworth, and the line was continued up to the quarries by a 6½-mile tramroad.

Construction of the canal and tramway and their 4 short tunnels was carried out by navvies directed by Benjamin Outram, a notable Derbyshire engineer and one of the founders of the famous Butterley Ironworks. The canal was completed in 1800, except for the flight of locks at Marple, which were not built until 4 years later. (A second, temporary, tramway bridged the gap in the meantime.)

Buxworth soon became a bustling interchange point where the horse-drawn wagons bringing the stone down from Doveholes tipped their load either into canal boats or into limekilns, for burning into lime. This traffic, and the boats bringing coal *up* the canal for firing the kilns at Buxworth, accounted for the greatest proportion of the canal company's revenue.

Like the Ashton Canal, the Peak Forest was greatly boosted by the opening of the Macclesfield Canal to Marple top lock in 1831. This made it (with the Ashton) part of a new through route from Manchester to the Potteries. In 1831 too, the Cromford & High Peak Railway was opened, joining up Whaley Bridge with the Cromford Canal on the far side of the Peak District.

By the early 1840s the Peak Forest Canal was suffering from keen competition on trade between Manchester, the Midlands and London. The competition came not only from the long-established Trent & Mersey Canal Company but also from 2 new railways. All the companies tried to undercut each other; the Peak Forest came off badly, so in 1846 the company leased the navigation in perpetuity to the Sheffield, Ashton-under-Lyne & Manchester Railway, which later became the Great Central. The canal declined slowly up to the present century. In 1922 the Buxworth traffic finished, while (through) traffic on the 'lower' Peak Forest Canal – from Marple Junction northwards – gradually disappeared by the last war.

Along with the Ashton, full navigation was restored in 1974, with the Buxworth line currently being restored.

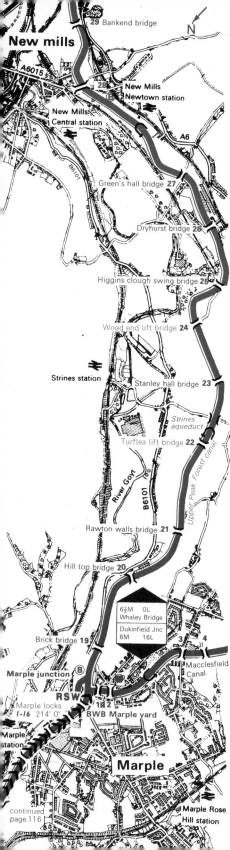

New Mills

As one passes from the Macclesfield Canal to the Upper Peak Forest Canal one enters at once dramatic, mountainous scenery. To the north and east, the land falls away sharply, with the Marple flight of locks emphasising the drop. The Upper Peak Forest Canal leads off to the south east; and it rapidly becomes apparent that this is a navigation set in a robust, handsome landscape. Clinging desperately to a wooded mountainside overlooking the steep, wide Goyt valley, it winds its precarious way to New Mills. The trains that traverse the opposite side of the valley look like tiny models on the distant, massive mountains. Near Disley, another railway pops out of the long Disley Tunnel, way below the canal; while yet another line appears above and beside the canal, from High Lane. Thus around New Mills the valley contains fully 3 operational and very picturesque railways. One of the pleasant features of this terrain is the easy co-existence of woods, fields and a canal on the one hand, and a certain amount of industrial urbanisation on the other. Usually, this mixture would tend to spoil the rural character of the area; but along this canal the steepness of the slope and the grandeur of the landscape leaves the canal's charm unimpaired. From here to Whaley Bridge the cut is very shallow – the slow progress gives time to fully appreciate the surroundings.

New Mills
Derbs. PO, tel, stores, garage, stations. A mostly stone-built town on the Cheshire/Derbyshire border: its industries include textile printing, engineering and engraving. One can still see the ruins of the extensive canal stables just east of bridge 28.

Disley
Ches. PO, tel, stores, garage, station. On the south bank of the canal. The centre of the village is quite pretty, slightly spoilt by the A6 traffic. The village is up the hill, south west of bridge 26. The attractive church stands among trees above the little village square. It was greatly renovated in the last century but the ancient tower with the griffin leering down at passers-by dates from the 16thC. Vehicular and pedestrian access to Lyme Park (see page 109) is from the A6 near Disley, 1½ miles south west of bridge 26.

BOATYARDS

Ⓑ **New Mills Marina** Hibbert Street, New Mills, near Stockport. (New Mills 45000). At bridge 28 Ⓡ Ⓦ Gas, boat sales & repairs, slipway, chandlery, moorings, winter storage, toilets.
BWB Marple Yard at Marple Junction, on the Macclesfield Canal. (061-427 1079). Ⓡ Ⓢ Ⓦ Toilet.

PUBS

🍺✕ **Ram's Head Hotel** Disley. Smart hotel with full restaurant. Baths available for boat crews who dine here.
🍺✕ **Dandy Cock** Disley. Bar lunches.
🍺 **Romper Inn** ½ mile uphill from bridge 21. Food.
🍺✕ **Ring O'Bells** Marple. Near the junction. (On the Macclesfield Canal). Good food: fine children's menu and real ale.

The Upper Peak Forest Canal. A very attractive, but shallow, waterway. *Derek Pratt*

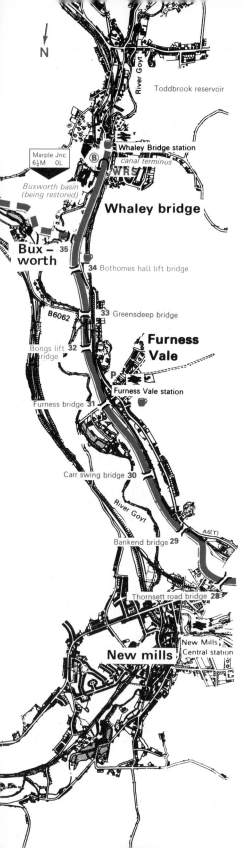

Whaley Bridge

The canal continues south east along the
mountainside towards Whaley Bridge. It is an
enchanting stretch, passing plenty of woods,
pastures and grazing horses. The A6 road and
the railway are always close to the navigation,
but they detract not at all from its isolation.
There are charming stations at New Mills,
Furness Vale and Whaley Bridge: from these
one may take a magnificent railway trip past 2
canal-feeding reservoirs and over the hills to the
summit, 1200ft above sea level, then down to
the old Roman town of Buxton, now
unfortunately the end of the line. As the canal
approaches Whaley Bridge, and the River Goyt
comes closer, there is a swing bridge and 2 lift
bridges to contend with – they can be hard
work. South of bridge 34 the canal splits: the
original main line, at present closed beyond the
bridge, turns east across the Goyt on an
aqueduct to Buxworth (changed from the
supposedly less desirable Bugsworth) with its
basin complex. The former Whaley Bridge
Branch continues for a short distance south to
Whaley Bridge, where it terminates in a small
basin, with a boatyard, at the north end of the
town. There is a building at the basin of great
interest to industrial archaeologists: it covers a
dock and was built in 1832 at this, the junction
of the Peak Forest Canal and the Cromford &
High Peak Railway. Here, transhipment
between canal, boat and railway wagon could
take place under cover. The former railway's
Whaley Bridge inclined plane (now a footpath)
rises to the south of this historic building
which, saved from demolition, now houses the
boatyard.

Coombs Reservoir
1½ miles south of Whaley Bridge. An 84-acre
canal reservoir with public access from the 3
highways round it. It is used extensively as a
sailing club centre and for angling.
Toddbrook Reservoir
Just south of Whaley Bridge. A very pleasant
area for picnicking and walking. Private sailing
club; fishing rights on this BWB reservoir are
exercised by an angling club.
Whaley Bridge
*Derbs. EC Wed. PO, tel, stores, garage, station,
banks.* Built on a steep hill at the end of the
canal, this village is now overwhelmed by the
traffic on the A6 road. There are a lot of shops
and pubs, and away from the main road it is a
quiet and pleasant place, with good views
across the Goyt valley. However the beautiful
nearby hills are more noteworthy than the
town.
The Cromford & High Peak Railway
In the early 1820s a physical connection was
planned between the Peak Forest Canal at
Whaley Bridge with the Cromford Canal, way
over to the south east on the other side of the
Peak District, using a junction canal. However
a canal would have been impracticable through
such mountainous terrain, and so a railway was
constructed. Known as the Cromford & High
Peak Railway, it was opened throughout in
1831, 33 miles long. With a summit level over
1200ft above the sea, this extraordinary
standard gauge goods line was interesting
chiefly for its numerous slopes and inclined
planes, up which the wagons were hauled by
either stationary or tenacious locomotive steam
engines. (The steepest gradient on the line was
1 in 7.) The C & HPR closed in 1967; much of
the route is now being turned into a public
footpath and bridleway. Around Whaley
Bridge one may still see the remains of the short
inclined plane (now a footpath) which brought
the goods down the hill, then through the town
to the wharf at the terminus of the Peak Forest
Canal.
Buxworth
Derbs. PO, tel, stores. The main feature in
Buxworth is the old terminal basin system.
This used to be a tremendously busy complex,
and is of great interest to industrial
archaeologists. The canal line to Buxworth
(once Bugsworth) was built to bring the canal
as near as possible to the great limestone
quarries at Doveholes, a plate tramway being
constructed in 1799 via Chapel Milton to
complete the connection. Known as the Peak
Forest Tramway, this little line 6½ miles long

brought the stone down the hills to Buxworth, where it was transhipped into waiting canal boats. Throughout the history of the line, the wagons on the tramway were drawn exclusively by horse power – except for a 500yd inclined plane in Chapel-en-le-Frith, where the trucks were attached to a continuous rope so that the descending trucks pulled empty ones up the 1 in 7½ slope. The tramway was closed by 1926, and the sidings and basins at Buxworth have been disused and overgrown since that time. However the Inland Waterways Protection Society is working towards a complete restoration of the complex by voluntary labour and already part of the basin is cleared and reopened. See the noticeboard by the bridge for the latest information.

Furness Vale
Derbs. PO, tel, stores, garage, station. A main road (A6) village, useful for supplies.

BOATYARDS

Ⓑ **Coles Morton Marine** Canal Wharf, Whaley Bridge. (3411). Ⓡ Ⓢ Ⓦ Ⓓ Pump-out, boat hire, crane, gas, boat building & repairs, mooring, chandlery, toilets, shop, telephone.

PUBS

🍺✕ **Jodrell Arms Hotel** Whaley Bridge. Lunches, dinners etc.
🍺✕ **Station Hotel** Whaley Bridge. Lunches and dinners.
🍺 **Navigation** Whaley Bridge. Near the canal terminus.
🍺 **Navigation** Buxsworth. By the canal terminus.
🍺 **Dog & Partridge** On A6, near swing bridge 34.
🍺 **Soldier Dick** Furness Vale.
🍺 **Station Hotel** Furness Vale.

Marple Aqueduct on the Lower Peak Forest Canal. The railway viaduct is in the background.

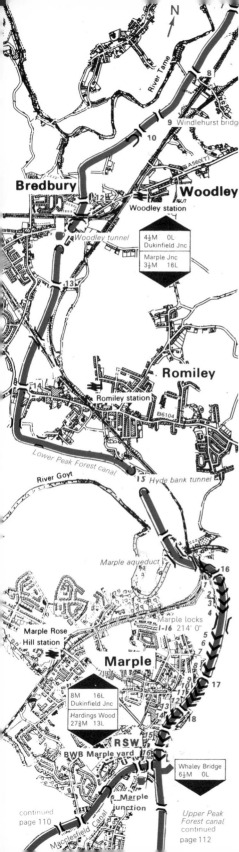

Marple Aqueduct

At Marple Junction the 16 narrow (standard 7ft beam) Marple Locks carry the Peak Forest Canal down 214ft past the Macclesfield Canal towards Manchester. The southernmost 5 miles of the Lower Peak Forest Canal (ie from Marple Junction northwards) are really very beautiful. The locks themselves, which are spaced out over 1 mile, have an unrivalled setting in an excellent combination of built-up area, parkland, tall trees and steep hillside; the River Goyt is hidden down in the wooded valley on the east. At the foot of the locks, where the River Goyt is crossed, one is treated to the double joys of a major canal aqueduct and an even bigger railway viaduct alongside. West of here, the canal traverses a wooded hillside before diving into the low, wide Hyde Bank Tunnel, 308yds long. The towpath is diverted over the hill, past a farm. The other side, a couple of minor aqueducts lead the canal northwards, away from the Goyt valley and past Romiley, Bredbury and Woodley. Here is a narrow 176-yd long tunnel, this time with the towpath continued through it. Beyond these not unattractive outer suburbs of Manchester, the canal runs again along a hillside in unspoilt countryside, overlooking the tiny River Tame. There are plenty of trees and the occasional textile mill to add interest to the rural scenery. One should relish this length of the canal – it is the last one sees of the countryside before one enters the vast conurbation of Manchester.

Marple Aqueduct
Deservedly scheduled as an ancient monument, this 3-arched aqueduct over the River Goyt is a very fine structure, in an exquisite setting almost 100ft above the river.

Marple Locks
The 16 locks at Marple were not built until 1804, 4 years after the rest of the navigation was opened. The 1-mile gap thus left was bridged by a tramway, while the Canal Company sought the cash to pay for the construction of a flight of locks. This was obviously a most unsatisfactory state of affairs, since the limestone from Doveholes had to be shifted from wagon to boat at Buxworth Basin, from boat to wagon at Marple Junction, and back into boat again at the bottom of the tramway. Not surprisingly, a container system was developed – using iron boxes with a 2-ton payload – to ease the triple transhipment. However, this was no long-term solution, and when the necessary £27,000 was forthcoming the company authorised construction of the flight of locks. Today they stand comparison with any flight on the network: note especially Samuel Oldknow's superb warehouse, by lock 9.

BOATYARDS
BWB Marple Yard At Marple Junction, on the Macclesfield Canal. (061-427-1079). R S W Toilet.

PUBS & RESTAURANTS
Navigation Woodley. At north end of tunnel. Robinsons real ale, garden.
the Foresters Greave, Romiley. (Known as 'The Piggy'.)
Spread Eagle Hatherlow, Romiley.
The Railway Romiley.
Waterside Restaurant Romiley. Near bridge 14. *Closed Sun evening and Mon.* PO, tel, stores, garage nearby.
Navigation By lock 13. Useful for 'lock wheelers' (no mooring on flight!) Chinese take-away close by.

The following labels appear on the map:

N

River Tame

8

9 Windlehurst bridge

10

A560(T)

Bredbury

Woodley

Woodley station

12

4½M 0L
Dukinfield Jnc

Marple Jnc
3½M 16L

Woodley tunnel

13

Romiley

Romiley station

B6104

Lower Peak Forest canal

River Goyt

15 Hyde bank tunnel

Marple aqueduct

16

Marple Rose Hill station

Marple locks
1-16 214' 0"

Marple

17

8M 16L
Dukinfield Jnc

Hardings Wood
27¾M 13L

R S W

BWB Marple yard

Whaley Bridge
6½M 0L

Marple junction

continued page 110

Macclesfield Canal

Upper Peak Forest canal continued page 112

Hyde

The canal continues northward through a landscape that becomes less rural, but in some ways more interesting. At bridge 7 the towpath changes sides; the building nearby is the Peak Forest Canal Society's headquarters. North of here the industrial tentacles of Hyde – outer Manchester – ensnare the canal traveller. Beyond Hyde, the canal traverses a great expanse of landscaped wasteland. There used to be 2 short branches along here; they are untraceable now. As one approaches Dukinfield, a powerful sewage works lies to the left near an incongruously attractive farm (Plantation Farm). Further on, beyond several railway bridges and Portland Basin is a small aqueduct over the River Tame and the junction with the Ashton Canal. There is a useful boatyard here, which keeps the anti-vandal keys needed for the locks and moveable bridges in this area. The Ashton Canal continues for a short distance to the right – north east – and then becomes the Huddersfield Narrow Canal. The latter has been infilled and piped for a short distance, beyond which many of the locks that used to lift boats on their way up and over the hills to Huddersfield have been filled in or weired. However the unnavigable Huddersfield Narrow Canal still fulfills the important function of carrying water down from its many reservoirs and streams high in the Pennines to feed the Ashton, Rochdale and Bridgewater Canals on the Lancashire side, and the Huddersfield Broad Canal and the Calder & Hebble on the Yorkshire side, as well as several factories along the way. It is with pleasant surprise that one finds the water in the upper part of the Ashton Canal crystal clear for many miles – a tribute to anti-pollution work done by BWB and the River Authority. However further towards the centre of Manchester, industrial pollution takes a heavy toll.

BOATYARDS

🚩 **Ruswell Canal Boats** 7 Princes Drive, Marple. (061-427 5121). R S W D Boat hire, gas, boat building & repairs, mooring, canal shop. Ashton keys and Rochdale licences available.

PUBS

🚩 **Globe** By bridge 2. Food.
🚩 **Cheshire Ring Hotel** A few yards east of bridge 6. Shops and station nearby.

The Ashton Canal, with central Manchester being left behind down the locks. *David Perrott*

Droylsden

From start to finish, the Ashton Canal passes
through a densely built-up area in which the
canal is conspicuous as an avenue of escape
from the oppressive townscape that flanks it. Its
clear water, its excellent towpath, its functional
but dignified old bridges and the peace that
surrounds it make it a potential haven for local
schoolchildren, anglers, walkers and idlers, and
for anyone else who enjoys an environment that
is quite separate from and unrelated to his
ordinary daily life. Regrettably parts have also
become a playground for gangs of unruly
youths, and some boaters have suffered as a
result of this. The rare pleasure, afforded only
by an English canal, stepping out of the noise
and bustle of everyday life in a city suburb, into
the peaceful and unpretentious atmosphere of
the 18thC is once again under threat. Leaving,
then, Dukinfield Junction – where substantial
old canal warehouses and docks face the Peak
Forest Canal – one turns west towards
Manchester. Electrified suburban railway lines
jostle the canal, which enters a cutting and
passes Guide Bridge. There are pubs, shops
and a railway station nearby, but it can be
difficult to scramble up the bank out of the
cutting. Droylsden is memorable for the
wonderful smell of a marmalade factory –
Fairfield Junction is the last 'safe' mooring this
side of Manchester – here the 18 locks begin the
descent to the Rochdale Canal. Shops and pubs
are all close to the junction, and there is a BWB
Sanitary Station. One can see the remains of
several old canal arms along the Ashton Canal:
one of the more important ones was the 5-mile
Stockport Branch, leaving from Clayton
Junction just below lock 11.

Navigational note
A BWB anti-vandal key is needed for all the
locks and moveable bridges on the Ashton, and
for the first lift bridge on the Lower Peak
Forest. Be very careful where you moor in this
area, and do not offer anyone a ride on your
boat.

BOATYARDS
BWB Fairfield Junction Ⓢ W Toilet, mooring.
(061-273 4686 from *07.45–16.30, nights*
061-330 8599). Anti-vandal keys for sale.
Ⓑ **Ruswell Canal Boats** 7 Princes Drive,
Marple. (061-427 5121). Ⓡ Ⓢ W Ⓓ Boat hire,
gas, boat building & repairs, mooring, canal
shop. Ashton keys and Rochdale licences
available.

PUBS
▪ **Inns Church** and **Bridge** Both by lock 11.
▪ **Crabtree** Canalside, at lock 13.
▪ **The Friendship** By lock 15.
▪ **Yew Tree** Near the first lift bridge east of
lock 16.
▪ **Cotton Tree** Droylsden.
▪ **Church Hotel** Droylsden.

Manchester

The canal now falls through the remaining 7 locks into Manchester. The surroundings are brightened by the well-cared for Beswick flight, but eventually become industrial until the canal is totally hemmed in by the back walls of tall factories – originally built there because of the canal's very presence – for ½ mile above the bottom 3 locks. The amount of rubbish in the canal increases steadily – through the clear water one may observe televisions, armchairs, various automobile parts among other less savoury objects. The necessary but tiresome chore of unlocking and locking the paddle gear tends to slow progress, which at times resembles a cross between 'It's a Knockout' and the Marx brothers. The Rochdale Canal, which is still privately owned, used to stretch for 33 miles over the Pennines from Manchester to Sowerby Bridge – where it joined the terminus of the Calder & Hebble Navigation. It has been closed to navigation, and in Manchester much of the canal has been reduced to a shallow, landscaped water channel. However the bottom mile of the canal is navigable, from the junction with the Ashton Canal at Ducie Street down to Castlefield and the junction with the Bridgewater Canal. This remaining mile of the Rochdale Canal is thus a vital link between the Bridgewater and Ashton canals in the 100-mile 'Cheshire Ring'. Persons wishing to navigate the 9 wide locks to the Bridgewater Canal should apply to the Head Office of the Rochdale Canal Company, 75 Dale Street, Manchester 1. (061-236-2456). A hefty charge is levied. The locks can accommodate vessels up to 74ft long and 14ft wide, drawing up to 4ft, with a height above water level of up to 9ft. This section suffers much unwelcome attention and is regularly short of water – check before you attempt a passage. A safe but isolated mooring can be made by Hulme Lock. If you've just come from Fairfield Junction in the day, you'll be too tired to go out, anyway. The Rochdale passage is described in full on page 22, in the Bridgewater section.

Manchester
See page 22.

Salford
See page 24.

BOATYARDS

BWB Section Office Vesta Street, Ancoats. (061-273 4686). Ⓦ

PUBS

🍺 **Navigation** Near lock 6, Ashton Canal.
🍺 **Alexandra** Mill Street. By bridge 9.

RIVER TRENT

Maximum dimensions

*Shardlow to Meadow Lane lock,
Nottingham*
Length: 81'
Beam: 14' 6"
Headroom: 8'
Meadow Lane lock to Gainsborough
Length: 165'
Beam: 18' 6"
Headroom: 13'

Mileage

DERWENT MOUTH to
Cranfleet lock: 2¾
Beeston lock: 7
Meadow Lane lock, Nottingham: 12
Gunthorpe Bridge: 22
Fiskerton: 29¾
Newark Castle: 35½
Cromwell lock: 40½
Dunham Bridge: 53
TORKSEY junction: 57
Littleborough: 60½
GAINSBOROUGH Bridge: 67
WEST STOCKWITH: 71¾
KEADBY Junction: 84¼
TRENT FALLS: 93¾

Locks: 12

The River Trent is an historic highway running for about 100 miles from the Midlands to the Humber ports and the North Sea. It has long been of prime economic and social importance to the areas through which it flows.

It is thought that as long ago as the Bronze Age the Trent was part of the trade route from the Continent to the metal-working industry in Ireland. The discovery of 2 dug-out canoes in the river bed near Nottingham, dating from about 1000BC and complete with bronze weapons, indicates that the Trent was probably being navigated at this time.

The Romans recognised the value of the river as a route to the centre of England from the sea. In about AD120, in the time of Emperor Hadrian, they built the Foss Dyke canal to link the Trent valley with Lindum Colonia (now Lincoln), the River Witham and the Wash. The Trent later acted as an easy route for the Danish invaders, who got past the guardian Knights of Torksey and penetrated as far as Nottingham. They wintered at Torksey in AD872 and, under King Swein Forkbeard, at Gainsborough in 1013.

In about AD924 Edward the Elder expelled the Danes from Nottingham and built the first bridge there. The second bridge at Nottingham was built in 1156 (some 20 years earlier than Old London Bridge) and lasted 714 years. Its remains can still be seen. The third bridge was built in 1871 and forms the basic structure of today's Trent Bridge. The traditional role of the Trent as a dividing line between 1 region of the country and another (many people still consider it to be a useful division between north and south England) is strengthened by the existence even today of only 7 road bridges in the 80 miles between Nottingham and the sea.

Although the first Act of Parliament to improve the Trent as a navigation was passed in 1699, the first important one was in 1783. This Act authorised the construction of a towpath, thus allowing for the first time the passage of sail-less barges. 10 years later the Trent Navigation Company's engineer drew up a comprehensive scheme to build locks and weirs, to increase the depth in certain reaches and build a number of training walls to narrow and thus deepen the channel. Some of these works were carried out, but the scheme was far from complete by 1906, when the Royal Commission on Inland Waterways adopted it as the official future plan. The Act of 1906 authorised for the first time locks at Stoke Bardolph, Gunthorpe, Hazleford and Cromwell; but owing to the shortage of available money caused by the Great War, the works were not completed until 1926. Trade soon increased fourfold.

At its peak in the 19th and early 20thC, the Trent formed the main artery of trade for the East Midlands, being connected with the Sheffield & South Yorkshire Navigations, the Chesterfield Canal, the Foss Dyke, the Grantham Canal, the Erewash Canal, the River Soar Navigation and the Trent & Mersey Canal. Although it remains so connected today to all but the Grantham Canal, the large trade between these waterways has dwindled away with railway competition, and in particular as a result of railway ownership of most of those connecting waterways. Today most of the commercial carrying is from the Humber ports to Gainsborough, as well as hundreds of thousands of tons of gravel from Carlton, below Newark. But there is not very much trade now on the non-tidal section, even to Nottingham.

The Trent remains a useful through route for pleasure craft, easy of navigation and with many interesting connections. Although it is notable for the numerous large power stations sited along its banks, the Trent is not otherwise an industrial waterway and has many attractive reaches.

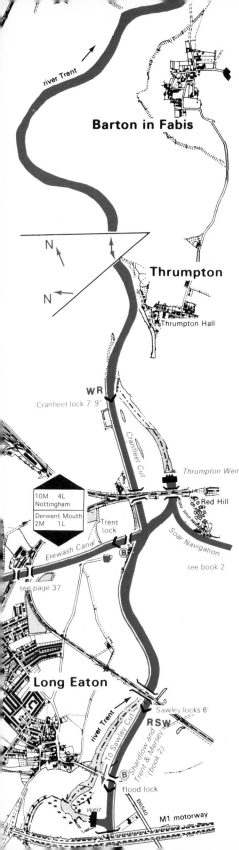

river Trent

Barton in Fabis

N

N

Thrumpton

Thrumpton Hall

W R
Cranfleet lock 7' 9"

Cranfleet Cut

Thrumpton Weir

10M	4L
4L Nottingham	
Derwent Mouth	
2M	1L

Red Hill

Trent lock

Erewash Canal

Soar Navigation

see book 2

B

see page 37

Long Eaton

Sawley locks 6'

R S W

river Trent

To Sawley Cut

Shardlow and Trent & Mersey (book 2)

B

flood lock

weir

M1 motorway

B6540

Thrumpton

Downstream from Derwent Mouth (see Book 2), the navigation goes through Sawley Cut, avoiding the weir to the north, by the M1 bridge. Near the head of the Cut is a flood lock, which under most conditions is open. Beyond this lock and the main road bridge is a wide stretch of waterway, where both banks are crowded with moored boats. Just at the tail of Sawley Locks (a pair) is a large railway bridge over the river; this line carries oil and coal trains to Castle Donington and Willington power stations. To the east can be clearly seen from this area the cooling towers of the huge Ratcliffe Power Station, but they are discreetly tucked away behind Red Hill and their intrusion into the landscape is thus minimised. Trent Lock marks the junction of the Erewash Canal with the River Trent, while at the wooded Red Hill is the mouth of the River Soar. It is important not to get lost here, for there is a large weir just downstream of the railway bridges. Boats aiming for Nottingham should bear left at the big sailing club house, entering Cranfleet Cut. They will pass a pair of protective flood gates, another railway bridge (the line disappearing into the decorative tunnel through Red Hill), another long line of moored motor cruisers (many belonging to the Nottingham Yacht Club) and an attractive white accommodation bridge. At the end of the Cut is Cranfleet Lock; from here one may enjoy a view of the woods hiding Thrumpton Park. The old lockhouse at Cranfleet is now the headquarters of the Nottingham Yacht Club. Steep wooded slopes rise behind Thrumpton, while the towers of the power station still overlook the whole scene. Below Thrumpton, the river winds through flat land, passing the village of Barton in Fabis.

Barton in Fabis
Notts. Tel. A small and isolated village, composed mainly of modern housing and set well back from the river. The 14thC church seems unbalanced in several respects; it has a great variety of styles. The building has however considerable charm; it is light, and attractively irregular. It contains several monuments to the Sacheverell family.
Thrumpton
Notts. PO, tel. This little village beside the Trent is, like so many other places on the river, a dead end. Motorists only go there if they have a good reason to. Hence Thrumpton is quiet, an unspoilt farming village, with new development only up at the far end. Although the impressive Hall is hidden away at the west end of the village, its large uncompromising gateway serves to remind the villagers what they are there for. The tiny church, with its narrow nave and a tower, was built in the 13thC but restored in 1872 by the well-known architect G. E. Street, at the expense of Lady Byron. The single street winds past it down to the river – there used to be a ferry here.
Thrumpton Hall Basically a James I mansion built around a much older manor house. The Hall is famous for its oak staircase, which dates from the time of Charles II. The ground floor rooms are well used, and elegantly decorated; the grounds are delightful, encompassing a backwater off the River Trent. The house is private.
Trent Lock
A busy and unusual boating centre at the southern terminus of the Erewash Canal. (*See page 37*). There is a boatyard and 2 pubs here.
Sawley
Notts. PO, tel, stores, garage. The tall church spire attracts one across the river to Sawley, and in this respect the promise is fulfilled, for the medieval church is very beautiful and is approached by a formal avenue of lime trees leading to the 600-year-old doorway. But otherwise Sawley is an uninteresting main road village on the outskirts of Long Eaton.
Sawley Cut
In addition to a large marina and a well-patronised BWB mooring site, the Derby Motor Boat Club have a base on the Sawley Cut. All kinds of boats are represented here: canal boats, river boats and even sea-going boats. It is certainly no place to be passing

through on a summer Sunday late-afternoon, for there will be scores of craft queueing up to pass through the locks after spending the weekend downstream. There are windlasses for sale at Sawley Lock, as well as the more conventional facilities.

BOATYARDS

Ⓑ **Sawley Bridge Marina** Long Eaton. (Long Eaton 4278/2343). 🅦🅓 Gas, chandlery, slipway, crane, moorings, boat building, provisions. Hire cruisers.

Ⓑ **Davison's** Trent Lock. Long Eaton. (Long Eaton 4643). 🆂🅦 Pump-out, hire cruisers, drydock, boat building and fitting out. On the Erewash Canal, just above the lock.

PUBS

🍺✕ **Steamboat Inn** Trent Lock. On the Erewash Canal. (Long Eaton 732606) Built by the canal company in 1791, when it was called the Erewash Navigation Inn, it is now a busy and popular venue. Handsome bars, restaurant and carvery, evening entertainment and Shipstones real ales. Garden, playground, children welcome. The beer is delivered by narrowboat.

🍺✕ **Trent Navigation Inn** Trent Lock. Large popular riverside pub with a garden.

🍺 **Harrington Arms** Sawley.

🍺 **White Lion** Sawley.

Trent Lock, the entrance to the Erewash Canal.

Lenton Chain

The river winds on towards Nottingham, passing the picturesque Barton Island (keep to the west of it), the old gravel pits of the Attenborough Nature Reserve and many sailing boats; this is clearly a popular stretch of the river. To the south runs a ridge of hills on which stands Clifton Hall. At the boatyard one should keep to the north side of the river to avoid the weir and enter Beeston Lock. This introduces the Beeston Canal or Beeston Cut, which bypasses an unnavigable section of the River Trent. The canal passes first a housing estate and then the industrial estate of Boots, before entering the less salubrious parts of Nottingham's outskirts – truly a drab wasteland, which is cheered only by the occasional glimpse of the newly-cleaned castle on its unlikely-looking rock cliff. East of the A614 bridge, the canal passes Lenton Chain. This marks the end of the short Beeston Canal, for at this point the Nottingham Canal used to flow in from the north. The junction is called Lenton Chain because the Trent Navigation Company used to lock their Beeston Canal (with a chain across it) from Saturday evening until Monday – without fail. The major part of the Nottingham Canal, from Lenton to the Erewash Canal at Langley Mill (see page 40) is now closed, but the rest of it forms the main line of through navigation from the Beeston Canal back to the River Trent at Meadow Lane Lock. The Nottingham Canal leads the traveller towards the town centre.

Beeston Lock
A splendidly kept lock where BWB facilities are available for boats. The pretty cottages and the little backwater off the canal are a hint of its past importance; there used until some years ago to be a lock down into the river here, at right angles to the present lock. The river channel used to be navigable – by shallow-draft vessels – from here down to Trent Bridge, the Beeston Canal being cut to connect with the Nottingham Canal and to afford access into the middle of the town. But now the river is unnavigable as a through route and the canal is the only way. It is a pity, since the scenery surrounding the canal is dismal compared to the riverside.

Attenborough Nature Reserve
Worked out gravel pits, once derelict and unsightly, are now providing an interesting habitat for plant and animal life. A comprehensive nature trail has been laid, and a wooden observation hide erected.

BOATYARDS

Ⓑ **Beeston Marina** Riverside. Beeston. (223168). WPD Slipway, gas, boat & engine repairs, mooring, chandlery, toilets, showers, winter storage, licensed club.

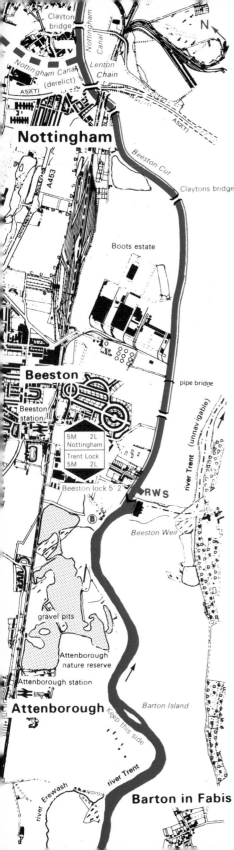

The River Trent in Nottingham. *Derek Pratt.*

Nottingham

East of Lenton Chain, the Nottingham Canal
continues towards Nottingham Castle, which is
clearly visible on its rocky cliff near the centre
of the city. The canal banks are fairly 'open'
and unobstructed by factories. At the shallow
Castle Lock is a pub and a waterways museum
in the old Fellows, Morton & Clayton
Warehouse; further on is the first of 3 BWB
yards as buildings pile up on either side,
forming a corridor for the canal. At the railway
station there is a bank, and the centre of
Nottingham is very close, but this is no place to
leave a pleasure boat unattended. Probably the
safest place to moor in Nottingham is at
Meadow Lane Lock, near Trent Bridge. At the
east end of the station there is a junction; boats
should turn right (south) here, for straight
ahead the Nottingham Canal is derelict, and
piled off after a couple of hundred yards. The
canal to the Trent runs beside a main road, the
little old brick canal bridges looking very much
out of scale with the dual carriageway. At the
end of this cut is a bend, then Meadow Lane
Lock, dropping into the River Trent.
Upstream is Trent Bridge and an attractive
stretch of river – but navigation is not
recommended. Near Meadow Lane Lock,
which is by the BWB freight depot, is the Notts
County football ground, while on the opposite
side of the river is the Trent Bridge cricket
ground, with Nottingham Forest football
stadium next to it. Below the latter is the
entrance to the now derelict Grantham Canal.
Downstream from the railway bridge, the wide
river soon leaves Nottingham behind and enters
pleasant countryside. On the north bank are
many boating centres and the Colwick
racecourse. On the south side, an exploration of
the landscaped area will reveal the magnificent
rowing course at Holme Pierrepont.
Downstream are Holme Locks and sluices
(Nottingham 811197). The locks are on the
south side – there is a small one for pleasure
boats next to the very big one.

Holme Pierrepont
Notts. An isolated village east of the Holme
Locks, this is an ancient, strange and virtually
private place, with no surfaced public roads at
all. The hall, once the home of the Pierreponts,
is an extensive stuccoed building with the little
17thC church next to it gently decaying. Inside
the church is a remarkably fine monument
carved from Italian alabaster commemorating
Sir Henry Pierrepont, a champion of Henry
Tudor. Well to the west of the village is the
international rowing course, parallel and close
to but quite separate from the river. This
award-winning recreational centre, completed
in the summer of 1972, was built from a string
of worked out gravel pits. A lot of wild birds
frequent this area, including yellow wagtails,
sand martins, little winged plover, common
terns, and great crested grebes.

The Grantham Canal
A long-disused but delightful canal from Trent
Bridge, Nottingham, to Grantham. The canal
was built purely to serve the agricultural
communities of eastern Nottinghamshire, so it
pursues a remarkably circuitous course through
pleasant farmland, including the Vale of
Belvoir (the subject of an inquiry regarding the
vast stocks of coal which lie beneath – to mine
or not to mine?). Belvoir Castle, seat of the
Duke of Rutland, is only about a mile from the
canal at one point, and a tramway was
constructed to connect them in order to carry
coal up to the castle, using wagons drawn by
horses. Traces can still be seen of this, 1 of
Nottinghamshire's earliest railways. The
Grantham Canal still feeds water down from
secluded reservoirs at Knipton and Denton to
the Trent, and a canal society has been formed
to campaign for its restoration. But it is
unlikely that through navigation could ever be
restored.

Nottingham
The city's prosperity derives largely from the
coal field to the north, and the long established
lace industry. John Player & Son make all their
cigarettes here and Raleigh Industries turn out
bicycles for the world. The city centre is busy
and not unattractive – there is an imposing

town hall in Slab Square – but little of the architecture is of note. Modern developments are encouraging, however, notably the superb Playhouse Theatre and the appearance of the Nottingham Festival in 1970, which revived in this country the gentle art of jousting. The Festival is now an annual event, taking place in the splendid Wollaton Park on the west side of the town. A big hot air balloon race starting in the park is one of its most spectacular features.
Nottingham Castle William the Conqueror's castle, which was notorious as the base of Robin Hood's unfortunate enemies while King Richard I was away crusading, has been destroyed and rebuilt many times during its tumultuous history. (It was a Yorkist stronghold in the Wars of the Roses and it was from here that Charles I raised his standard in 1642, starting the Civil War.) Though the original secret caves beneath the castle still exist and can be visited by appointment, the present building dates only from 1674. It now houses the city's museum and art gallery which include a fine display of English pottery and textiles, and special collections of the works of Bonington and Sandby, artists from the Nottingham area. *Open daily, and Sun afternoons.*
Nottingham Goose Fair The traditional Goose Fair is now a conventional funfair, but on a gigantic scale. It features traditional entertainments like boxing bouts (challengers

invited to fight the 'house champ'), as well as the usual mechanical fairground delights. The fair's original site was in the town centre, but now it is out on the Forest Recreation Ground, a mile to the north east (served by buses). The fair takes place in the *first week of Oct*; it is advisable to get there before the Saturday, when the prices are doubled.
Waterways Museum Below Castle Lock in the old Fellows, Morton & Clayton Warehouse. Local and general waterways history. *Open Wed–Sat and Sun afternoons in summer, Wed, Thur, Sat and Sun afternoons in winter.*

BOATYARDS

BWB 24 Meadow Lane, Nottingham. The Nottingham Area Engineer's office is here. (Nottingham 862411) Navigation notes for users of the Trent between Nottingham and Gainsborough may be obtained here.
Ⓑ **M.B. Park Marine** Trent Lane, Nottingham. (56550). Caters mainly for speed boats. ⓇⓌ Chandlery. Boats and outboard motor sales & repairs. Hard standing for winter storage.

PUBS

🍺 **Castle Inn** Canalside at Castle Lock.
🍺 **Salutation Inn** Near the Castle Inn.
🍺 **Trip to Jerusalem** Set into the cliff face below Nottingham Castle. This is allegedly the oldest pub in England.

Commercial traffic on the River Trent.

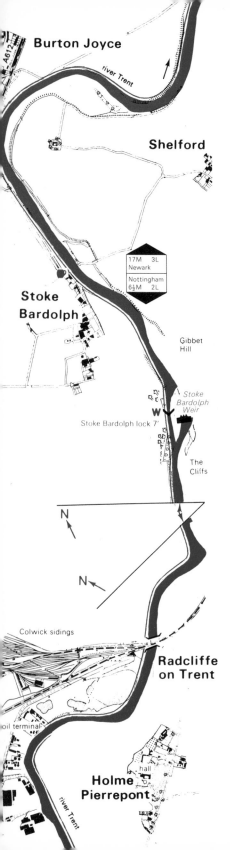

Stoke Bardolph

This section serves to establish the Trent's
attractive rural character as it continues to
sweep along through Nottinghamshire. Passing
under a railway bridge (the Nottingham–
Grantham line), one sees a very steep
escarpment of tree-covered hills, effectively
cliffs, rising out of the water. Radcliffe on
Trent is concealed in the woods by the bend,
but access is difficult. It is better to move on,
down to the delightfully secluded Stoke
Bardolph Lock. (Nottingham 248110), where
there is a water point. The lock island is
covered with trees. Below the lock, the river
bends northwards and crosses over to the other
side of the valley, leaving behind the woods and
cliffs. At Stoke Bardolph there is a sailing club,
an attractive riverside pub and a ferry (a white
rowing boat). At Burton Joyce the river
rebounds from the side of the valley and turns
east again. The water meadows that accompany
the river serve to keep at bay any inroads by
modern housing.

Shelford
Notts. PO, tel, stores. A flood bank protects this
quiet and isolated village from the waters of the
Trent. The old church has a wide
Perpendicular tower which commands the
Trent valley. There is a pub, but there is no
obvious mooring place for boats to be left on
the river. Shelford Manor is 1½ miles north
east of the village. (See next page.)

Burton Joyce
Notts. All services. A long village extending
along the very busy A612. There is a railway
station by the river (Nottingham–Lincoln
line). The cricketer Alfred Shaw – the
'Emperor of Bowlers' – was born here. Access
from the river is via semi-submerged boulders.

Stoke Bardolph
Notts. Tel. Most of the village, which is of little
interest, is away from the river. But the focal
point is the riverside pub, the sailing club is
based here, and it can be a busy spot. This pub
is one of several on the river in
Nottinghamshire which, by their very presence
(invariably on the site of a ferry) have caused
the development of a tiny isolated colony of
houses. They are a magnet for local
day-trippers and anglers.

Radcliffe on Trent
Notts. Access to Radcliffe from the river is
extremely difficult, even from the chic
residential caravan site at the foot of the cliffs.
In fact this caravan site reflects the smart,
suburban atmosphere of Radcliffe.

PUBS
🍺 **Earl of Chesterfield Arms** Shelford.
🍺 **Ferry Boat Inn** Stoke Bardolph. Riverside.
Good temporary moorings here by the ferry.
(Ask in the pub for permission to tie up to the
wooden jetty.)
🍺 **Manvers Arms** Radcliffe. Meals.

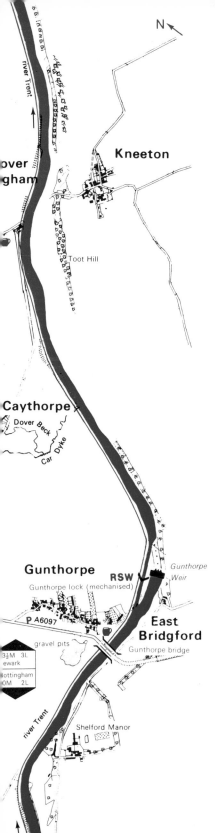

Gunthorpe

This is a stretch in which the presence of big old riverside pubs has far more effect on the river scene than do the villages that they represent. Passing Shelford Manor, one arrives at the sleek arches of Gunthorpe Bridge – the only road bridge over the river in the 24 miles between Nottingham and Newark. To the east of the bridge are the grand houses up on the hills of East Bridgford. Boats heading downstream should keep left to enter the mechanised Gunthorpe Lock (Lowdham 2621) and avoid the foaming weir. What looks like a small boatyard just above the weir is in fact just a private mooring site. The next 5 or 6 miles below Gunthorpe are probably the most beautiful and certainly the most dramatic on the whole river. On the east side, the wooded cliffs rise almost sheer from the flat valley floor to a height of 200ft, allowing here or there the presence of a strip of fertile land on which cattle graze. Only at 2 places does a track manage to creep down the perilous slope to the river; otherwise, access is impossible. On the west side, by contrast, the ground is flat for miles, across to the other side of the valley. The Elm Tree, a riverside pub at Hoveringham, is a popular place from which to launch sailing and motor boats.

Hoveringham
Notts. PO, tel, stores, garage. The well known Hoveringham Gravel Company is based nearby, although its gravel pits are not easily seen from the river. Outside the company's head office is a very striking sheet metal sculpture representing a mammoth, the company's symbol. Next to the building is a superbly landscaped example of what can be done with worked-out gravel pits.

East Bridgford
Notts. PO, tel, stores, garage. Accessible via a pleasant shady lane up the hill from the river, this village has many comfortable Georgian houses. The church is pleasantly light and has several monuments of the Hacker family. Rector Oglethorpe, one time incumbent of this parish, crowned Queen Elizabeth I.
Margidunum 1½ miles south east of East Bridgford is the site of Margidunum, a Roman town on the Fosse Way (the straightest road in England). Margidunum was probably located here to guard the ford at East Bridgford, which in Roman times was one of the very few easy crossings on the Trent.

Gunthorpe
Notts. PO, tel, stores, garage. Gunthorpe has been an important river crossing point for over 2000 years. The bridge built in 1875 was replaced by the present one in 1927. Prior to this, a ferry operated here. The riverside near the bridge and the pubs is a pleasant situation, backed by the hills of East Bridgford, although often crowded with motorists and trippers, speed boats buzz about on certain days when BWB relax the speed limit Byelaw for particular clubs. The vast mechanised lock; surrounded by trees, seems to lend a tone of sobering functionalism.

Shelford Manor
Near the river just west of Gunthorpe Bridge. The old manor was burnt down in 1645 after 2000 Roundheads attacked this Royalist stronghold. They forced an entrance and massacred 140 of the 200 men inside. The manor was rebuilt in 1676. *Not open to the public.*

PUBS
Elm Tree Hoveringham. Large riverside pub standing quite alone opposite the hills concealing Kneeton. Often used for dances.
Marquess of Granby Hoveringham.
Reindeer Hoveringham and East Bridgford.
Black Horse Caythorpe.
Anchor Inn Gunthorpe. By the river.
Unicorn Gunthorpe. Near the river.

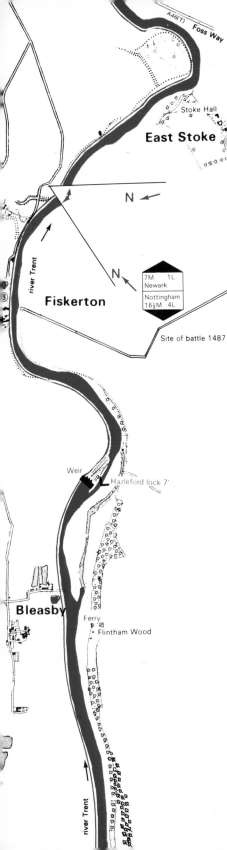

Fiskerton

The river continues along its superb isolated course, with the forested cliffs of the Trent Hills striding along the river's east bank, while on the other side the flat plain of the valley rolls away through green fields and quiet Nottinghamshire villages. Unseen up on the plateau to the east is the big Syerston Airfield, now little used. A solitary hut on the east bank houses a ferryman, who plies across the river at weekends for the fishermen. The Star and Garter pub is on the left bank near an island in the river; boats should keep west of the island to reach Hazleford Lock (Newark 830312). This lock is the only one between Nottingham and the North Sea that is not mechanised, so the lock keeper usually appreciates a helping hand. He lives in isolation on the rabbit-infested lock island, for there is no bridge over the adjacent weir, and his sole access is by boat. Beyond this lock, the steep Trent Hills dwindle away and the river leaves the woods (near the battlefield of East Stoke) for Fiskerton. There is a splendid wharf here – one of the few good places on the whole of this river navigation where it is easy to tie up. Downstream of Fiskerton, the river sweeps round past the parkland at Stoke Hall. The site of a 4-acre Roman fort is on the nearby Fosse Way.

East Stoke
Notts. Tel. The village is nearly a mile from the river, and mooring is difficult. The dark and gloomy lane by the church and hall seems to brood on Stoke's violent past. For in 1487 the concluding battle in the Wars of the Roses was fought here. 2 years after the Battle of Bosworth Field (fought on a site near the Ashby Canal), where Henry Tudor defeated King Richard III and was proclaimed King Henry VII, the Earl of Lincoln set up Lambert Simnel – a 10-year-old lad – as the Earl of Warwick and proclaimed him King Edward VI. (The real Earl of Warwick was in fact locked up in the Tower of London.) With a 9000-strong army, comprising mainly German and Irish mercenaries, the rebels engaged the Crown's army at Stoke Field as the Earl of Oxford led Henry's 12,000 men away from Nottingham. The battle was short but sharp. After 3 hours most of the rebel leaders were dead and their army in total disarray. This effectively terminated the Wars of the Roses, although the last Yorkist claim to the throne was not extinguished until the real Earl of Warwick was executed in 1499. The appropriately named Red Gutter in Stoke is a reminder of the battle, although there is no physical trace.
Fiskerton
Notts. PO, tel, stores, station. A charming riverside village with excellent access for boats. Although the normal river level is well below the wharf, all the buildings along the splendid front are carefully protected from a possible flood by stone walling or a bank of earth. The wharf is definitely the most interesting part of Fiskerton.
Southwell
Notts. 3 miles north west of Fiskerton, this very attractive country town is well worth visiting in order to see its Minster. The Minster was founded at the beginning of the 12thC by the Archbishop of York, and is held by many to be

one of the most beautiful Norman ecclesiastical buildings in England. Its scale is vast for Southwell, but it is set well back from the houses and is in a slight dip, so it does not overawe the town centre, in spite of the 2 western towers and the massive central tower. Chief among the treasures inside the building are the naturalistic stone carvings in the late 13thC chapter house, and the wooden carvings of the choir stalls.

BOATYARDS

Ⓑ **Fiskerton Wharf** Fiskerton, Newark. (830695). Ⓡ Ⓢ Ⓦ Ⓓ Pump-out, boat hire, boat building & repairs, mooring, toilets. *Closed Sun.*

PUBS

🍺 **Pauncefote Arms** East Stoke. On the Fosse Way.
🍺 **Bromley Arms** Fiskerton. Riverside. Food sometimes.
🍺 **Star & Garter** Hazleford Ferry. Huge, heavily gabled house on the river opposite the Trent Hills and the head of the mile-long lock island. Not everyone will enjoy the gnome-filled toy garden, and model village. Meals here by arrangement.
🍺✗ **Saracens Head Hotel** Southwell. Old timbered coaching house with interesting associations with events in the Civil War. Restaurant and Buttery meals. Bed & breakfast.

River Trent in Newark. *Derek Pratt.*

Newark Castle. *Derek Pratt*

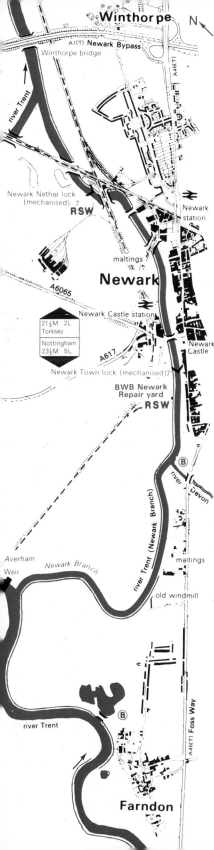

Newark-on-Trent

Farndon is a pleasant riverside village, with
sailing clubs on either side and a small ferry.
The boat population is further increased by the
use of some old gravel pits just north of
Farndon as a mooring site for pleasure boats.
For a mile or two, the flat landscape is
dominated by the great Staythorpe Power
Station, which is beside the river and is visible
for miles; this common feature of the gentle
river landscape will by now be familiar to those
cruising on the Trent. Navigators must be
especially careful to avoid the large Averham
Weir which takes the main channel of the Trent
to Kelham and round the north side of Newark.
Boats heading downstream should keep right,
steering by the 240ft spire of Newark church.
The waterway immediately becomes narrower
east of this weir. This is the Newark Branch
which takes boats straight into the middle of
the town. On the way into Newark, the
navigation passes an old windmill, a boatyard at
the mouth of the River Devon (pronounced
'Deevon'), some extensive old maltings, and a
gently decaying warehouse with the words
'Trent Navigation Company' in faded lettering
on the side. Opposite is the BWB Repair Yard,
and just beyond it is Newark Town Lock
(Newark 702226). This is a large, mechanically
operated lock. The remains of the old one are
alongside, half of which is now used as a
mooring for pleasure boats while the rest is a
covered drydock. The townscape at this point is
dominated by the northwest wall of the ruined
Newark Castle. Hard by is a splendid old
5-arched stone bridge. The size of the arches
limits the width of boats which can use the
navigation, but this bridge is listed as an
ancient monument and so cannot be altered to
accommodate bigger vessels. Just through the
bridge is Town Wharf, which is the best
temporary mooring site in Newark. Beyond
here the navigation passes the oldest and most
interesting industrial buildings in Newark – an
old ironworks, a maltings, a brewery and a
glueworks giving off a smell of old leather. A
weir follows this to the left, then a right bend
under a railway bridge, and one arrives at
Newark Nether Lock (Newark 703830) with a
smart new lock keeper's cottage nearby. East of
the lock, the navigation rejoins the main
channel of the River Trent and proceeds
north-eastward under the graceful modern road
bridge carrying the Newark bypass.

Winthorpe
Notts. Tel. Access from the river is not easy.
Winthorpe is an attractive village. Bypassed by
the A1, it is free from all through traffic and the
abundance of mature trees gives it a peaceful
air. The pub is inviting and the church, in an
ostentatious Victorian style, was entirely rebuilt
between 1886 and 1888, at the sole cost of its
patron, the Reverend Edward Hadley.

Newark

Notts. EC Thur. MD Wed, Sat. 2 stations.
Newark is magnificent, easily the most interesting and attractive town on the Trent, and it is very appealing from the navigation. Situated at the junction of 2 old highways, the Great North Road and the Fosse Way, the town is of great historical significance. During the Civil War it was a Royalist stronghold which was besieged 3 times by the Roundheads between March 1645 and May 1646. The defensive earthworks or 'sconces' constructed by the Royalists are still visible. Today Newark, like everywhere else, is large, busy and surrounded by industry and modern housing. But the town centre is intact and still full of charm.

The Market Square It is worth making a point of visiting Newark on market day to view the scene in the colourful old market. In opposite corners of the square are 2 ancient pubs: 1 of them, the White Hart, was built in the 15thC and is the oldest example of domestic architecture in the town.

The parish church of St Mary Magdalene The enormous spire is all that one can see of this elegant church from the market place, for the buildings on one side of the square hide the body of the structure. Inside, the church is made light and spacious by soaring columns and great windows containing little stained glass. The building was begun in 1160 and completed about 1500. It is rich in carving, both within and without, but 1 of the church's most interesting features is a brass made in Flanders to commemorate Alan Fleming, a merchant who died in 1375. The monument is made up of 16 pieces of metal and measures 9ft 4in by 5ft 7in – one of the biggest of its type in England.

Newark Castle Only a shell remains, the 1 intact wall overlooking the river. The first known castle on this site was constructed around 1129, probably for Alexander, Bishop of Lincoln. The present building was started in 1173, with various additions and alterations in the 14th, 15th and 16thC – notably the fine Oriel windows. King John died here in October 1216, soon after his traumatic experience in the Wash. The castle was naturally a great bastion during the Civil War sieges and battles that focused on Newark. When the Roundheads eventually took the town in 1646, they dismantled the castle. The ruins and the grounds are *open daily*.

Newark Museum & Art Gallery Appleton Gate. An historical collection of local items, which includes several Civil War relics, a lead Roman coffin (and its original contents) and W. E. Gladstone's advertisement board ('Gladstone and the Conservative Cause') which he used at elections. During the early part of his career, Gladstone spent 14 years as MP for Newark. Half of the museum is in a schoolroom which is much as it was when built by Archbishop Magnus in 1529. *Open daily except Sun.*

Governor's House A late 16th or early 17thC half-timbered house where successive Governors of Newark lived during the Civil War. It is thought that the quarrel between Charles I and Prince Rupert in 1645 took place here. It resulted in Rupert losing his position as Army General and Governor of Newark. It is obvious from the size and style of the house that it was built for someone of distinction, and further evidence of this is the line of cobble paving running from the house across the square to the south porch of the church.

Farndon

Notts. PO, tel, stores. A pleasant riverside village; with the sailing boats and riverside pub this is a busy place in summer. The 14thC church is tucked away in the trees near the older houses of the village.

BOATYARDS

Ⓑ **BWB Newark Repair Yard** Above Newark Town Lock. (Newark 704106). Ⓡ Ⓢ Ⓦ at the lock.

Ⓑ **Farndon Harbour** Farndon, near Newark. (705483). Ⓡ Ⓢ Ⓦ Ⓓ Moorings, gas, chandlery, slipway, winter storage. Boat building and repairs, salvage work carried out, toilets.

Ⓑ **Newark Marina** Farndon Road, Newark. (704022). At the mouth of the River Devon. Ⓡ Ⓦ Gas, chandlery, slipway, moorings, winter storage. Dinghy building, boats, inboard and outboard engines sales and repairs.

PUBS

🍺 **Admiral Nelson** Winthorpe.

🍺 **Castle Barge** Floating pub at Newark Town Wharf, in a 94ft former Spillers grain barge.

🍺 **White Hart** Market Place, Newark. 15thC pub.

🍺✕ **Queen's Head** Market Place, Newark.

🍺 **Britannia** Farndon. Riverside, by the ferry. Snacks etc.

🍺✕ **Rose & Crown** Farndon. Near the river.

A 'pusher' tug entering Newark Town Lock.

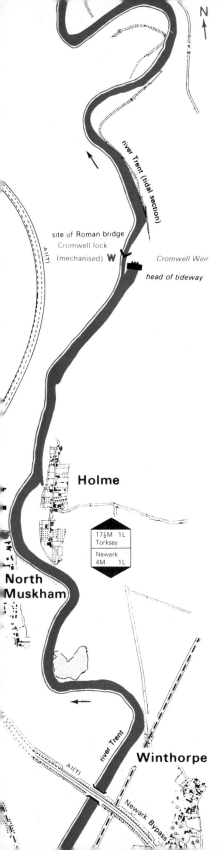

Cromwell Lock

From Newark, the Trent follows a generally
northerly course towards the Humber, which is
still over 50 miles away owing to the very
sweeping and tortuous line of the river. The
villages of North Muskham and Holme face
each other across the water; neither has a good
landing stage, but the former has a waterside
pub and thus beckons more strongly. There
used to be a ferry between the 2 villages. A mile
or more below Holme is Cromwell Lock and
Weir. The weir is the largest on the Trent, and
is thankfully now buoyed and has a safety boom
so all boats should keep to the west side of the
river. The lock too is truly enormous; it is
mechanised, and there is a lock keeper on duty
every day (Newark 821213). Cromwell has
always been a significant place on the river; the
Romans built a bridge across at this point.
More importantly, this lock marks the
beginning of the tidal section of the Trent, so
navigation north of here requires a very
different approach.

Navigating the tidal Trent
A suitable boat is essential: proper navigation
lights (compulsory on all the navigable Trent)
and safety equipment (including an anchor and
cable) is compulsory. A chart should be
obtained (from D. Sissons, Worksop Guardian,
31 Bridge Street, Worksop) and a copy of the
BWB Navigation Notes (SAE to BWB, 24
Meadow Lane, Nottingham). Deep-draughted
boats should beware of shoals at low water and
should avoid the inside of bends. The river
banks are unsuitable for mooring and there are
few wharves. Navigators who are more used to
canals and non-tidal rivers will be more likely to
treat the tidal Trent as a link route with the
Fossdyke & Witham Navigation, the
Chesterfield Canal, the Sheffield and South
Yorkshire Canal or the Humber estuary. They
should plan their trip with an eye to the
tide-table. The best approach is either to use a
Hull tide-table (available from G. A. & J. Fisk,
College Street, Beverley Road, Hull) bearing in
mind that the Trent floods for only about $2\frac{1}{4}$
hours and ebbs for the remainder of the 12 hour
period or, if in doubt, to ask the BWB lock
keepers at the various junctions along the river.
The relevant telephone numbers are listed
below.
Cromwell Lock: Newark 821213
Torksey Lock: Torksey 202
West Stockwith Lock: Gainsborough 890204
Keadby Lock: Scunthorpe 782205

Holme
Notts. Tel. Separated from the river by a flood
bank and a line of trees. Holme is really more of
a large farming hamlet than a village. The
church is a delightfully irregular shape; it has a
tiny stub of a spire, and a 15thC porch that
resembles an Elizabethan gatehouse. In fact the
porch has an upper room. During the Great
Plague a woman called Nanny Scott took refuge
in it, but when she emerged to get more food
after a prolonged stay she found that she and 1
man were the only people alive in the whole
village, so she returned to the room and spent
the rest of her life there. There is no proper
landing place on the river for this village.
North Muskham
Notts. PO, tel, stores. A small, quiet village
right on the river bank. The church was built
mainly in the 15thC, and has large clerestory
windows. The village used to be in the same
parish as Holme, because previously the 2
villages were on the same side of the river.
However in Elizabethan times the river
changed its course and since then it has
separated them. No proper landing place from
the river.

PUBS
⬤ **Newcastle Arms** North Muskham.
Riverside.

Sutton on Trent

This is a typical stretch of the upper section of the tidal Trent. The river meanders along its northward course. It is flanked by flood banks and there are no bridges. There is little to see except the occasional barge. A relatively interesting place is Carlton Wharf, where there are still working barges to be seen, but the moorings here are not for pleasure boats. The village of Sutton on Trent is near this wharf; so is a big derelict windmill. On the east bank is Besthorpe Wharf, which is used for feeding gravel from the adjacent pits into the river barges. These 2 wharves handle several hundred thousand tons of gravel every year. Mooring along the tidal Trent is not recommended.

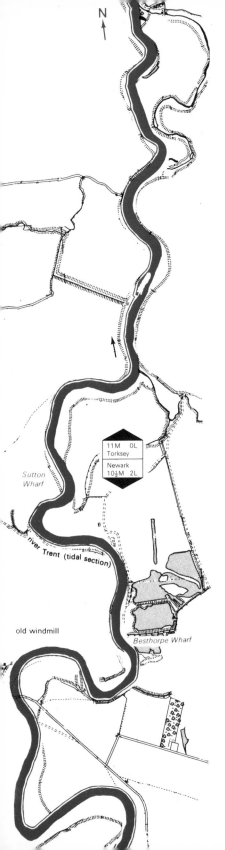

N

11M   0L
Torksey

Newark
10½M   2L

Sutton
Wharf

river Trent (tidal section)

old windmill

Besthorpe Wharf

Dunham Bridge

Passing the nearby villages of High Marnham, Low Marnham and South Clifton, the river reaches the big cooling towers of High Marnham Power Station. There is a foot bridge carrying a pipe across the river here; just north of it is the iron railway viaduct that carries the line supplying the power station. Near the viaduct is an isolated church. 1½ miles further, the river describes a sharp S-bend as it passes a welcome little ridge of hills, pleasantly wooded. But the ridge fades away as one reaches Dunham Toll Bridge (built in 1832) and the iron aqueduct that precedes it. The countryside resumes its flat and rather featureless aspect, while the river now forms the border between Nottinghamshire and Lincolnshire (as far downstream as West Stockwith). From Stapleford to Dunham the river is a birdwatcher's paradise of water meadows, pools and marshes. Mooring along the tidal Trent is not recommended.

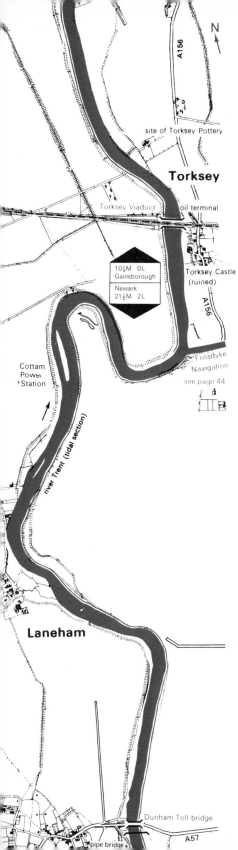

Torksey

At Laneham the traveller will enjoy a little
relief from the Trent's isolation. Here there is a
church and a few houses on a slight rise near the
river. There is also a sailing club. To the north
of the village, yet another power station –
Cottam – appears as the river turns back on
itself to the south before swinging northwards
again at the junction with the Fossdyke
Navigation (marked by a new pumping
station). The lock up into the Fossdyke is just
through the road bridge; there is a small
mooring jetty below the bridge, and a pub,
petrol station and shop are all near the lock.
There is also a good restaurant in the village –
but further information on Torksey can be
found on page 44. Nearing the railway viaduct
at Torksey, one sees the gaunt ruin of Torksey
Castle standing beside the river. As at Newark,
the façade that faces the Trent is the most
complete part of the building, for the rest has
vanished. (The castle has been abandoned since
the 16thC.) For the first 15ft or so from the
ground, the castle is built of stone – above this
it is dark red brick. The railway viaduct at
Torksey is disused, although, curiously
enough, the line on either side is much used;
from the west, coal trains supply Cottam Power
Station, while from the east oil trains bring fuel
from Immingham to an oil terminal on the
river. From here it is taken away by lorries,
mostly to the numerous air bases around
Lincolnshire. Mooring on the tidal Trent is not
recommended.

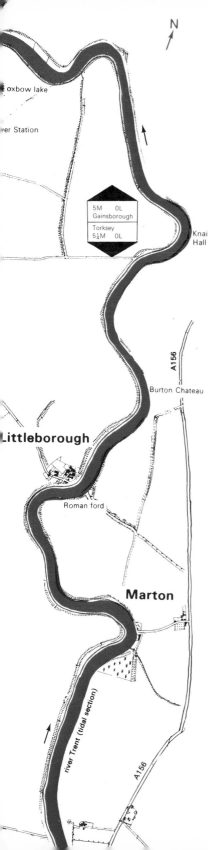

Littleborough

From Cottam, the river continues to wind
northwards towards Gainsborough. This is not
as dull a stretch as those further south. A
windmill marks the exaggeratedly named Trent
Port, which is in fact the wharf for the small
village of Marton. Speed boats operate from
here, but owners of any larger boats will once
again find it difficult to land. The next place of
interest is Littleborough, a tiny riverside
settlement. Fortunately boats may moor
temporarily at the floating jetty. Below
Littleborough is a beautiful reach, with steep
wooded hills rising from the water's edge on the
Lincolnshire side. The attractive timbered
building set in the parkland is called Burton
Château. A little further downstream, another
clump of trees on the east bank at Knaith
conceals a former nunnery and chapel, but
mooring is only just possible here. On towards
Gainsborough, the cooling towers of West
Burton Power Station stand out prominently in
the flat landscape on the west side of the river.

Knaith
Lincs. Temporary mooring just possible.
Among the trees are the hall and an interesting
old church, with its Jacobean pulpit. Both were
part of a nunnery dissolved in 1539. The hall
was the birthplace of Thomas Sutton, who
founded Charterhouse School and Hospital.
Littleborough
Notts. An attractive hamlet with reasonably
good access from the river. The little church
stands on a slight rise; it is a delightfully simple
Norman structure and incorporates much
herringbone masonry. It is assumed from
various finds, including the perfectly preserved
body of a woman dug up in the graveyard, that
this was the site of the Roman camp
Segelocum. The paved ford dating from the
time of Emperor Hadrian became visible
during a drought in 1933. King Harold's army
crossed this ford on their way to Hastings in
1066.

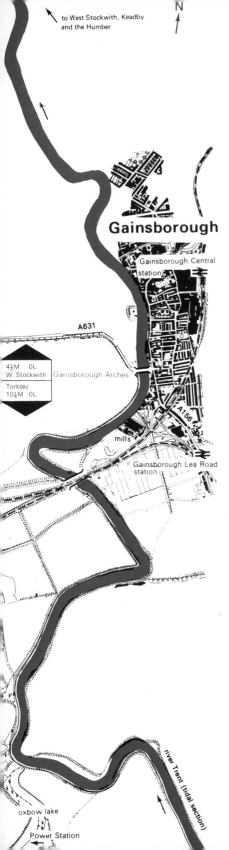

to West Stockwith, Keadby
and the Humber

N

Gainsborough

The river moves away from the wooded slopes,
passes the power station (the northernmost on
the river) and heads for Gainsborough, which is
clearly indicated by a group of tall flour mills.
Below the railway bridge, the river bends
sharply before reaching the flour mills, the
bridge at Gainsborough and the busy wharves,
where it is possible to tie up (seek permission
first). The town is set entirely on one side of the
river, and is worth visiting.

Navigational note
Below Gainsborough the river is covered at a
much reduced scale on the general map of the
North East Waterways. The entrance to the
Chesterfield Canal at West Stockwith is just 4½
miles below Gainsborough Bridge; Keadby, the
entrance to the Stainforth & Keadby Canal, is a
further 13 miles downstream from Stockwith.
Those proceeding from Gainsborough to either
of these places are advised to warn the
respective lock keepers of their impending
arrival. (see page 135).

Gainsborough
*Lincs. EC Wed, MD Tue/Sat. All services, 2
stations.* Gainsborough is best seen from the
river, where the old wharves and warehouses
serve as a reminder of the town's significance as
a port in the 18th and 19thC. Possibly Britain's
furthest inland port, it now handles vessels of
850 tonnes deadweight, carrying animal
feedstuffs, grain, fertilisers and scrap.
Elsewhere industrial sprawl and Victorian red
brick housing tend to obscure the qualities of
the old market town. There are several
Victorian churches, but All Saints retains its
Perpendicular tower. Gainsborough was a
frequent battleground during the Civil War and
George Eliot described it as St Ogg's in 'The
Mill on the Floss.'
The Old Hall An attractive manor house of the
15thC and 16thC in the centre of the town: it
contains a medieval kitchen and Great Hall.
Here Henry VIII met Catherine Parr, later his
sixth wife, who was the daughter-in-law of the
house. Now a folk museum. *Open weekday
afternoons all year; Sun Easter–Oct only.*

Gainsborough

Gainsborough Central
station

A631

4½M   0L
W. Stockwith

Torksey
10¼M   0L

Gainsborough Arches

A156

mills

Gainsborough Lea Road
station

river Trent (tidal section)

oxbow lake

Power Station

TRENT & MERSEY

Maximum dimensions

Harding's Wood to Middlewich
Length: 72'
Beam: 7'
Headroom: 5' 9"
Middlewich to Anderton
Length: 72'
Beam: 14' 6"
Headroom: 7'
Anderton to Preston Brook
Length: 72'
Beam: 7'
Headroom: 7'

Mileage

HARDING'S WOOD, junction with
Macclesfield Canal to King's Lock,
Middlewich, junction with Middlewich
Branch: 10½
Anderton Lift, for River Weaver: 22¾
PRESTON BROOK, north end of tunnel and
Bridgewater Canal: 29¾

Locks: 36

This early canal was originally conceived partly as a roundabout link between the ports of Liverpool and Hull, while passing through the busy area of the Potteries and mid-Cheshire, and terminating either in the River Weaver or in the Mersey. One of its prime movers was the famous potter Josiah Wedgwood (1730–1795). Like the Duke of Bridgewater a few years previously, he saw the obvious enormous advantages to his – and others' – industry of cheap, safe and rapid transport which a navigation would offer compared with packhorse carriage (the only alternative then available). Wedgwood was greatly assisted in the promotion of the canal by his friends, notably Thomas Bentley and Erasmus Darwin. Pamphlets were published, influential support was marshalled; and in 1766 the Trent & Mersey Canal Act was passed by Parliament, authorising the building of a navigation from the River Trent to Runcorn Gap, where it would join the proposed extension of the Bridgewater Canal from Manchester.

The ageing James Brindley was – of course – appointed engineer of the new canal. Construction began at once and much public interest was excited in this remarkable project, especially in the great 2900yd tunnel under Harecastle Hill.

Once opened in 1777 the Trent & Mersey Canal was a great success, attracting much trade in all kinds of commodities. Vast tonnages of china clay and flints for the pottery industry were brought by sea from Devon and Cornwall,

then transhipped into canal boats on the Mersey and brought straight to the factories around Burslem, taking finished goods away again. Everyone near the canal benefited: much lower freight costs meant cheaper goods, healthier industries and more jobs. Agriculture gained greatly from the new supply of water, and of stable manure from the cities.

The Trent & Mersey soon earned its other name (suggested by Brindley) as the Grand Trunk Canal – in the 67 miles between Fradley Junction and Preston Brook Junction, the Trent & Mersey gained connection with no less than 8 other canals or significant branches.

By the 1820s the Trent & Mersey was so busy that the narrow and slowly-sinking tunnel at Harecastle had become a serious bottleneck for traffic. Thomas Telford was called in; he recommended building a second tunnel beside Brindley's old one. His recommendation was eventually accepted by the company, and a tremendous burst of energy saw the whole tunnel completed in under 3 years, in 1827. A much-needed towpath was included in this tunnel.

Although the Trent & Mersey was taken over in 1845 by the new North Staffordshire Railway Company, the canal flourished until the Great War as a most important trading route. The complete canal is covered in Book 2 – this section, Harding's Wood to Preston Brook, is included to complete the coverage of the 'Cheshire Ring' canal circuit within this volume.

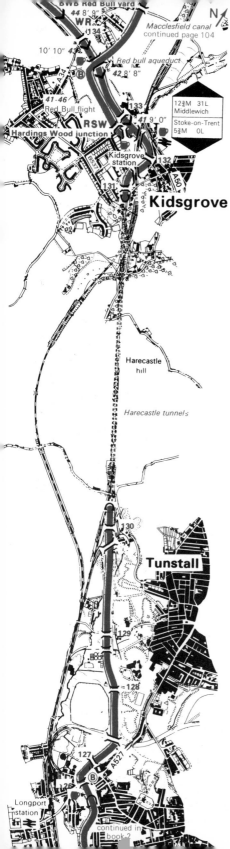

Macclesfield canal
continued page 104

BWB Red Bull yard

WR

Red bull aqueduct

RSW

Hardings Wood junction

Kidsgrove
station

12¾M	31L
Middlewich	
Stoke-on-Trent	
5¾M	0L

Kidsgrove

Harecastle
hill

Harecastle tunnels

Tunstall

Longport
station

continued in
book 2

Harding's Wood Junction

The Trent & Mersey from Harding's Wood to Preston Brook Tunnel is included in this book to complete the coverage of the 'Cheshire Ring'. Those on the ring with time to spare may wish to have a look at the northern entrance of the Harecastle Tunnel, only a short walk from Harding's Wood Junction, or even make a 'through and back' journey, winding at Longport Wharf (bridge 126). Operating times for the tunnel are given on a board at the entrance. Those who make the passage will not regret it. At Harding's Wood Junction there are two pubs and a grocer. The Trent & Mersey proceeds to descend from the summit level through a flight of paired narrow locks. Just below the second lock, the Macclesfield Canal crosses the T & M on Red Bull Aqueduct.

Kidsgrove
Staffs. All services. Originally a big iron and coal producing town, Kidsgrove was much helped in its growing size and prosperity by the completion of the Trent & Mersey Canal, which gave the town an outlet for these goods. James Brindley is buried in the town in a churchyard at Newchapel.
St Saviour's church Butt Lane. This building is unusual in looking quite unlike a church. Built in 1878, it was designed in black and white Tudor style.
The three Harecastle tunnels There are altogether 3 parallel tunnels through Harecastle Hill. The first, built by James Brindley, was completed in 1777, after 11 years work. To build a 9ft wide tunnel 1¾ miles long represented engineering on a scale quite unknown to the world at that time, and the world was duly impressed.
Since there was no towpath in the tunnel the boats – which were of course all towed from the bank by horses in those days – had to be 'legged' through by men lying on the boat's cabin roof and propelling the boat by 'walking' along the tunnel roof. (The towing horse would have to be walked in the meantime over the top of the hill.) This very slow means of propulsion, combined with the great length of the narrow tunnel and the large amount of traffic on the navigation, made Harecastle a major bottleneck for canal boats. So in 1822 the Trent & Mersey Canal Company called in Thomas Telford, who recommended that a second tunnel be constructed alongside the first one. This was done: the new tunnel was completed in 1827, with a towpath, after only 3 years work. Each tunnel then became one-way until in the 20thC Mr Brindley's bore had sunk so much from mining subsidence that it had to be abandoned. An electric tug was introduced in 1914 to speed up traffic through Telford's tunnel; this service was continued until 1954. Subsidence has necessitated the removal of much of the towpath, although some parts remain, at water level and below.
The 3rd tunnel through Harecastle Hill was built years after the other 2, and carried the Stoke–Kidsgrove railway line. It runs 40ft above the canal tunnels and is slightly shorter. This tunnel was closed in the 1960s: the railway line now goes round the hill and through a much shorter tunnel. Thus 2 out of the 3 Harecastle tunnels are disused.

BOATYARDS

🛥 **BWB Red Bull Yard** North of bridge 134 (Kidsgrove 5703). R W

🛥 **David Piper** Red Bull Basin. Church Lawton, Stoke-on-Trent. Staffs (Kidsgrove 4754). On Macclesfield Canal W D Pump-out. Slipway, moorings, winter storage, boat building, sales, boat & engine repairs.

🛥 **Black Prince Narrow Boats** Longport Wharf, Station Street, Stoke-on-Trent. (813831). R S W D Pump-out. Boat hire, slipway, gas, boat & engine repairs, boat building, mooring, chandlery, toilets, winter storage. *Closed winter weekends*. Shops and pub close by.

PUBS

🍺 **Red Bull** Canalside, in the Red Bull flight of locks. Garden, food.

🍺 **Blue Bell** at junction with Macclesfield Canal. Real ale.

🍺 **Canal Tavern** opposite the Blue Bell.

🍺 **Duke of Bridgewater** near bridge 126. The lounge is full of narrow boat parts. Bass real ale.

🍺 **Pack Horse** Station Street. Near bridge 126. Ansells and Ind Coope real ale.

The northern entrance to the Harecastle Tunnel – Brindley's disused bore is to the right.

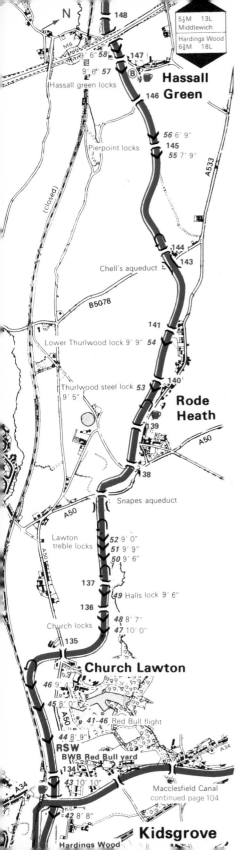

Rode Heath

Leaving behind the spire of Church Lawton, the canal continues to fall through a heavily locked stretch sometimes called, unfairly, 'heartbreak hill'. The countryside is entirely rural and pleasant, slightly hilly and wooded. Two minor aqueducts are encountered, but the locks are more interesting: they are all pairs of narrow locks, side by side. Some of the duplicate locks are unusable or even filled in, but many of them are in good condition, so that a boatman can choose whichever lock is set for him. One of the strangest locks on the whole canal system is Thurlwood Steel lock, a gigantic and complicated affair with a massive steel superstructure, constructed in 1957 to combat local brine-pumping subsidence. There is a conventional lock adjoining, which is the one to use. At Hassall Green a *PO, tel and stores* incorporating a canal shop and boatyard services can be found just by the new concrete bridge. The M6 motorway crosses noisily nearby.

Rode Heath
PO, tel, stores. A useful shopping area right by bridge 139.

BOATYARDS

🛥 **Vistra Marina** Hassal Green (Sandbach 2266). ⓌⒹ Pump-out, mooring, gas, general store, canal shop, coffee and tea. Superb meat and potato pies.
BWB Red Bull Yard north of bridge 134. ⓌⓇ

PUBS

🛥 **Romping Donkey** Hassall Green. A pretty country pub. Leave your wellington boots in the boat. Snacks, garden.
🛥 **Broughton Arms** Rode Heath. Canalside. Snacks.

Elton moss bridge **160**

N

N

159 Rookery bridge

Sandbach station

addys wood

(closed)

B5079

157

156

155

A533

A534

Sandbach

154

153 aqueduct

4

WRS

152

Vheelock

66

65

golf
course

64

59-66 Wheelock flight 79' 6"

151

Malkins
bank

63

62

150

61

149

60

59

148

closed

M6

6M	5L
Middlewich	
Hardings Wood	
6¾M	26L

Wheelock

The canal now descends the Wheelock flight of
8 locks, which are the last paired locks one sees
when travelling northwards. The countryside
continues to be quiet and unspoilt but
unspectacular. The pair of locks halfway down
the flight has a curious situation in the little
settlement of Malkin's Bank: overlooked by
terraced houses, the boatman can get the
distinct feeling that his lock operating routine is
a very public performance. The boatman's
Co-op used to be here, but the small terrace of
cottages is now to be demolished. At the bottom
of the flight is the village of Wheelock: west of
here the navigation curls round the side of a hill
before entering the very long-established
salt-producing area that is based on
Middlewich. The 'wild' brine pumping and
rock-salt mining that has gone on hereabouts
has resulted in severe local subsidence: the
effect on the canal has been to necessitate the
constant raising of the banks as lengths of the
canal bed sink. This of course means that the
affected lengths tend to be much deeper than
ordinary canals. Non-swimmers beware of
falling overboard.

Sandbach
*Ches. EC Tue. MD Thur. PO, tel, stores, garage,
bank, station.* 1½ miles north of Wheelock. An
old market town that has maintained its charm
despite the steady growth of its salt and
chemical industries.
Ancient Crosses in the cobbled market place
on a massive base stand two superb Saxon
crosses, believed to commemorate the
conversion of the area to Christianity in the
7thC. They suffered severely in the 17thC when
the Puritans broke them up and scattered the
fragments for miles. After years of searching for
the parts, George Ormerod succeeded in
re-erecting the crosses in 1816, with new stone
replacing the missing fragments.
St Mary's Church High Street. A large, 16thC
church with a handsome battlemented tower.
The most interesting features of the interior are
the 17thC carved roof and the fine chancel
screen.
The Old Hall Hotel An outstanding example of
Elizabethan half-timbered architecture, which
was formerly the home of the lord of the manor,
but is now used as an hotel.
Wheelock
*Ches. EC Tue. PO, tel, stores, garage, fish &
chips.* Busy little main road village on the canal.

PUBS
● **Cheshire Cheese** Wheelock. Canalside.
Food, garden.
● **Nag's Head** Wheelock.
● **Market Tavern** The Square, Sandbach.
Opposite the crosses. Food, garden.

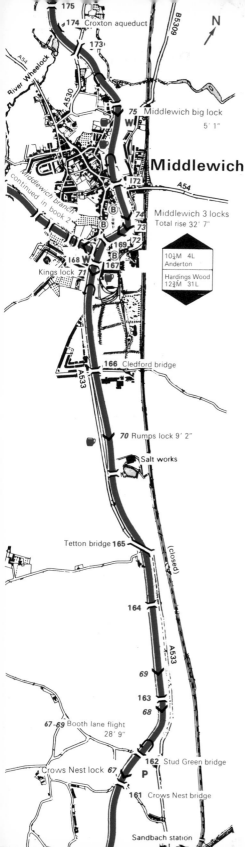

Middlewich

The navigation now begins to lose the rural
character it has enjoyed since Kidsgrove.
Falling through yet more locks, the canal is
joined by a busy main road (useful for fish and
chips and Chinese take away) which
accompanies it into increasingly flat and
industrialised landscape, past several salt works
and into Middlewich, where a branch of the
Shropshire Union leads off westwards towards
that canal at Barbridge. The Trent & Mersey
skirts the centre of the town, passing lots of
moored narrow boats and through 3
consecutive narrow locks, arriving at a wide
(14ft) lock (which has suffered from
subsidence) with a pub beside it. This used to
represent the beginning of a wide, almost
lock-free navigation right through to Preston
Brook, Manchester and Wigan (very
convenient for the salt industry when it shipped
most of its goods by boat), but Croxton
Aqueduct had to be replaced many years ago,
and is now a steel structure only 8ft 2ins wide.
The aqueduct crosses the River Dane, which
flows alongside the navigation as both water
courses leave industrial Middlewich and move
out into fine open country.

Middlewich
Ches. EC Wed. PO, tel, stores, bank, garage. A
town that since Roman times has been
dedicated to salt extraction. Most of the salt
produced here goes to various chemical
industries. Subsidence from salt extraction has
prevented redevelopment for many years, but a
big new renewal scheme is now in progress.
The canalside area is a haven of peace below the
busy streets. Tourist Information is by bridge
172.
St Michael's Church A handsome medieval
church which was a place of refuge for the
Royalists during the Civil War. It has a fine
interior with richly carved woodwork.

BOATYARDS

ⓑ **Anderson Boats** Wych House, St Annes
Road, Middlewich. (3668). Ⓡ Pump-out, boat
hire, gas, groceries, gifts.
ⓑ **Middlewich Narrow Boats** Canal Terrace,
Lewin Street, Middlewich (2460) Ⓡ Ⓢ Ⓦ Ⓟ Ⓓ
Pump-out. boat hire, gas, drydock, boat
building & repairs, mooring, chandlery, toilets,
trip boat. *Closed Nov–Feb.* Have a look at the
beautifully decorated house and garden round
the back.
ⓑ **Kings Lock Boatyard** at the junction,
Middlewich (3234). Hire cruisers.

PUBS

🍺 **Big Lock** Middlewich. Canalside. Food.
🍺 **Newton Brewery Inn** Canalside above big
lock. Garden.
🍺 **Cheshire Cheese** Lewin Street,
Middlewich. Food.
🍺 **Kings Lock** Middlewich. Canalside. Fish
& chips opposite.
🍺 **Kinderton Arms** Close to canal 1 mile south
of Middlewich, by lock 70. Ignore its dour
appearance and walk in.

Dane Valley

Initially, this is a stretch of canal as beautiful as any in the country. Often overhung by trees, the navigation winds along the side of a hill as it follows the delightful valley of the River Dane. The parkland on the other side of the valley encompasses Bostock Hall, a school for subnormal children.

At Whatcroft Hall (privately owned), the canal circles around to the east, passing under a derelict railway before heading for the industrial outskirts of Northwich and shedding its beauty and solitude once again. The outlying canal settlement of Broken Cross acts as a buffer between these 2 very different lengths of canal.

Navigational note
There are several privately-owned wide 'lagoons' caused by subsidence along this section of the Trent & Mersey, in some of which repose the hulks of abandoned barges and narrowboats, lately being salvaged. Navigators should be wary of straying off the main line, since the offside canal bank is often submerged and invisible just below the water level.

Northwich
Ches. EC Wed, MD Fri, Sat. All services. Regular buses from Barnton. A rather attractive town at the junction of the Rivers Weaver and Dane. (The latter brings large quantities of sand down into the Weaver Navigation, necessitating a heavy expenditure on dredging.) As in every other town in this area, salt has for centuries been responsible for the continued prosperity of Northwich. (The Brine Baths in Victoria Road are still open throughout the year for the benefit of salt-water enthusiasts.) The Weaver Navigation has of course been another very prominent factor in the town's history, and the building and repairing of barges, narrow boats, and small seagoing ships has been carried on here for over 200 years. Nowadays this industry has been almost forced out of business by foreign competition, and the last private shipyard on the river closed down in 1971. (This yard – Isaac Pimblott's – used to be between Hunt's locks and Hartford bridge. Their last contract was a tug for Aden.) However the big BWB yard in the town continues to thrive; some very large maintenance craft are built and repaired here. The wharves by Town bridge are empty, and are an excellent temporary mooring site for anyone wishing to visit the place. The town centre is very close, much of it has been completely rebuilt very recently. There is now an extensive shopping precinct. Although the large number of pubs has been whittled down in the rebuilding process, there are still some pleasant old streets. The Weaver and the big swing bridges across it remain a dominant part of the background.

PUBS
🍺 **Old Broken Cross** Canalside, at bridge 184. An attractive old canal pub. Shops and launderette a short way past the pub.

Anderton Lift

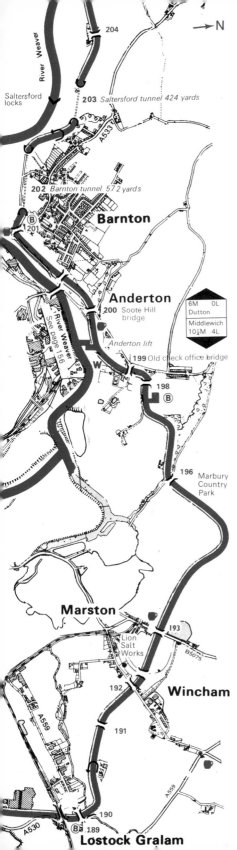

This is another length in which salt mining has
determined the nature of the scenery. Part of it
is heavily industrial, much of it is devastated
but rural (just), some of it is nondescript, and
some of it is superb countryside. Donkey
engines can still be seen in surrounding fields
pumping brine. Leaving the vicinity of Lostock
Gralam and the outskirts of Northwich, one
passes Marston and Wincham (*PO, tel, stores*).
Just west of the village, one travels along a ½
mile stretch of canal that was only cut in 1958,
as the old route was about to collapse into –
needless to say – underground salt workings.
Beyond the woods of Marbury Country Park
(attractive short stay mooring) is Anderton
(*PO, tel, stores*) – the famous boat lift down into
the Weaver Navigation is on the left. The main
line continues westward, winding along what is
now a steep hill and into Barnton Tunnel. At
the west end one emerges onto a hillside
overlooking the River Weaver, with a
marvellous view straight down the huge
Saltersford Locks. Now Saltersford Tunnel is
entered: beyond it, one is in completely open
country again.

Navigational note
Both Barnton and Saltersford Tunnels are
crooked; two boats cannot pass in the tunnel so
take care they are clear before proceeding.

Anderton Lift
An amazing and enormous piece of machinery
built in 1875 by Leader Williams (later
engineer of the Manchester Ship Canal) to
connect the Trent & Mersey to the flourishing
Weaver Navigation, 50ft below. As built, the
lift consisted of 2 water-filled tanks
counterbalancing each other in a vertical slide,
resting on massive hydraulic rams. It worked
on the very straightforward principle that
making the ascending tank slightly lighter – by
pumping a little water out – would assist the
hydraulic rams (which were operated by a
steam engine and pump) in moving both tanks,
with boats in them, up or down.
In 1908 the lift had to have major repairs, so it
was modernised at the same time. Electricity
replaced steam as the motive power. One of the
most fascinating individual features of the canal
system, it draws thousands of sightseers every
year although its operational future is
uncertain. If you plan to use it, ring Northwich
74321 and check beforehand.

Marston
Ches. Tel. A salt-producing village, suffering
badly from its own industry. The numerous
gaps in this village are presumably caused by
the demolition or collapse of houses affected by
subsidence. Waste ground abounds. The Lion
Salt works is open on *summer afternoons*, and is
well worth visiting. You can buy natural brine
salt 'in the lump' here.

BOATYARDS
Ⓑ **Clare Cruisers** Tunnel Road, Barnton,
Northwich (77199) Ⓡ Ⓦ Ⓓ Pump-out,
narrowboat hire, gas, repairs.
Ⓑ **Masterfleet Anderton Marina** (Inland
Marine Leisure) Uplands Road, Anderton.
(Northwich 79642). Ⓡ Ⓢ Ⓦ Ⓓ Water borne
pump-out ('Two-loos Lautrec'), narrowboat
hire, gas, slipway, mooring, boat and engine
repairs, boat sales, chandlery, gifts, coffee
shop, toilets. *Closed winter weekends.*
Ⓑ **Colliery Narrow Boat Co** Wincham Wharf
(bridge 189) Lostock Gralam, Northwich
(44672). Ⓓ Ⓜ Ⓔ Pump-out, gas, trip boat, day
boat hire, drydock, repairs and servicing, boat
building, chandlery. Off-licence and groceries
close by.

PUBS
🍺 **Red Lion** Barnton, just east of bridge 201.
Food, garden, children's room.
🍺 **Stanley Arms** Canalside, overlooking the
Anderton Lift. Real ale, food, putting green.
🍺 **New Inn** Marston.
🍺 **Black Greyhound** ½ mile east of bridge 192.
Good food, garden, children welcome
lunchtime.

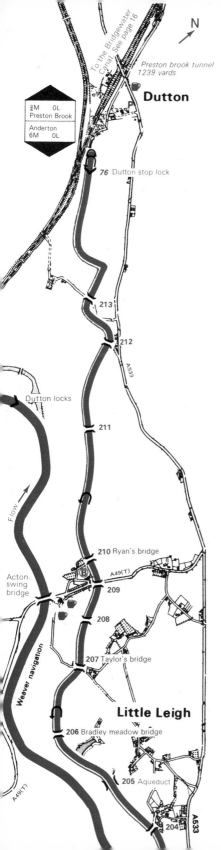

Dutton

This, the northernmost stretch of the Trent &
Mersey, is a very pleasant one and delightfully
rural. Most of the way the navigation follows
the south side of the hills that overlook the
River Weaver. From about 60ft up, one is often
rewarded with excellent views of this splendid
valley and the large vessels that ply up and
down it. At one point one can see the elegant
Dutton railway viaduct in the distance; then the
2 waterways diverge as the Trent & Mersey
enters the woods preceding Preston Brook
Tunnel. There is a stop lock just south of the
tunnel, it has only one gate. At the north end of
the tunnel a notice announces that from here
onwards one is on the Bridgewater Canal.

Dutton
Ches. PO, tel, stores, garage. Small settlement
on top of Preston Brook Tunnel, at the end of
the lane uphill from the south end of the
tunnel. There is a large hospital up the road,
and a pub.
Preston Brook Tunnel 1239yds long and
forbidden to unpowered craft. No towpath. *On
summer weekends and B. Hols* entry is as posted
on the notices at each end. It is crooked, like
Barnton and Saltersford Tunnels, and 2 boats
cannot pass, so at other times, make sure it is
clear before entering.

BOATYARDS

Ⓑ **Black Prince Narrowboats** Bartington
Wharf, Acton Bridge, Northwich (Weaverham
852945) Ⓢ Ⓦ Ⓓ Pump-out. boat hire, gas, boat
& engine repairs, mooring, chandlery, toilets,
provisions. Trip boat 'Lapwing'.

PUBS

🍺✕ **Horns** 200yds south of bridge 209 on A49.
Food lunchtime and evenings.
🍺 **Leigh Arms** ¼ mile south of bridge 209,
beside the Weaver. Sandwiches.
🍺 **Talbot Arms** Dutton. Food, garden.

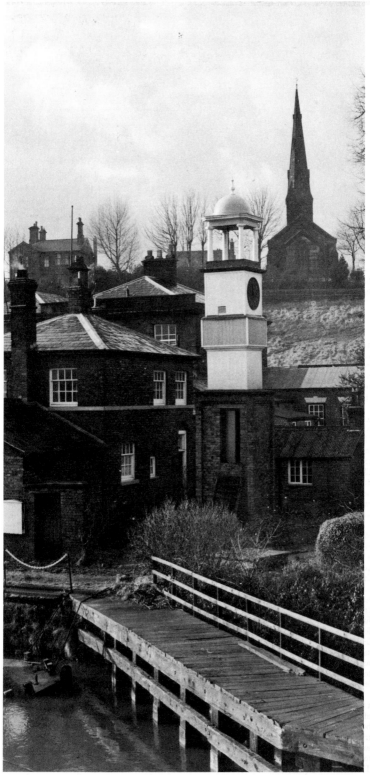

Mellow riverside architecture at Northwich, on the Weaver. *Derek Pratt*

WEAVER NAVIGATION

Maximum dimensions

Winsford to Winnington
Length: *150'*
Beam: *30'*
Headroom: *29'*
Winnington to Weston Point
Length: 176'
Beam: 30'
Headroom: 56'

Mileage

WINSFORD BRIDGE to
Northwich: 5½
Anderton Lift (Trent & Mersey Canal): 7
Acton Bridge: 11
Sutton Bridge: 17
WESTON POINT DOCKS (Manchester Ship Canal) 20

Locks: 5

The Weaver Navigation still carries a large amount of commercial traffic. In general terms, this must be due to its fortunate position in the centre of the salt and chemical industries, its endless supply of water, and the enterprising attitude of its past (and present) administrators.

The river itself, which rises in the Peckforton Hills and proceeds via Wrenbury, Audlem, Nantwich, Church Minshull and Winsford to Northwich and Frodsham, is just over 50 miles long. Originally a shallow and tidal stream, it was for long used for carrying salt away from the Cheshire salt area. The mineral was carried down by men and horses to meet the incoming tide. The sailing barges would load at high water, then depart with the ebbing tide. It was a somewhat unsatisfactory means of transport.

In the 17thC the expansion of the salt industry around Northwich, Middlewich and Winsford gave rise to an increasing demand for a navigation right up to Winsford. In 1721, 3 gentlemen of Cheshire obtained an Act of Parliament to make and maintain the river as a navigation from Frodsham to Winsford, 20 miles upstream. Plans were drawn up, labourers were organised, and by 1732 the Weaver was fully navigable for 40-ton barges up to Winsford. It was naturally a great boost to the salt industry near Winsford, which now exported salt and imported coal via this splendid new navigation. And clay was also brought upstream to Winsford: it was then carted up to the Potteries by land.

When the Trent & Mersey was planned in 1765 to pass along the River Weaver the trustees of the Weaver were understandably alarmed; but in the event the new canal provided much traffic for the river, for although the 2 waterways did not join, they were so close at Anderton that in 1793 chutes were constructed on the Trent & Mersey directly above a specially built dock on the River Weaver, 50ft below. Thereafter salt was transhipped in ever increasing quantities by dropping it down the chutes from canal boats into 'Weaver flats' (barges) in the river. This system continued until 1871, when it was decided to construct the great iron boat lift beside the chutes at Anderton. This remarkable structure (which still operates) thus effected a proper junction between the 2 waterways. Trade improved accordingly.

The Weaver Navigation did well throughout the 19thC, mainly because continual and vigorous programmes of modernisation kept it thoroughly attractive to carriers, especially when compared to the rapidly dating narrow canals. The Weaver locks were constantly reduced in number and increased in size; the river was made deeper, and the channel wider; the docks at Weston Point (built in 1806 along with the canal from Frodsham cut to the docks) were duplicated and enlarged. Eventually coasters were able to navigate the river right up to Winsford. Much of this progress was due to the efforts of Edward Leader Williams, who was the engineer of the Weaver Navigation from 1856 to 1872, when he left to become engineer of the new Manchester Ship Canal.

In spite of this constant improvement of the navigation, the Weaver's traditional salt trade was affected by 19thC competition from railways and the new pipelines. However the chemical industry began to sprout around the Northwich area at the same time, so the salt and clay traffic was gradually replaced by chemicals. Today, ICI's chemical works at Winnington and BWB's Anderton Depot supply all the traffic on the river: coasters up to 1000 tonnes deadweight capacity ship cargoes through the Manchester Ship Canal and to various ports in the UK and Europe. Meanwhile Weston Point Docks profit from being beside the Manchester Ship Canal (opened in the 1890s) and continue to flourish.

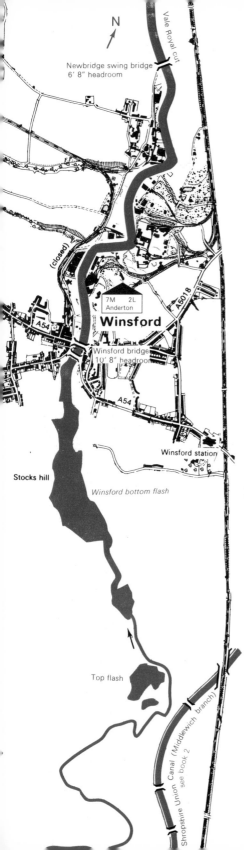

Winsford

Although Winsford Bridge (fixed at 10ft 8in) is
the upper limit of navigation for shipping and
the limit of BWB's jurisdiction, canal boats can
easily slip under the bridge and round the bend
into the vast, wonderful and deceptively
shallow Winsford Bottom Flash (controlled by
Winsford UDC). Navigation upstream of the
Bottom Flash is unreliable, for the channel is
shallow and winding, but can apparently be
done by adventurous persons with small craft.
The Top Flash is situated just beside and below
the Middlewich Branch of the Shropshire
Union Canal; but there is no junction between
them here. Downstream of Winsford Bridge,
there are some disused wharves – a good place
to tie up. Further down is a winding stretch of
little interest: each bank is piled high with the
industrial leftovers of chemical industries. But
soon the horizon clears as one arrives at
Newbridge, beyond which is the superb stretch
known as Vale Royal Cut.

Navigational note
Boats with a headroom greater than 6ft 8in will
not clear the swing bridge known as
Newbridge. Crews of such boats which are
proceeding downstream should first telephone
the BWB office at Northwich 74321 to arrange
for the bridge to be opened.

Winsford
Ches. MD Sat. All services. A busy salt-mining
town astride the Weaver. The centre of town
used to be very close to the river, but now a
huge new shopping precinct has shifted the
heart of the town well away from it.
Winsford Bottom Flash This very large
expanse of water in an attractive setting among
wooded slopes, was created by subsidence
following salt extraction in the vicinity. It is a
unique asset for the town, whose citizens
obviously appreciate it to the full. 3 caravan
sites and a sailing club are based along its
banks, anglers crouch in the waterside bushes,
and at the northern end (nearest to Winsford)
one may hire dinghies and runabouts by the
hour. It is, however, quite shallow in places –
those in canal craft beware!

PUBS
🍺 **Red Lion** Winsford. Riverside, at Winsford
Bridge.
🍺 **The Ark** Winsford.
🍺 **Bees Knees** Winsford. Riverside, above
Winsford Bridge.

Navigating the Weaver

The Weaver is a river navigation that carries a substantial traffic – transported not in canal boats or barges, but in small seagoing ships displacing up to 1000 tonnes, which use the navigation at all times of day or night. The locks are correspondingly large and often paired. The locks and bridges are all operated by keepers, and are open to pleasure craft *Mon–Fri 08.00–16.30, with a break for lunch 12.00–13.00. They are not open B. Hols. They also operate on some summer weekends –* contact the area office at Northwich 74321 for details.

The bridges are either very high, or are big swing bridges operated by BWB staff. With the exception of Town Bridge in Northwich and Newbridge below Winsford (6ft 9in) none of these bridges needs to be swung for any boat with a height above water of less than 8ft. Those craft which do require the bridges to be opened should give prior notice to the BWB Area Office. Unless there has been heavy rain, the current is quite gentle – however, as on any river navigation, an anchor and warp should be carried, and the set rules should be adhered to. There are few facilities for pleasure craft.

Winsford Bottom Flash, at the head of the Weaver Navigation.

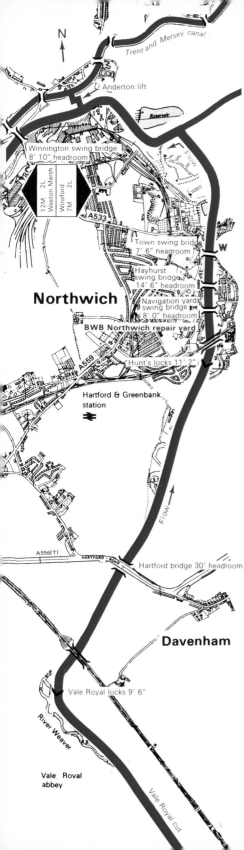

Northwich

The Vale Royal Cut typifies the Weaver at its most attractive. The river flows along a closely-defined flat green valley floor, flanked by mature woods climbing the steep hillsides that enclose the valley. No buildings or roads intrude upon this very pleasant scene. Vale Royal Locks are at the far end of the cut; the remains of the old Vale Royal Abbey (believed to have been founded by Edward I and dissolved by Henry VIII) is just up the hill nearby. It is now much changed, and is a summer school for an electronics firm. Beyond is a tall stone railway viaduct, then Hartford Road Bridge, a steel girder construction offering to ships a headroom of only 30ft – by far the lowest fixed bridge between Winsford and the Mersey. Another stretch of pleasant water meadows leads to Hunts Locks, another railway viaduct and the 3 swing bridges that are so much a feature of the town of Northwich. The trip through Northwich is pleasant enough, but north of the town the river twists and turns through a repetition of the industrial landscape that predominates outside Winsford. This stretch does not last long, and as the Anderton Lift (see page 148) comes into view one rounds the bend to be confronted by the shipping tied up at the Winnington wharves.

Northwich
Ches. EC Wed. MD Fri, Sat. All services. A rather attractive town at the junction of the Rivers Weaver and Dane. (The latter brings large quantities of sand down into the Weaver Navigation, necessitating a heavy expenditure on dredging.) As in every town in this area, salt has for centuries been responsible for the continued prosperity of Northwich. The town's motto is *Sal est Vita*, Salt is Life, and there is a salt museum in London Road. The Brine Baths in Victoria Road are still open throughout the year for the benefit of salt-water enthusiasts. The Weaver Navigation has of course been another very prominent factor in the town's history, and the building and repairing of barges, narrow boats, and small seagoing ships has been carried on here for over 200 years. Nowadays this industry has been almost forced out of business by foreign competition, and the last private shipyard on the river closed down in 1971. (This yard – Isaac Pimblott's – used to be between Hunt's Locks and Hartford Bridge. Their last contract was a tug for Aden.) However the big BWB yard in the town continues to thrive; some very large maintenance craft are built and repaired here. The wharves by Town Bridge are empty, and are an excellent temporary mooring site for anyone wishing to visit the place. The town centre is very close; much of it has been completely rebuilt very recently. There is now an extensive shopping precinct. Although the large number of pubs has been whittled down in the rebuilding process, there are still some pleasant old streets. The Weaver and the big swing bridges across it remain a dominant part of the background.
Tourist information Northwich 41510.

BOATYARDS

BWB Northwich Area Offices and Repair Yard (Northwich 74321). Alongside the extensive workshops is the Area Engineer's office – formerly the Weaver Navigation Trustee's offices. From here are controlled the Weaver Navigation, the Trent & Mersey Canal and a string of other BWB canals in the north west. Wet and dry docks for hire. As usual, this yard contains many mellow 18thC buildings. There is also an elegant clock tower on the office block.

PUBS

Northwich pubs include:
- Beehive.
- Crown Hotel.
- Sportsman.

Anderton Lift from the River Weaver. Both tanks are raised to the Trent & Mersey Canal level.

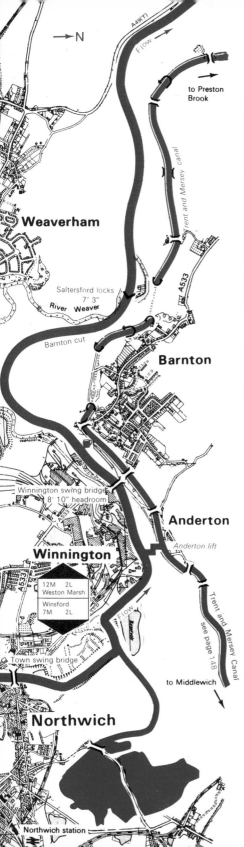

Barnton Cut

North of Northwich, the river begins to meander extravagantly in a generally westerly direction. The amazing structure that is Anderton Lift is on one side of the river: this is on the way up to the Trent & Mersey Canal (see page 148), which runs along the Weaver valley as far as Dutton Locks. Beside the lift is the thriving BWB Anderton Depot, which can handle ships of up to 1000 tonnes deadweight capacity. Opposite Anderton Lift is Winnington. Here are a large ICI chemical works and extensive wharves, where several ships are usually to be seen. These ships take their cargoes of potassium, caustic soda and soda ash (used for making glass) to many countries around Europe – and to Israel. With these ships about, pleasure boats should keep a good lookout from Winnington onwards to Weston Point, especially on the bends. (The rule of the road is of course 'keep to the right' and out of the deep-water channel.) It is also important to give correct sound signals. Below Winnington, the river runs again along a peaceful green valley, lined by hills on its north side, and is inaccessible to motor cars. Part of the route is canalised, leading to Saltersford Locks. The town of Weaverham is on the hills to the south.

Weaverham
Ches. PO, tel, stores, garage. The heart of this town contains many old timbered houses and thatched cottages – but these are now heavily outnumbered by council housing estates. The church of St Mary is an imposing Norman building containing several items of interest.

PUBS
Red Lion Barnton. Between the river and canal.

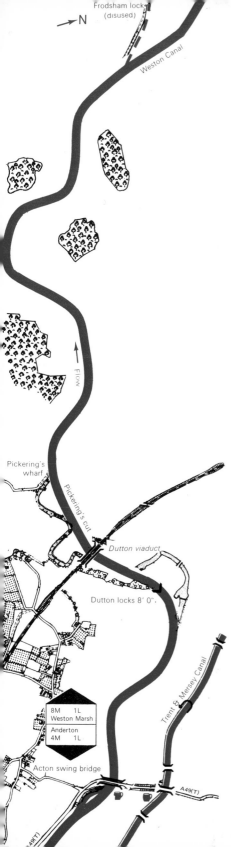

Acton Bridge

The A49 joins the river for a while, crossing at
Acton Bridge. A backwater here houses a boat
club, pubs and a riverside restaurant are
nearby. A mile further on, Dutton Locks lead
to the Dutton railway viaduct, whose elegant
stone arches carry the main electrified West
Coast line. Beyond the viaduct one comes to
Pickering's Wharf, the site of a swing bridge
long gone. From here down to Frodsham, the
Weaver valley is a beautiful green, narrow
cutting reminiscent of Vale Royal. Woods are
ranged along the hills on either side. There are
no roads, and no houses except for 1 farm. It is
a delightfully secluded rural setting. As the
valley gradually widens out to reveal the
impending industrialism that stretches along
the river from Sutton Bridge, one may notice a
branch off to the left. This is where a cut from
the navigation leaves to fall through a shallow
lock before rejoining the river course. This was
the old line of navigation until 1827, when the
Weston Canal was constructed to take the main
line of the Weaver Navigation to Weston Point.
One may still venture down the old cut to a
swing bridge, now fixed, and the derelict lock.
(The size of the lock reveals how much the
navigation has been improved and enlarged in
the past 100 years.)

Acton Swing Bridge
An impressive structure weighing 650 tons,
which uses a very small amount of electricity to
open it; 560 tons of its weight is borne by a
floating pontoon. It was built in 1933.

PUBS & RESTAURANTS
Horns Acton Bridge. Between the bridge
and the Trent & Mersey Canal. Food at
lunchtime and evenings.
Leigh Arms Acton Bridge. Riverside, at the
bridge. Food. Note the 'painted' windows.
Rheingold Restaurant Acton Bridge.
Riverside, on south side of the river. *Evenings.*

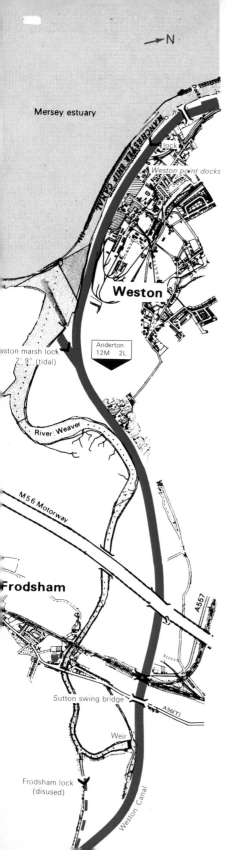

Weston Point

Passing the former Sutton flood lock, now completely disused, the Weston Canal section of the Weaver Navigation now runs along the side of the valley, while the river follows its own twisting course down towards the Mersey. By Sutton (Frodsham) swing bridge one leaves for good the charming pastures that flank the Weaver; chemical works line 1 side of the canal all the way from here to Weston Point. The wooded hills and grassy fields of the Weaver suddenly seem very distant. At Weston Marsh there is a lock down into the Manchester Ship Canal (see navigational note below). Beyond here the navigation goes right alongside the Ship Canal from which it is separated by a tall bank. Eventually, after passing the entrance lock up into the abandoned Runcorn & Weston Canal one arrives at a low (about 5ft) swing bridge. Beyond it are the Weston Point Docks and another lock into the Ship Canal. There are shops, fish & chips and pubs at Weston Point. through the dock gates.

Navigational note
Those wishing to pass through Weston Marsh Lock should give the BWB advance notice (Northwich 74321) and get clearance from the Manchester Ship Canal Company (061-872 2411).

Weston Point Docks
The docks, at the junction of the Weaver Navigation's Weston Canal and the Manchester Ship Canal, are an industrial centre. The docks have been modernised and their facilities expanded to handle ships up to 3000 tonnes.

Christ Church
Situated between Weston Point Docks and the Manchester Ship Canal, this church was built by the Weaver Navigation Commissioners. Known as 'the island church', its tall spire is a distinctive landmark.

The North East Waterways

This is predominantly a commercial network, the major parts of which have been recently modernised and upgraded. Where it is possible to establish a series of routes such as this, the desirability of the movement of goods by water can be clearly seen – less use of fuel, less road traffic and less pollution. It is to be hoped that rivers such as the Severn and the Trent may also soon see a revival of commercial carrying, the merits of which are clearly appreciated by our European neighbours.

Certain parts of these waterways are both attractive and interesting – a refreshing diversion from the mainstream holiday areas. If you are considering a cruise in the area, the relevant navigation authority can answer any specific queries you may have.

Aire & Calder Navigation

The River Aire was navigable to Knottingley in medieval times. In 1699 an Act was passed to construct navigation works, and in 1700 boats reached Leeds Bridge. A great trade soon developed, taking coal out of the Yorkshire coalfield, and bringing back raw wool, corn and agricultural produce. This success led to improvements; to avoid the difficult and lengthy lower reaches, a canal was built in 1788 from Haddlesey to Selby. Selby became Yorkshire's principal inland port. Later Goole took over this position when, in 1826, a large canal from Knottingley to the Ouse at Goole was built, 16 miles down-river from Selby. This then became the main line of the canal. A number of tributory canals were built to feed the A & C, but these soon disappeared with the coming of the railways. The A & C survived, and still prospers, due in part to the invention of 'Tom Puddings', square barges propelled in trains and emptied by being lifted up bodily and tipped. The opening of the New Junction Canal in 1905 further contributed to the success of this waterway, which now has an annual traffic amounting to 2½ million tonnes (mainly coal and petroleum products).

Maximum dimensions
Goole to Leeds
Length: 142′
Beam: 17′ 9″
Headroom: 12′
Castleford to Wakefield
Length: 132′
Beam: 17′ 9″
Headroom: 12′
Mileage
Main line: GOOLE Docks to
New Junction Canal: 7¼
Castleford Junction: 24
LEEDS: 24
Locks: 12
Wakefield Branch: CASTLEFORD to
WAKEFIELD Fall Ing Lock: 8
Locks: 4

NEW JUNCTION CANAL
Maximum dimensions
Length: 195′
Beam: 17′ 6″

Headroom: not limited
Mileage
5½ miles long, 1 lock

Navigation authority:
British Waterways Board

Calder & Hebble Navigation

The construction of the Aire & Calder Navigation early in the 18thC resulted in pressure to improve the Calder above Wakefield. After much opposition, the Canal Bill received Royal Assent in 1758 – the Wakefield Cut was opened in 1761, and boats finally reached Sowerby Bridge in the 1770s.

The Calder & Hebble was never as successful as the Aire & Calder to which it fed traffic. But its position improved due to modernisation of the textile industries and the opening up of a coalfield which the lower part of the navigation passed. Trade also came from various connecting navigations – the Huddersfield Broad Canal, opened in the 1770s, and the Huddersfield Narrow and Rochdale Trans-Pennine Canals which opened in 1811.

Although improvements were continually made to the C & H, the maximum capacity boat has remained at 70 tons, and the disparity between the sizes of the various connecting canals was a continual handicap to its success. After nationalisation in 1947, traffic declined rapidly; at present the coal barges trading to Thornhill Power Station have stopped, but it is hoped that other commercial traffic will soon replace this. However, its fascinating and often beautiful upper reaches are attracting many pleasure cruisers, exploring the Yorkshire waterways for the first time.

Maximum dimensions
Wakefield Fall Ing Lock to Broad Cut
Length: 120′
Beam: 17′ 6″
Headroom: 12′
Broad Cut to Sowerby Bridge
Length: 57′ 6″
Beam: 14′ 2″
Headroom: 9′ 6″
Mileage
WAKEFIELD Fall Ing Lock to
Cooper Bridge flood lock: 13
SOWERBY BRIDGE Basin: 21½
Locks: 27 (excluding flood locks)

HUDDERSFIELD BROAD CANAL
Maximum dimensions
Cooper Bridge to Huddersfield
Length: 57′ 6″
Beam: 14′ 2″
Headroom: 9′ 6″
Mileage
3¾ miles long, 9 locks
It is advisable to inform the lock keeper of the Huddersfield flight if you intend to navigate this canal. His telephone number is Huddersfield 36732.
Navigation authority
British Waterways Board

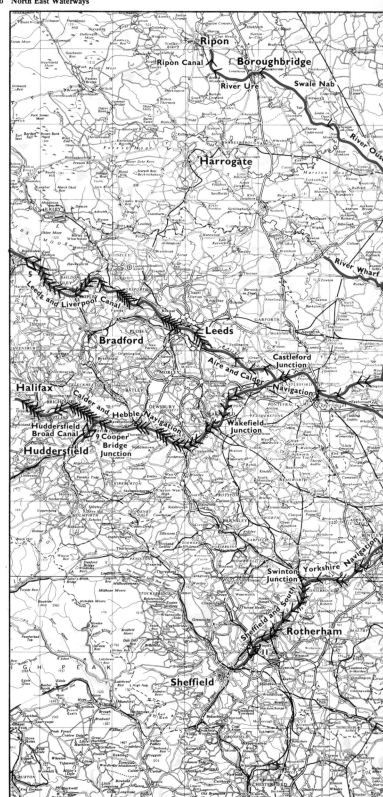

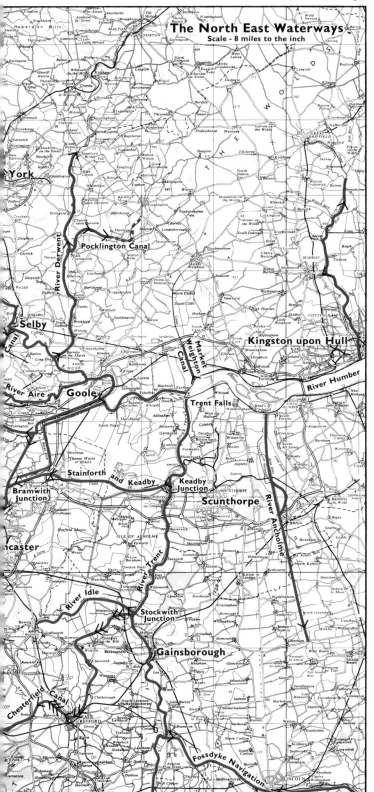

The North East Waterways
Scale - 8 miles to the inch

River Derwent

A navigation since 1701, the River Derwent joins the Ouse near Barmby-on-the-Marsh and is navigable at present to Stamford Bridge, with isolated stretches between the as yet unusable locks above here carrying some craft. There are launching and mooring facilities at Malton. The Yorkshire Derwent Trust has been busy restoring the disused locks, but it may be some time before this work is completed.

Maximum dimensions
Length: 55'
Beam: 14'
Headroom: 10'
Mileage
BARMBY-ON-THE-MARSH to
East Cottingwith, junction with
Pocklington Canal: 11½
STAMFORD BRIDGE: 18½
Locks: 1 in use.

Navigation authority
There is no *navigation* authority as such, but the river is controlled by the Yorkshire Water Authority, and their Recreation and Amenities Division can supply information to prospective navigators (67 Albion Street, Leeds. Leeds 448201). No licence is required, but powered craft, and those with sea toilets, must register with the YWA (£5) in the interests of pollution control. Those intending to navigate the Derwent from Selby Lock should take advice from the lock keeper (Selby 703182) and also inform the lock keeper at Barmby (Selby 638579).

River Ouse

In 1462 the city of York was granted responsibility for the River Ouse and the first navigation works were started, which led to the river navigation reaching Swale Nab and beyond. The Ure, which together with the Swale, forms the Ouse, was made navigable to Ripon by an Act of 1767, the last 2 miles of this route being canal. Today only half of this remains, terminating near Littlethorpe. The Ouse is tidal to Naburn Lock, and commercial traffic still reaches York.

Although remote from the main cruising network, the reaches above York are much used by local pleasure craft. Below Naburn the tidal river, and commercial traffic, should be treated with the greatest respect.

Maximum dimensions
Naburn to York
Length: 150'
Beam: 25' 6"
Headroom: 25' 6"
York to Swale Nab
Length: 60'
Beam: 15' 4"
Headroom: 16' 4"
Mileage
TRENT FALLS to
Goole, junction with Aire & Calder: 8
Barmby-on-the-Marsh, junction with River
Derwent: 17¼
Junction with River Wharfe: 32¾
York: 43
SWALE NAB: 60¾
Locks: 2

Navigation authority
The Ouse and Foss Navigation Trustees control the river from 2 miles south of Linton Lock to 100yds short of Skelton Railway Bridge, Goole. Those who require information should contact The River Manager, Captain W. C. Rimmer, Naburn Lock, Naburn, N. Yorks (Escrick 229 or Selby 708949). There is no licence fee but craft are charged for passage through Naburn Lock.

RIVER URE & RIPON CANAL
Maximum dimensions
Ure Navigation
Length: 59'
Beam: 15'
Headroom: 10'
Ripon Canal (navigable section)
Length: 57'
Beam: 14' 3"
Headroom: 8' 6"
Mileage
SWALE NAB to
Boroughbridge: 2¾
Oxclose Lock: 8
LITTLETHORPE LOCK: 9
Locks: 3

Navigation authority
British Waterways Board

Pocklington Canal

By the end of the 18thC, prosperous local farmers were in need of a cheap means of transporting their produce to the rapidly expanding industrial towns of the West Riding. In 1814 a bill was put forward to build a canal from the River Derwent at East Cottingwith to Street Bridge on the York to Hull turnpike, 1 mile from Pocklington. George Leather jnr of Leeds drafted the plans, and the canal was opened in 1818, having been completed for less than the estimated cost. For 30 years the canal prospered, but with its sale to the York & North Midland Railway Company in 1847, trade began to decline. Tolls increased and maintenance was neglected. By the turn of the century the upper reaches of the canal were becoming unnavigable, and in 1932 the last traffic used the canal. Local support for the upkeep of the canal has always been strong, and proposals in 1954 to use it as a dumping ground for chalk sludge were happily suppressed. The Pocklington Canal Amenity Society are aiming for complete restoration of the canal with the cooperation of the BWB.

Maximum dimensions
Navigable section
Length: 57'
Beam: 14' 3"
Headroom: 9'
Mileage
RIVER DERWENT to
Melbourne: 5
Bielby: 7
CANAL HEAD: 9½
Locks: 9

Navigation authority
British Waterways Board

Sheffield & South Yorkshire Navigation

First attempts in 1697 to make the River Don navigable were unsuccessful. But following Acts passed in 1726 and 1727, work began, and in 1731 boats reached Aldewarke, below Rotherham. They had access to Rotherham in 1740, and in 1751 the uppermost section to Tinsley was opened. From here a toll road connected with Sheffield. The Navigation prospered, and in 1793 two independent canals were joined to it – the Dearne & Dove and the Stainforth & Keadby. After the Napoleonic Wars, the Sheffield Canal was built from Tinsley to Sheffield but it was financially unsuccessful. The coming of the railways brought an amalgamation in 1850, and ownership by the new Manchester, Sheffield and Lincolnshire Railway Company in 1864. Later the Sheffield and South Yorkshire Navigation Company was established to remove the entire Don-based waterway system from railway interests, but it was never able to raise sufficient capital to purchase majority interest in the waterways, and improvement was not possible. In 1905 however, the New Junction Canal was built to connect with the Aire & Calder, and provide access to the port of Goole.

Between Bramwith and Rotherham the waterway has been the subject of a £16 million improvement scheme. 7 locks have been improved, bridges have been underpinned and in one case removed, and extensive bank protection has taken place. The maximum size craft able to use the navigation is 700 tonnes, with lock mechanisation halving transit times.

Maximum dimensions
SHEFFIELD & SOUTH YORKSHIRE BELOW ROTHERHAM
Length: 232'
Beam: 21'7"
Draught: 8'
ROTHERHAM TO SHEFFIELD
Length: 61'6"
Beam: 15'6"
Draught: 3'
Headroom: 10'
STAINFORTH & KEADBY
Length: 61'6"
Beam: 17'6"
Headroom: 10'
Mileage
KEADBY to
Thorne Lock: 10¼
Swinton Junction: 31
SHEFFIELD Basin: 43
Locks: 28

Navigation authority
British Waterways Board

A motor barge on the Aire & Calder Navigation at Castleford. *Derek Pratt*

A BRIEF HISTORY OF BRITISH CANALS

River navigations, that is rivers widened and deepened to take large boats, had existed in England since the Middle Ages: some can even be traced back to Roman times. In 1600 there were 700 miles of navigable river in England, and by 1760, the dawn of the canal age, this number had been increased to 1300. This extensive network had prompted many developments later used by the canal engineers, for example, the lock system. But there were severe limitations; generally the routes were determined by the rivers and the features of the landscape and so were rarely direct. Also there were no east-west, or north-south connections.

Thus the demand for a direct inland waterway system increased steadily through the first half of the 18thC with the expansion of internal trade. Road improvements could not cope with this expansion, and so engineers and merchants turned to canals, used extensively on the continent.

One of the earliest pure canals, cut independently of existing rivers, was opened in 1745, at Newry in Northern Ireland, although some authorities consider the Fossdyke, cut by the Romans to link the rivers Trent and Witham, to be the first. However, the Newry is more important because it established the cardinal rule of all canals, the maintenance of an adequate water supply, a feature too often ignored by later engineers. The Newry canal established the principle of a long summit level, fed by a reservoir to keep the locks at either end well supplied. Ten years later, in England, the Duke of Bridgewater decided to build a canal to provide an adequate transport outlet for his coal mines at Worsley. He employed the self-taught James Brindley as his engineer, and John Gilbert as surveyor, and launched the canal age in England. The Bridgewater canal was opened in 1761. Its route, all on one level, was independent of all rivers; its scale of operations reflected the new power of engineering and the foresight of its creators. Although there were no locks, the engineering problems were huge; an aqueduct was built at Barton over the River Irwell, preceded by an embankment 900yds long; 15 miles of canal were built underground, so that boats could approach the coal face for loading – eventually there were 42 miles underground, including an inclined plane – the puddled clay method was used by Brindley to make the canal bed watertight. Perhaps most important of all, the canal was a success financially. Bridgewater invested the equivalent of £3 million of his own money in the project, and still made a profit.

Having shown that canals were both practical and financially sound, the Bridgewater aroused great interest throughout Britain. Plans were drawn up for a trunk canal, to link the 4 major rivers of England: the Thames, Severn, Mersey and Trent. This plan was eventually brought to fruition, but many years later than its sponsors imagined. Brindley was employed as engineer for the scheme, his reputation ensuring that he would always have more work than he could handle. The Trent and Mersey, and the Staffordshire and Worcestershire Canals received the Royal Assent in 1766, and the canal age began in earnest.

Canals, like the railways later, were built entirely by hand. Gangs of itinerant workmen were gathered together, drawn by the comparatively high pay. Once formed these armies of 'navigators' – hence 'navvies' – moved through the countryside as the canal was built, in many cases living off the land. All engineering problems had to be solved by manpower alone, aided by the horse and the occasional steam pump. Embankments, tunnels, aqueducts, all built by these labouring armies kept under control only by the power of the section engineers and contractors.

The Staffordshire and Worcestershire canal opened in 1770. In its design Brindley determined the size of the standard Midlands canal, which of course had direct influence on the rest of the English system as it was built. He chose a narrow canal, with locks 72ft 7in by 7ft 6in, partly for reasons of economy, and partly because he realised that the problems of an adequate water supply were far greater than most canal sponsors realised. This standard, which was also adopted for the Trent and Mersey, prompted the development of a special vessel, the narrow boat with its 30-ton payload. Ironically this decision by Brindley in 1766 ensured the failure of the canals as a commercial venture 200 years later, for by the middle of this century a 30-ton payload could no longer be worked economically.

The Trent and Mersey was opened in 1777; 93 miles long, the canal included 5 tunnels, the original one at Harecastle taking 11 years to build. In 1790 Oxford was finally reached and the junction with the Thames brought the 4 great rivers together. From the very start English canal companies were characterised by their intense rivalries; water supplies were jealously guarded, and constant wars were waged over toll prices. Many canals receiving the Royal Assent were never built, while others staggered towards conclusion, hampered by doubtful engineering, inaccurate estimates, and loans that they could never hope to pay off. Yet for a period canal mania gripped British speculators, as railway mania was to grip them 50 years later. The peak of British canal development came between 1791 and 1794, a period that gave rise to the opening of the major routes, the rise of the great canal engineers, Telford, Rennie and Jessop, and the greatest prosperity of those companies already operating. At this time the canal system had an effective monopoly over inland transport: the old trunk roads could not compete, coastal traffic was uncertain and hazardous, and the railways were still a future dream. This period also saw some of the greatest feats of engineering.

A contemporary view of canal promoters. *Eric de Maré.*

The turn of the century saw the opening of the last major cross-country routes; the Pennines were crossed by the Leeds and Liverpool Canal between 1770 and 1816, while the Kennet and Avon (opened in 1810) linked London and Bristol via the Thames. These 2 canals were built as broad navigations: already the realisation was dawning on canal operators that the limits imposed by the Brindley standard were too restrictive, a suspicion that was to be brutally confirmed by the coming of the railways. The Kennet and Avon, along with its rival the Thames and Severn, also marks the introduction of fine architecture to canals. Up till now canal archictecture had been functional, often impressive, but clearly conceived by engineers. As a result, the Kennet and Avon has an architectural unity lacking in earlier canals. The appearance of architectural quality was matched by another significant change, canals became straighter, their engineers choosing as direct a route as possible, arguing that greater construction costs would be outweighed by smoother, quicker operation, whereas the early canals had followed the landscape. The Oxford is the prime example of a contour canal, meandering across the Midlands as though there were all the time in the world. It looks beautiful, its close marriage with the landscape makes it ideal as a pleasure waterway, but it was commercial folly.

The shortcomings of the early canals were exploited all too easily by the new railways. At first there was sharp competition by canals. Tolls were lowered, money was poured into route improvements; 14 miles of the Oxford's windings were cut out between 1829 and 1834; schemes were prepared to widen the narrow canals; the Harecastle tunnel was doubled in 1827, the new tunnel taking 3 years to build (as opposed to 11 years for the old). But the race was lost from the start. The 19thC marks the rise of the railways and the decline of the canals. With the exception of the Manchester ship canal, the last major canal was the Birmingham and Liverpool Junction, opened in 1835. The system survived until this century, but the 1914 –18 war brought the first closures, and through the 1930s the canal map adopted the shape it has today. Effective commercial carrying on narrow canals ceased in the early 1960s, although a few companies managed to survive until recently. However, with the end of commercial operation, a new role was seen for the waterways as a pleasure amenity, a 'linear national park 2000 miles long'.

Water supply has always been the cardinal element in both the running and the survival of any canal system. Locks need a constant supply of water – every boat passing through a wide lock on the Grand Union uses 96,000 gallons of

The rudimentary tools of the early 'navvies'. *Hugh McKnight.*

Worcester and Birmingham Canal Company toll ticket, dated 1816. *Hugh McKnight.*

water. Generally 2 methods of supply were used: direct feed by rivers and streams, and feed by reservoirs sited along the summit level. The first suffered greatly from silting, and meant that the canal was dependent on the level of water in the river; the regular floods from the River Soar that overtake the Grand Union's Leicester line shows the dangers of this. The second was more reliable, but many engineers were short-sighted in their provision of an adequate summit level. The otherwise well-planned Kennet and Avon always suffered from water shortage. Where shortages occurred, steam pumping engines were used to pump water taken down locks back up to the summit level. The Kennet and Avon was dependent upon pumped supplies, while the Birmingham Canal Navigations were fed by 6 reservoirs and 17 pumping engines. Some companies adopted side ponds alongside locks to save water, but this put the onus on the boatman and so had limited success. Likewise the stop locks still to be seen at junctions are a good example of 18thC company rivalry; an established canal would ensure that any proposed canal wishing to join it would have to lock *down* into the older canal, which thus gained a lock of water each time a boat passed through.

Where long flights or staircase locks existed there was always great wastage of water, and so throughout canal history alternative mechanical means of raising boats have been tried out. The inclined plane or the vertical lift were the favoured forms. Both worked on the counterbalance principle, the weight of the descending boat helping to raise the ascending. The first inclined plane was built at Ketley in 1788, and they were a feature of the west country Bude and Chard canals. The most famous plane was built at Foxton, and operated from 1900–10. Mechanical failure and excessive running costs ended the application of the inclined plane in England, although modern examples work very efficiently on the continent, notably in Belgium. The vertical lift was more unusual although there were 8 on the Grand Western

Canal. The most famous, built at Anderton in 1875, is still in operation, and stands as a monument to the ingenuity shown in the attempts to overcome the problems of water shortage.

Engineering features are the greatest legacy of the canal age, and of these, tunnels are the most impressive. The longest tunnel is at Standedge, on the now derelict Huddersfield Narrow Canal. The tunnel runs for 5456yds through the Pennines, at times 600ft below the surface. It is also on the highest summit level, 656ft above sea level. The longest navigable tunnel is now Dudley Tunnel, 3154yds, which was reopened in 1973 after being closed for many years. Others of interest include the twin Harecastle Tunnels on the Trent and Mersey, the first 2897yds, and now disused, the second 2926yds; Sapperton, which carried the Thames and Severn Canal through the Cotswolds and Netherton on the Birmingham Canal navigations. This last, built 1855–58, was the last in England, and was lit throughout by gas lights, and at a later date by electricity.

The Netherton Tunnel was built wide enough to allow for a towing path on both sides. Most tunnels have no towing path at all, and so boats had to be 'legged', or walked through.

The slowness and relative danger of legging in tunnels led to various attempts at mechanical propulsion. An endless rope pulled by a stationary steam engine at the tunnel mouth was tried out at Blisworth and Braunston between 1869 and 1871. Steam tugs were employed, an early application of mechanical power to canal boats, but their performance was greatly limited by lack of ventilation, not to mention the danger of suffocating the crew.

An electric tug was used at Harecastle from 1914 to 1954. The diesel engine made tunnel tug services much more practical, but diesel-powered narrow boats soon put the tugs out of business: by the 1930s most tunnels had to be navigated by whatever means the boatman chose to use. Legging continued at Crick, Husbands, Bosworth and Saddington until 1939.

Until the coming of the diesel boats, the

Islington Tunnel during construction. *Hugh McKnight.*

horse reigned supreme as a source of canal power. The first canals had used gangs of men to bow-haul the boats, a left over from the river navigations where 50–80 men, or 12 horses, would pull a 200-ton barge. By 1800 the horse had taken over, and was used throughout the heyday of the canal system. In fact horse towage survived as long as large-scale commercial operation. Generally 1 horse or mule was used per boat, a system unmatched for cheapness and simplicity. The towing path was carried from one side of the canal to the other by turnover bridges, a common feature that reveals the total dominance of the horse. Attempts to introduce self-propelled canal boats date from 1793, although most early experiments concerned tugs towing dumb barges. Development was limited by the damage caused by wash, a problem that still applies today, and the first fleets of self-propelled steam narrow boats were not in service until the last quarter of the 19thC. Fellows, Morton and Clayton, and the Leeds and Liverpool Carrying Co ran large fleets of steam boats between 1880 and 1931, by which time most had been converted to diesel operation. With the coming of mechanical power the butty boat principle was developed: a powered narrow boat would tow a dumb 'butty' boat, thereby doubling the load without doubling the running costs. This system became standard until the virtual ending by the late 1960s of carrying on the narrow canals. Before the coming of railways, passenger services were run on the canals; packet boats, specially built narrow boats with passenger accommodation, ran express services, commanding the best horses and

the unquestioned right of way over all other traffic. Although the railways killed this traffic, the last scheduled passenger service survived on the Gloucester and Berkeley Canal until 1935.

The traditional narrow boat with its colourful decoration and meticulous interior has become a symbol of English canals. However this was in fact a late development. The shape of the narrow boat was determined by Brindley's original narrow canal specification, but until the late 19thC boats were unpainted, and carried all male crews. Wages were sufficient for the crews to maintain their families at home. The increase in railway competition brought a reduction in wages, and so bit by bit the crews were forced to take their families with them, becoming a kind of water gipsy. The confines of a narrow boat cabin presented the same problems as a gipsy caravan, and so the families found a similar answer. Their eternally wandering home achieved individuality by extravagant and colourful decoration, and the traditional narrow boat painting was born. The extensive symbolic vocabulary available to the painters produced a sign language that only these families could understand, and the canal world became far more enclosed, although outwardly it was more decorative. As the canals have turned from commerce to pleasure, so the traditions of the families have died out, and the families themselves have faded away. But their language survives, although its meaning has mostly vanished with them. This survival gives the canals their characteristic decorative qualities, which make them so attractive to the pleasure boater and to the casual visitor.

FISHING

Many anglers start their fishing careers on the canals and navigable rivers, mainly because our system of waterways has always offered excellent opportunities for the thousands of angling enthusiasts throughout Great Britain.

Most of these cross-country waterways have natural reed-fringed and grassy banks, and in addition to the delightful surroundings the fishing is generally good. In most areas there has been a steady improvement in canal fishing in recent years and in many places new stocks of fish have been introduced. The popular quarry are roach, perch and bream, but the canals also hold dace, tench, chub and carp in places, in addition to pike and other species in particular areas.

Canals afford good hunting grounds for those seeking specimen fish (that is, fish above average size) and these are liable to be encountered on almost any water. The canals also make good venues for competition fishing, and in most places nowadays matches are held regularly at weekends throughout the season.

The Statutory Close Season for coarse fish is March 15 to June 15 inclusive, but in some areas, notably the Yorkshire River Authority, the Close Season is from February 28 to May 31. The Close Season for pike in some areas is March 15 to September 30.

Permits and fishing rights.

Most parts of the waterways systems are available to anglers. The big angling associations – e.g. the London AA, Birmingham AA, Reading & District AA, Coventry & District AA, Nottingham AA plus many smaller clubs – rent fishing rights over extensive areas on the system. In most cases, day tickets are available.

On arrival at the water-side it is always advisable to make enquiries as to who holds the fishing rights, and to obtain a permit if one is required *before* starting to fish. Remember, also, that a River Authority rod licence is usually required in addition to a fishing permit. It is essential to obtain this licence from the relevant River Authority *before* starting to fish. Some fishing permits and licences are issued by bailiffs along the bank, but local enquiry will help to determine this.

A canalside pub or a local fishing tackle shop are good places to enquire if permission or day tickets are required for the local stretch of water. Canal lock keepers are usually knowledgeable about the fishing rights in the immediate locality, and often a lock keeper may be found who issues day tickets on behalf of an angling association, or owner. It is likely that he will also know some of the better fishing areas, as well as local methods and baits which may be considered most successful.

The fishing rights on most canals are owned by the British Waterways Board and many miles of good fishing are leased to clubs and angling associations. They also issue day tickets on certain lengths, so it is worth enquiring at the local British Waterways office when planning a trip. Special arrangements are made for fishing from boats; again, enquire with the BWB locally.

'Private fishing' notices should *not* be ignored. If the owner's name and address is on the board then application can be made for permission for a future occasion. Once permission has been obtained it would be advisable to find out if there are any restrictions imposed, since some clubs and associations ban certain baits, or have restrictions on live baiting for pike: and on some fisheries pike fishing is not allowed before a specified date.

Other restrictions may concern size-limits of fish, and this certainly applies to the London AA canal fisheries. Some River Authority bye-laws prohibit the retention of under-sized fish in keep nets. A local club holding the fishing rights may have imposed their own size-limits in order to protect certain species. Such restrictions are generally printed on permits and licences.

Tackle

In the slow moving, sluggish waters of canals the float tackle needs to be light and lines fine in order to catch fish. When fishing for roach and dace lines of 1½lb to 2lb breaking strain are the maximum strength normally needed in order to get the fish to take a bait – particularly when the water is clear, or on the popular reaches that are 'hard-fished'.

Fine tackle also means small hooks, sizes 16 and 18 – or even as small as 22 at times. Such light gear is also effective when fishing for the smaller species, such as gudgeon and bleak. This tackle will require a well-balanced float to show the slightest indication of a bite.

Bait

Baits should be small, and maggots, casters (maggot chrysalis), hempseed, wheat, tiny cubes of bread crust, or a small pinch of flake (the white crumb of a new loaf) may take fish. It always pays to experiment with baits; bait that is effective on one occasion will not necessarily prove to be as effective the next. With slight variations, similar fishing methods can be used effectively on the majority of waterways.

Northern anglers who regularly compete in contests on canals use bloodworms as bait. They have become extremely skilful in using this tiny bait and often take fish on bloodworms when all other baits fail. Bloodworms are the larvae of a midge, and are a perfectly natural bait. The anglers gather the bloodworms from the mud and, apart from a wash in clean water, the baits are ready for use.

A popular groundbait that has had great success is known as 'black magic'! This is a mixture of garden peat and bread crumbs mixed

Barbel

Bleak

Bullhead

Common Bream

Common Carp

Chub

Dace

Freshwater Eel

Gudgeon

River Lamprey

Perch

Minnow

Roach

Pike

Ruffe

Rudd

Stickleback

Tench

Brown Trout

dry and carried to the water. When dampened and mixed it can be thrown in in the usual way. The basis of most groundbaits is bread, and many other materials may be added, although stodgy mixtures should be avoided when canal fishing. Canals are not waters which respond to heavy groundbaiting tactics. It is far better to use a cloud-bait, and this can be purchased ready for use. Some successful Midland anglers wet their cloud-bait with milk instead of water to increase the cloud effect.

Methods

Once the swim – that is the area of water to be fished – has been decided upon, and the tackle set up, use a plummet to find the depth and adjust the float, but be cautious when doing so in clear waters. At times it may be best to find the depth by trial and error. Often most fish will be caught from around mid-water level, but always be prepared to move the float further up the line in order to present the bait closer to the bottom, where the bigger fish are usually to be found. At frequent intervals toss a few samples of the hook-bait into the top of the swim to keep the fish interested.

Fish in different waters may vary in the way they take a bait and this creates a different bite registration. It may be found that fish take the hook-bait quickly, causing the float to dip sharply or dive under the surface. The strike should be made instantly, on the downward movement. On some canals the fish are even quicker – and perhaps, gentler – not taking the float under at all, and in this case the strike should be made at the slightest unusual movement of the float.

Roach and dace abound in many lengths and although working the float tackle down with a flow of water takes most fish, better quality fish – including bream – are usually to be taken by fishing a laying-on style, with the bait lying on the bottom. This method can often be best when fishing areas where there is no flow at all. This is done with float tackle, adjusted to make the distance from float to hook greater than the depth of water, so that when the float is at the surface the bait and lower length of line are lying on the bottom.

The alternative method of fishing the bottom is by legering, the main difference in the methods being in the bite indicator. Without a float a bite is registered at the rod-tip where, if need be, a quiver-tip or swing-tip may be fitted. These bite detectors are used extensively on Midland and Northern waters. Legering is a method often used in the south, where in some southern canals barbel and chub are quite prolific. These species grow to good sizes in canal waters – chub up to 7lb and barbel up to 14lb have been taken – but these are exceptional and the average run of fish would be well below those weights. Nevertheless, both species are big fish and big baits and hooks may be used when fishing for them.

Many bigger than average fish – of all species – have been taken by fishing the bait on the bottom. Whatever the style of leger fishing, always choose the lightest possible lead weight, and position it some 12 to 18in up from the hook. There are no hard and fast rules governing the distance between lead and hook, so it pays to experiment to find the best to suit the conditions.

Anglers who regularly fish the Northern and Midland canals invariably use tiny size 20 and 22 hooks, tied to a mere ¾lb breaking strain line, and when float-fishing use a tiny quill float – porcupine or crow quill. A piece of peacock quill is useful because it can be cut with scissors to make it suit prevailing conditions. Such small floats only need a couple of dust-shot to balance them correctly, and usually the Midland anglers position this shot on the line just under the float so that the bait is presented naturally. Once the tackle has been cast out, the bait falls slowly through the water along with hook-bait samples, which are thrown in at the same time. This is called 'fishing on the drop'. A fine cloud-bait is also used with this style.

Canals which have luxuriant weed growth harbour many small fish, which are preyed upon by perch. These move in shoals and invariably the perch in a shoal are much the same size. Usually the really big perch are solitary, so it pays to rove the canal and search for them. They are to be caught from almost any canal and although they may be caught by most angling methods, the most effective is usually float-fishing. The fishing depth can vary according to conditions, time of year, and actual depth of the canal, so it pays to try the bait at varying depths. The usual baits for perch are worms, small live-baits (minnows etc) and maggots. Close by wooden lock gates is often the haunt of large perch.

In certain places canals and rivers come together and take on the characteristics of the river (ie with an increased flow) and different methods are required for splendid chub (and sometimes barbel) in addition to roach and other species. Trotting the stream is a popular and effective fishing style.

Weather

Weather conditions have to be taken into consideration. Canals usually run through open country and catch the slightest breeze. Even a moderate wind will pull and bob the float, which in turn will agitate the baited hook. If bites are not forthcoming under such conditions then it may be best to remove the float and try a straightforward leger arrangement.

When legering, the effects of the wind can be avoided by keeping the rod top down to within an inch or two of the water level – or even by sinking the rod-tip below the surface. Anglers in the North and Midlands have devised a wind-shield for legering that protects the rod-tip from the wind and improves bite detection. Nevertheless, in some circumstances a slight wind can be helpful because if a moderate breeze is blowing it will put a ripple on the water, and this can be of assistance in fishing in clear waters.

Where to fish

Most canals are narrow and this makes it possible to cast the tackle towards the far bank, where fish may have moved because they had been disturbed from the near bank. Disturbance will send the fish up or downstream and often well away from the fishing area. So always approach the water quietly, and remember to move cautiously at all times. When making up the tackle to start fishing it is advisable to do so as far back from the water as possible to avoid scaring the fish. It pays to move slowly, to keep as far from the bank as possible, and to avoid clumping around in heavy rubber boots. If there is cover along the bank – shrubs, bushes, tall reeds and clumps of yellow flag iris – the wise angler will make full use of it.

There are some canals that are no longer navigable, and these are generally weedy. At certain times in the season the surface of the water disappears under a green mantle of floating duckweed, which affords cover and security for the fish. It is possible to have the best sport by fishing in the pockets of clear water that are to be found.

Some canals have prolific growths of water lilies in places, and are particularly attractive for angling. They always look ideal haunts for tench, but they can also be rather difficult places from which to land good fish. Tench are more or less evenly distributed throughout the canals and the best are found where weed growth is profuse. It may be best to fish small areas of clear water between the weeds. Groundbait can encourage tench to move out from the weed beds, and to feed once they are out. Sometimes it is an advantage to clear a swim by dragging out weeds or raking the bottom. This form of natural groundbaiting stirs the silt, which clouds the water and disturbs aquatic creatures on which the fish feed.

Bream seem to do well in canals and some fairly good fish up to 5lb may be taken. Any deep pools or winding holes (shown as ⌒ on map) are good places to try, particularly when fishing a canal for the first time.

Other places worth fishing are 'cattle drinks' regularly used by farm animals. These make useful places to fish for bream, roach and dace. The frequent use of these drinking holes colours the water, as the animals stir up the mud, and disturb the water creatures. The coloured water draws fish into the area – on the downstream side of the cattle drink when there is the slightest flow.

Pike are to be found in every canal in the country – they are predators, feeding on small fish (which gives a sure indication of the most effective baits). Any small live fish presented on float tackle will take pike. The best places to fish are near weed beds and boats that have been moored in one place a long time.

Many of our canals are cut through pleasant and peaceful countryside, and this enables anglers to spend many delightful hours along the banks – and always with the chance of making a good catch. As a general rule, never fish in locks on navigable canals, or anywhere that could obstruct the free passage of boats. Remember that you will inconvenience yourself as well as the boatman if you have to move in a hurry, or risk a broken line. Never leave discarded line or lead weights on the bank, and never throw these items into the water. Waterfowl become entangled in the line, and are poisoned by lead shot, which they swallow when grubbing for food. All responsible anglers take their spoilt tackle home with them, where it can be disposed of safely.

The BWB Fisheries Officer at Watford welcomes specific enquiries about fishing on BWB canals from individuals, associations and clubs. He will also supply the name and address of the current Secretary of each Angling Association.

FURTHER READING

Reference works:

Canals and Rivers of Britain	Andrew Darwin	Dent
Shell Book of Inland Waterways	Hugh McKnight	David & Charles
Canal Architecture in Britain	Frances Pratt	BWB
Inland Waterways of Great Britain and Northern Ireland	L. A. Edwards	Imray
A General History of Inland Navigation (reprint from 1805)	J. Phillips	David & Charles
Historical Account of Navigable Rivers & Canals of Great Britain (reprint from 1831)	J. Priestley	David & Charles
Bradshaw's Canals & Navigable Rivers of England and Wales (reprint from 1904)	Henry de Salis	David & Charles

General books:

British Canals	Charles Hadfield	David & Charles
The Canals of the East Midlands	Charles Hadfield	David & Charles
The Canals of the West Midlands	Charles Hadfield	David & Charles
The Canals of South & East England	Charles Hadfield	David & Charles
The Canals of Yorkshire & East England (2 volumes)	Charles Hadfield	David & Charles
The Canals of North West England (2 volumes)	Charles Hadfield	David & Charles
The Canals of Eastern England	Charles Hadfield	David & Charles
The Canals of South Wales and the Border	Charles Hadfield	David & Charles
James Brindley Engineer, 1716–1772	C. T. G. Boucher	Goose & Son
The Decorative Arts of the Mariner	G. F. Cook (ed.)	Cassell
Slow Boat Through England	Frederic Doerflinger	Allan Wingate
English Canals (3 volumes)	D. D. Gladwin & J. M. White	Oakwood Press
The Canal Age	Charles Hadfield	David & Charles and Pan Books
Canals and Their Architecture	Robert Harris	Hugh Evelyn
A Tour of the Grand Junction Canal in 1819 (reprinted 1968)	J. Hassell	Cranfield & Bonfiel
Journeys of the Swan	John Liley	Allen & Unwin
The Canals of England	Eric de Maré	The Architectural Press
Discovering Canals	L. Metcalf & J. Vince	Shire Publications
Narrow Boat	L. T. C. Rolt	Eyre & Spottiswoode
Navigable Waterways	L. T. C. Rolt	Longmans
The Inland Waterways of England	L. T. C. Rolt	Allen & Unwin
Thomas Telford	L. T. C. Rolt	Longmans
James Watt	L. T. C. Rolt	Batsford
Lost Canals of England and Wales	R. Russell	David & Charles
Voyage into England	John Seymour	David & Charles
Lives of the Engineers (3 volumes – reprint) from 1862)	Samuel Smiles	David & Charles
Maidens Trip	Emma Smith	Penguin
The Flower of Gloster (reprint from 1911)	Temple Thurston	David & Charles
River Navigation in England 1600–1750	T. S. Willan	F. Cass
The Kennett & Avon Canal	Kenneth R. Clew	David & Charles
Waterways to Stratford	C. Hadfield & J. Norris	David & Charles
London's Lost Route to Basingstoke	P. A. L. Vine	David & Charles
London's Lost Route to the Sea	P. A. L. Vine	David & Charles

*Not all of these books are in print – your local
library will help you obtain those not readily
available.*

**There are also 3 more volumes in this series,
providing complete coverage of all the
popular cruising waterways.**

**1: South
2: Central
River Thames and Wey**

BRITISH WATERWAYS BOARD OFFICES

Headquarters
Melbury House, Melbury Terrace, London NW1 6JX. (01-262 6711). General and official enquiries. Willow Grange, Church Road, Watford, Herts WD1 3QA. (Watford 26422). Pleasure craft licences and registration, mooring permits and angling enquiries.

Area Offices
Will deal with enquiries regarding stoppages, long term moorings and specific problems on a particular canal in their area.

Nottingham Area Amenity Assistant 24 Meadow Lane, Nottingham. (Nottingham 862411).
Chesterfield Canal
Erewash Canal
Fossdyke & Witham Navigations
River Trent

Wigan Area Amenity Assistant Swan Meadow Road, Wigan, Gt. Manchester. (Wigan 42239).
Ashton Canal
Lancaster Canal
Leeds & Liverpool Canal

Northwich Area Amenity Assistant Navigation Road, Northwich, Cheshire. (Northwich 74321).
Macclesfield Canal
Peak Forest Canal
Trent & Mersey Canal (west)
River Weaver

Castleford Area Amenity Assistant Lock Lane, Castleford, Yorks. (Castleford 554351).
The north east waterways

Other navigation authorities are listed in the appropriate place in the text.

INDEX